A GUIDE TO
AUSTRALIAN
FOLKLORE

A GUIDE TO
AUSTRALIAN
FOLKLORE

From Ned Kelly to Aeroplane Jelly

Gwenda Beed Davey and Graham Seal

Kangaroo Press

A GUIDE TO AUSTRALIAN FOLKLORE
First published in Australia in 2003 by Kangaroo Press,
an imprint of Simon & Schuster (Australia) Pty Limited,
20 Barcoo Street, East Roseville NSW 2069

A Viacom Company
Sydney New York London

Visit our website at www.simonsaysaustralia.com

Cataloguing-in-Publication data:

Davey, Gwenda, 1932–
    A guide to Australian folklore: from Ned Kelly to Aeroplane Jelly.

    Bibliography.
    Includes index
    ISBN 0 7318 1075 9.

    1. Folklore - Australia. 2. Australia - Social life and
    customs. I. Seal, Graham, 1950- . II. Title.

398.0994

Cover and internal design by Avril Makula GRAVITY AAD
Illustrations by Edwina Riddell
Cover illustration of Ned Kelly in Spring by Sidney Nolan, 1955
Typeset in Goudy 11pt on 14pt
Printed in Australia by Griffin Press

10 9 8 7 6 5 4 3 2 1

CONTENTS

PREFACE

This book is a guide to the many folk traditions that enrich our culture. It is selective rather than comprehensive, but within the limits of available space we have tried to suggest at least a little of all aspects of Australian folklore, past and present.

The term 'folklore' often makes people think of the past. Bush songs, old tales, traditional sayings and beliefs and the like. But as this Guide shows, folklore is just as much a part of modern life, encompassing such things as electronic lore, urban legends, colloquial speech and the many and varied customs observed by groups of Australians, large and small. While many of these traditions have their roots in the past, they are still very much part of the way we live in modern Australia. In this book we have tried to show both the old and the new in Australian folklore.

The relationship between cultural identity and folklore is a strong one in all nations. In Australia's case this is especially true. In the relatively brief history of European occupation we have developed a view of what is characteristically Australian that draws heavily upon the traditions of the convicts, the pioneers, bushranging, the pastoral industry and the tradition, of the digger. In addition to these elements of historical tradition this national folklore has been influenced by interaction with indigenous people and increasingly, particularly in the years since World War II, by contact with people of many different ethnic, religious and cultural backgrounds. Australian-English language folk tradition is very much an amalgam of all these varying influences.

Any consideration of cultural heritage in Australia must take account of the great diversity of our multicultural population. At the time of writing, the 2001 Australian Census figures are very revealing. This Census shows that in the last fifty years Australia more than doubled its population to almost 20 million, and nearly 2.5 million of these, or about one person in seven, speak a language other than English at home. The main other languages spoken are Italian, Chinese languages, Greek, Arabic and Vietnamese, and some linguists refer to more than one hundred languages being spoken in Australia. At the 2001 Census, our indigenous populations totalled 460,000, or 2.4% of the Australian population as a whole. This cultural diversity is, however, neither fixed nor unchanging. Writing in *The Oxford Companion to Australian Folklore*, Jerzy Zubrzycki notes 'the ever-increasing rate of inter-marriage' in Australia, and comments that the folk culture which immigrants bring to the country is not only transported but frequently transformed.

As well, each of the many groups speaking languages other than English also have their own extensive traditions. These too are now part of our folklore, though the English-speaking majority are only just beginning to discover their riches. Where possible, we have referred to these traditions while acknowledging that this Guide is mainly restricted to English-language lore. We would like to think that future generations of folklorists will take up the considerable challenge of collecting and studying the many individual folklores of the Australian people. This is only likely to happen if substantial amounts of funding are made available for the necessary fieldwork and expertise. Given the reluctance of Australian governments to provide adequate facilities for the retrieval and study of English-language folklore, as the Chronicle we have included demonstrates, we are not optimistic that this will happen.

This Guide has a number of sections, designed to help the reader find out as much, or as little, about a topic as required. Following the Introduction is a section on Definitions of Folklore, then a Chronicle or history of the documentation and study of folklore in Australia. Next is an A–Z Dictionary, then a Calendar of the Australian folk year, and a Gazetteer of traditions that organises the entries according to their relevant state or territory. The final sections are a select Bibliography for readers in search of more detailed information, and an Index that allows access to topics, themes and issues as they occur throughout the work.

Throughout these sections of the Guide you will find entries on a great variety of Australian folk traditions, including yarns, folk speech, customs, dance, music, song, belief, urban legends, convict lore, war lore, work lore, ghost stories, bush stories, eco-lore, e-lore, lost treasures and much more. There is also information about the collection and preservation of folklore, about its uses and misuses, and about the influences of migrant and indigenous groups on English language lore.

We hope that this Guide will be useful for the general reader wishing to find out more about Australian folklore, for those wanting to look up an unfamiliar reference, and as a useful work for teachers, librarians, media professionals and anyone else needing information about Australia's diverse folk traditions. In it we have tried to provide information about people, events, places and the many other allusions and references that occur in our folklore. Readers wishing to locate a custom, a song, an area of folklore can look for an entry in the A–Z Dictionary. Entries all have one, and usually more, cross-references to other relevant entries to help expand their search. The Index is also designed to allow readers to look up whatever interests them and to find relevant references in the Dictionary as well as anywhere else they may occur in the Guide.

Finally, we would like to acknowledge the many people who have assisted in the development and completion of this project, including Angelo Loukakis, Fran Bryson, Emma Costantino, Joanne Cook, Jodie Jongeling, Barry York, June Factor and Bill Scott.

INTRODUCTION

What is Folklore?

On the second Tuesday in November almost everybody in Australia will bet on a horse in the Melbourne Cup. For many people, this will be their only bet for the year. Almost every workplace will hold a 'sweep' for the Melbourne Cup. Every day in Australia somebody will tell a joke, spin a yarn, recite a nursery rhyme, or cook a meal. Every day in Australia somebody will celebrate a birthday or saint's day, or take part in a local festival. Every day somebody will knit a jumper, build a letter-box or 'run up a dress'.

Who teaches you to do these things? You might have learned some of them in school, but not many. You probably learned them at home, or from friends. You might not know where some of them came from.

This is folklore, the unofficial culture of everyday life. It's unofficial because there are no laws saying that you must learn it. In Australia there are laws saying that you must drive a car on the left-hand side of the road and wear a seat belt, but there are no laws telling you to hang two dice, or a toy kangaroo, or a St Christopher medal in the front or the back window of your car. These are folk customs, which you probably learned from seeing other people do the same thing.

As well as learning by watching other people, a great deal of folklore is learned by word of mouth, or what folklorists call oral transmission. This is how most of us learn the words of the great Australian folk song, 'Waltzing Matilda'. The first folklore you learn this way might be a hand-clapping routine such as 'Pat-a-cake Pat-a-cake' or a lullaby or nursery rhyme such as 'Baa Baa Black Sheep'.

Nursery rhymes, children's games and folk tales (often called fairy tales) are some of the oldest continuous traditions we have. The great Flemish artist Pieter Brueghel's painting *Children's Games* (1560), an international treasure held in the Art History Museum in Vienna, shows more than eighty children's games, such as chasing, dressing up, knucklebones and hoops. Almost all of these games are still played today.

Sometimes oral transmission receives a little help from the printed word. The 'father of English printing', William Caxton, produced *Aesop's Fables* in the late fifteenth century as one of his first publications. This collection of tales, said to have been written by the Greek slave Aesop in the sixth century BC, imparts moral lessons, such as not to be greedy or too proud, and to watch out for trickery, which are told through animal fables such as 'The fox and the crow'. These stories are still known today: possibly the best known is 'The hare and the tortoise', where the slow and steady tortoise beats the fast but lazy hare in a race.

Where does the word 'folklore' come from? Most scholars accept that the English antiquary William Thoms introduced the word 'folklore' to English scholarship in 1846 in a letter written to the London *Athenaeum* magazine. Thoms wrote about the need to gather 'the few ears... remaining' of 'the manners, customs, observances, superstitions, ballads, proverbs, etc., of the olden time'.

Like other nineteenth-century scholars such as E.B. Tylor, Thoms saw folklore in terms of survivals from the past. Today, folklorists recognise that folklore is alive and well in the modern era, and both continuous and changing .

There have been many attempts to define the meaning and significance of folklore in the modern world, by international bodies such as the United Nations Educational, Scientific and Cultural Organisation (UNESCO), and by Australian bodies such as the Committee of Inquiry into Folklife in Australia. This committee published its report in 1987 under the title *Folklife in Australia: Our Living Heritage*.

What is the difference between the terms 'folklore' and 'folklife'? In practice, the answer is 'not much', as many folklorists use the terms interchangeably. But there are reasons why one term is sometimes used rather than the other. 'Folklore' refers to the actual lore itself, the great body of unofficial customs and knowledge held in all societies. In Chapter 3 of its report, the Committee of Inquiry listed some of the major categories of folklore in Australia, namely:

* Making Things
* Oral Folklore
* Music and Dance
* Customs, Pastimes and Beliefs
* Occupational Folklore
* Children's Folklore.

But folklorists are not only interested in *what* people do, think and believe. They are also interested in the *how*, *where* and *when* about folklore. They are not only interested in the colourful words and phrases Australians use as part of their folk speech (or slang), such as 'I'm flat out like a lizard drinking', or 'it's better than a poke in the eye with a burnt stick'; they are also interested in what these amusing sayings mean in everyday life. This living culture of everyday life is folklife.

The term 'folklife' comes from Scandinavia, where countries such as Finland have long been international leaders in the study of folklore and folk customs. The term became well known in English-speaking countries in the 1970s. As part of its bicentennial celebrations, and in an effort to protect and preserve its folk traditions, the United States Congress passed the American Folklife Preservation Act, which established the American Folklife Center in the Library of Congress. The 1976 Act defined folklife as follows, and this definition could equally apply to Australian folklife:

> The term 'American folklife' means the traditional expressive culture shared within the various groups in the United States: familial, ethnic, occupational, religious, regional; expressive culture includes a wide range of creative and symbolic forms such as custom, belief, technical skill, language, literature, art, architecture, music, play, dance, drama, ritual, pageantry, handicraft; these expressions are mainly learned orally, by imitation, or in performance, and are generally maintained without benefit of formal instruction or institutional direction.

It is a great pity that Australia has no national body similar to the American Folklife Center to take overall responsibility for the protection and preservation of Australian folklore and folklife; the National Library of Australia does do a great deal in this regard.

There have been many Australian attempts to define both 'folklore' and 'folklife'. In Australia, one of the earliest was Hugh Anderson's *Colonial Ballads* (1955), which discussed several contentious aspects of the definition of folksong, including oral transmission, communal origin, authorship, and comparisons with British folk song and American frontier songs. In 1987, the report of the Committee of Inquiry into Folklife in Australia drew on the 1976 American Folklife Preservation Act and a 1985 definition by UNESCO, as well as on the many public submissions to the Inquiry:

> *Folklife is tradition-based and/or contemporary expressive culture repeated and shared within a community, and accepted by it as an adequate reflection of its cultural and social identity. It embraces a wide range of creative and symbolic forms such as custom, belief, mythology, legend, ritual, pageantry, language, literature, technical skill, play, music, dance, song, drama, narrative, architecture, craft. Its expressions are mainly learned orally, by imitation or in performance, and are generally maintained without benefit of formal instruction or institutional direction.*

For some years UNESCO has been encouraging its signatory nations, including Australia, to act on behalf of their national folk culture. The 1989 UNESCO Recommendation on the Safeguarding of Traditional Culture and Folklore urged that member states take action with regard to 'identification, protection, and conservation, preservation and dissemination' of folklore, and also to international relations. In 1999 UNESCO conducted an international review of the 1989 Recommendation, and produced an Action Plan for the Safeguarding and Revitalisation of Intangible Cultural Heritage. Among the plan's many features, it recommended that UNESCO should declare a World Day for Safeguarding Traditional Culture and Folklore.

Some countries such as Japan and South Korea have massive programs to ensure that their traditional folk culture survives. In both countries, traditional performers in music, dance and ritual, or craft workers with a high degree of skill, may be called 'Living National Treasures'. They are given great honour, recognition and financial rewards and, in return, are required to pass on their skills to a younger generation. In South Korea, this is taken with such seriousness that young men apprenticed to a Living National Treasure may be exempted from military service.

Does official recognition such as that given by the American Folklife Center or the Japanese or Korean Living Treasures systems mean that officialdom is 'taking over' folk culture, and therefore destroying its unofficial, truly folk nature? It is true that folklore develops without assistance, but it cannot always survive without help. In modern societies dominated by commercial media and business, it is hard for traditional singers (for example) to pass on their songs, or for traditional boat-builders to pass on their skills, without some assistance. The American Folklife Center regularly honours traditional musicians by sponsoring concerts on the steps of the Library of Congress, and the National Library of Australia has presented traditional music in its entrance foyer on a number of occasions. UNESCO, in its 1989 Recommendation, began its list of actions needed to safeguard traditional culture and folklore with 'identification', meaning that it is necessary to start by identifying what folklore is. That is the aim of this book.

As well as the terms 'folklore' and 'folklife', there is another useful term which was introduced into folk culture studies by the American folklorist Richard Dorson. This is the term 'fakelore', which refers to a whole range of crafts, performances and customs which may borrow some traditional elements, but which are truly 'fake'. A great deal of what is often called folk art falls into this category, featuring quaint or cute designs, often highly coloured, and painted onto wooden household objects of varying degrees of usefulness. Some so-called 'folkloric' concerts or performances are also fakelore, since they feature highly stylised or simplified dances and songs. They do not tell whose folklore this is, nor where it came from, nor what its meaning and significance were in its original setting.

Despite these examples of fakelore, not all 'invented traditions' can be dismissed. Some widely accepted traditions with known or dubious origins, such as Scottish tartans or some English folk tales and nursery rhymes, have passed into folklore. The key process is acceptance by a community. If 'the folk' accept and continue to practise such traditions, they become folklore. *See also The Documentation of Australian Folklore, Folk Festivals, Folklore, Folklorism, Folk Revival*

CHRONICLE

The Documentation of Australian Folklore

T he earliest known attempt to document what we now call folklore in Australia was made by James Hardy Vaux. He was an English-born convict who 'during his solitary hours of cessation from hard labour' in prison in Newcastle, New South Wales, in the early years of the nineteenth century, wrote his memoirs, and included a 'Vocabulary of the Flash Language'. The 'Vocabulary' was a dictionary of the slang (or folk speech) used by his fellow convicts, and was published in the second volume of his Memoirs in 1819. Many of the words in Vaux's 'Vocabulary' are still used today, in all walks of life: for example, *bash, bolt, dollop, fence, frisk, grub, racket* and *sting*.

Although a number of publications claiming to be 'folklore' appeared in Australia during the late nineteenth and early twentieth century, these were what would today be considered anthropological or pseudo-anthropological collections of various aspects of indigenous culture, especially myths and legends. Some examples include the Rev. George Taplin's *The Folklore, Manners, Customs and Languages of the South Australian Aborigines* (1879), Katharine Langloh Parker's *Australian Legendary Tales* (1896), and the still controversial works of Daisy Bates, among many others. While indigenous cultures have extensive folklore, these early efforts treated all aspects of those cultures as unofficial and informal, implicitly reducing them to the status of the European notion of 'superstition'. Although some of these collections have provided important documentation of aspects of indigenous belief and practice, they are generally considered today to be seriously partial, biased and ultimately poor reflections of the depth and complexity of indigenous cultures.

Beginning with A. B. Paterson's *The Old Bush Songs: Composed and sung in the Bushranging, Digging, and Overlanding Days* (1905), compiled mainly in the 1890s, the anthologisation and collection of settler lore, mainly the bush ballad, began in earnest. Banjo Paterson's compilation includes well-known Australian folk songs such as 'The Old Bullock Dray', 'The Old Bark Hut', 'Flash Jack from Gundagai', 'The Wild Colonial Boy' and 'The Dying Stockman'. It is worth noting that at the time *The Old Bush Songs* was published, Banjo Paterson was at the height of his fame in Australia, and the collection of his own poems entitled *The Man from Snowy River* had been a best-seller when published by Angus Robertson in 1895. Paterson, himself a journalist and writer, was one of the earliest members of those professions to make a contribution to the collection of Australian folklore. He was followed by numerous writers of a later generation, including Bill Wannan, Bill Beatty, Alan Marshall, Nancy Keesing, Bill Hornadge, Frank Hardy, Taffy Davies, John Lahey and others, with an interest in one or more aspects of folklore.

No attempt was made in the early, or even many later, compilations of folklore to examine or speculate on the cultural significance of the material. It was generally presented as an interesting echo of what was usually thought to be a golden age of pioneering, gold digging, overlanding and shearing, what would today be described as 'nostalgia'. Nor was very much attention given to the bearers of these traditions, the folk.

The English itinerant worker and later folklorist and performer A. L. Lloyd made the next substantial documentation of Australian folk song, in the 1920s and 1930s. Lloyd came to Australia at the age of fifteen, and worked as a station hand in New South Wales, Queensland and Victoria for approximately nine years. During that time he learned some hundreds of old bush songs from drovers, shearers and other work-mates. Lloyd noted down the words of these songs and sang them in a style he had learnt from his fellow bush workers. Unfortunately, these notebooks appear to be lost. But in 1957 Wattle Recordings (Peter Hamilton and Edgar Waters) produced an annotated recording of Lloyd singing songs he had collected, called *The Banks of the Condamine and Other Bush Songs*. The recording includes songs such as 'Flash Jack from Gundagai', 'The Overlander' and 'Bold Jack Donahue'.

Between 1932 and 1947 Alexander Vennard published *The Bowyang Reciters*, booklets of bush recitations and ballads, under the pseudonym of 'Bill Bowyang'. A number of these 'Reciters' are held in the National Library of Australia, which is Australia's principal institution concerned with the documentation of Australian folklore. Recitation was a popular pastime in many walks of Australian life until the onset of radio (wireless), and it is interesting to note that many of the booklets were sold door to door by returned servicemen – presumably those unemployed in the economic depression of the 1930s. Vennard's collections of recitations included dramatic ballads such as 'Starlight's Last Stand', items which were also songs such as 'The Drover's Dream' and 'The Bank of the Reedy Lagoon', as well as comic numbers.

Important collectors of folk ballads and songs in the 1940s were Will Lawson and Dr Percy Jones. Percy Jones was a musician and priest whose collected items included 'Click Go the Shears', 'Springtime it Brings on the Shearing', 'Botany Bay' and 'Wild Rover No More'. Percy Jones told this writer that he believed that many Australians lacked interest in these collected songs until the American folksinger Burl Ives sang and recorded them 'when he came out to Australia on his first tour after the war' for a series of hugely popular concerts. The songbook *Burl Ives' Folio of Australian Folk Songs* (1953) contained ten songs collected by Dr Jones, and was of great importance because it was commercially published and achieved widespread sales and circulation. During the 1950s, numerous writers, collectors and enthusiasts including Vance Palmer, continued to seek out and publish Australian folk songs. Other such publications of this decade were produced by Stewart and Keesing, Ron Edwards and Russel Ward.

Generally these people focused more on the lore than the folk who carried it. It was not until the post-World War II period that a rising interest in Australian identity impelled John Meredith (1920–2001) and a number of other collectors to go into the bush with sound recording equipment to collect, document and preserve what were feared to be the fast-fading traditions of the bush and its people. Rather than concentrating only on the texts, tunes and dances, Meredith also interviewed and documented the performers and bearers of the material he collected, an important development in the study of Australian folklore reflected in the sub-title of his and Hugh Anderson's *Folk Songs of Australia* – 'and the men and women who sang them' (1967). Meredith recorded not only folk songs but also dance music, recitations, children's playground chants, customs, oral history and yarns from the 1950s onwards, principally in New South Wales. What is now known as the Meredith Collection at the National Library of Australia includes numerous photographs of musicians and their instruments, as well as more than twenty books and other publications. The National Film and Sound Archive also holds a number of 8 mm films of traditional performers made by John Meredith.

Another of the many significant collections of tapes held in the National Library is the O'Connor Collection, recorded in Victoria and Tasmania by Norm and Pat O'Connor and Maryjean Officer. The National Library and state libraries also hold the work of many other collectors; and museums, universities and other institutions around the country also hold important folklore collections. A National Register of Folklore Collections has been initiated by the Australian Folklore Network to locate and make accessible these holdings.

Meredith's approach, and that of most other collectors of bush lore during this period, was conceived essentially as a rescue mission in which the lives, communal experiences and folkloric expressions of informants were preserved for posterity as a social historical record of Australian life. Time has proved their concerns largely justified.

As well as these collectors of folklore, a number of individuals have made significant contributions to folklore scholarship in Australia, Around the same time as Meredith began his work, the poet John Manifold (1915–1985), also inspired by a nationalistic vision, began collecting bush ballads and tunes. Like Meredith and others, Manifold was concerned to rescue folk material from oblivion, and was also interested in the social and cultural significance of the materials he collected. He published his study of Australian folklore, *Who Wrote the Ballads? Notes on Australian Folksong* in 1964.

Another major figure is Hugh Anderson, who has published prolifically on many aspects of the field, especially folksong and the balladry of convictism, his *Farewell to Judges and Juries: The Broadside Ballad and Convict Transportation to Australia, 1788–1868* (2000) being a major contribution in this area. Like a number of folklorists, Anderson is also known in other fields; he is a social historian and writer. Ron Edwards, also an artist, has collected and published extensively and intensively, his work covering many genres of folklore, including folksong, yarns, crafts, foodways. Edwards' work has also included indigenous material from remote communities. The writer Bill Scott is another noted collector and researcher, having collected and published both rural and urban folklore and pioneered research into Australian urban legends. Warren Fahey has collected throughout Australia and published many collections of folklore as part of his ongoing effort to draw attention to the wealth of Australian traditions.

All this collecting, documentation and theorising went on outside universities and colleges, mostly in small organisations such as the Sydney Bush Music Club, the Victorian Folk Music Club, the Folk Song and Dance Society of Victoria and the Folk Lore Council of Australia. The early collectors, including Maryjean Officer, Joy Durst, Norm O'Connor, Allan Scott, Bill Scott, Ron Edwards, Wendy Lowenstein, Bob Michell and, a little later, Warren Fahey, were enthused by their work and largely self-funded, supporting both their own extensive and intensive fieldwork as well as publications such as those of Ron Edwards, Hugh Anderson, Bill Scott and Brad Tate. Other material was published in the journals and newsletters of the various organisations, such as the Bush Music Club and the Folklore Society of Victoria. In addition, Hugh Anderson's Red Rooster Press published an ongoing series titled 'Studies in Australian Folklore'. By and large universities were not interested in studying folklore, especially Australian folklore. There was even a strong opinion in intellectual circles that Australia had little or no folklore, though writers such as Douglas Stewart, Nancy Keesing and Alan Marshall, together with academics such as Ian Turner, Edgar Waters, June Factor, Barry Andrews and G. A. Wilkes had strong interests in various aspects of the subject. As early as 1947 literary critic Brian Elliott had published *Singing to the Cattle and Other Essays* in which he discussed elements of the bush tradition seriously, and John Manifold published a brief but scholarly essay on the instruments of bush music, *The Violin, the Banjo and the Bones*, in 1957.

In 1958 Russel Ward published the first academic study of aspects of Australian folklore. *The Australian Legend* treated folk songs and ballads as primary evidence for his thesis on the origins and development of the Australian 'character'. The oral and, to some extent, the musical traditions of the bush (though few other forms of lore) were now able to be treated as important 'documents', and there was a growth of interest by critics in the bush ballad as literature. It was occasionally possible to study such matters in some literary and history courses at universities and, later, Colleges of Advanced Education, but it was not possible to study folklore as a discipline in the way that you could in many other countries of the world.

Interest in folklore – mainly in its bush music, yarn-spinning and recitative forms – continued through the 1960s folk revival, and the collection of bush music and dance traditions went on, as it does today, through the work of a small but dedicated group of collectors, sometimes funded by the National Library of Australia, by Screensound Australia (formerly the National Film and Sound Archive), and occasionally by other cultural institutions, such as the Australian Institute for Aboriginal and Torres Strait Islander Studies (AIATSIS). Hugh Anderson continues to collect, research and publish many important works on Australian folklore. Much of the work of this group is focused in the Australian Folklore Society which, mainly under the aegis of Ron Edwards, publishes a journal.

Researchers from other parts of the world have also been interested in aspects of Australian folklore. In 1972 the American folklorist John Greenway published *The Last Frontier: A Study of Cultural Imperatives in the Last Frontiers of America and Australia*, a work based on his earlier fieldwork in this country. In the 1950s Dorothy Howard visited Australia on a Fulbright Scholarship and conducted fieldwork on children's folklore, inspiring a number of local scholars to work in this field. Building on her work, academics such as June Factor and Gwenda Beed Davey established the Australian Children's Folklore Collection in 1979 at the Institute of Early Childhood Development, as well as the *Australian Children's Folklore Newsletter* (since 1997 *Play and Folklore*) in 1981. Work in this area is one in which Australia has a strong record, producing, among other outcomes, Ian Turner's *Cinderella Dressed in Yella: Australian Children's Play-Rhymes* (1969, rev. ed. 1978 by Turner, Factor and Lowenstein), along with a good number of research projects relating to children's folklore by the scholars already mentioned and Judy McKinty, Heather Russell, Kathryn Marsh and others. More recently June Factor published a work on the folk speech of Australian children, *Kidspeak* (2000).

American interest in Australian folklore continued with the arrival of John Marshall in the early 1980s, and the eminent scholar and collector Kenneth Goldstein, who made a number of field excursions in Australia in the 1980s and early 1990s. Folklorists from Canada, Ireland and

China have visited Australia under the auspices of the National Library of Australia Harold White Fellowship scheme and some universities. A number of local and North America-trained scholars, mostly anthropologists, have also been active in musicological fieldwork, especially concentrating on indigenous traditions. Many of these have links with the journal *Perfect Beat*, emanating from Macquarie University.

From the 1970s there have been increasing efforts to document the traditions of cultural and language groups other than Anglo-Celtic. These efforts continue, with Noris Iannou's *Barossa Journeys: Into a Valley of Tradition* (1997) being an example of a regional study of the traditions of a well-defined ethnic group. There has also been considerable study of indigenous tradition undertaken (increasingly) by indigenous people themselves rather than by anthropologists from other cultural groups, as had been the case in the past. Work was also carried out on Maltese, German and Greek traditions by Barry York, Ian Harmstdorf and the Greek Studies Department of Melbourne University, respectively.

Collectors and performers of bush and old-time music have developed a network of publications and productions, many on an ongoing basis, including the energetic Wongawilli Colonial Dance Club and its offshoots, and other such publications. These have been extended in recent years through utilisation of the Internet, which has also generated such publications as *Simply Australia* and many other websites related to the collection of and research into Australian folk musical traditions.

Beginning in 1984, a number of conferences have been held in various states. The Australian Folklore Society was formed in 1979 to represent the views of the collectors of folklore, and the Australian Folklore Association was founded in 1988 to promote the study of Australian folklore and, subsequently, to publish the scholarly journal *Australian Folklore*, founded by Graham Seal and Dave Hults in the Western Australian Folklore Archive at Curtin University of Technology in 1987. Since 1992, *Australian Folklore* has been edited by John Ryan at the University of New England.

In 1985 the Australian government commissioned a three-member Committee of Inquiry into Folklife in Australia made up of Hugh Anderson, Gwenda Davey and Keith McKenry. The Committee carried out extensive investigations into the nature and status of folk culture in Australia, and received 245 written submissions from members of the public. The Committee published its report in 1987 under the title

Folklife: Our Living Heritage, and in its chapter on 'The Nature and Diversity of our Folklife' identified Oral Folklore, Music and Dance, Customs, Pastimes and Beliefs, Occupational Folklore, Children's Folklore and Making Things (folk crafts and vernacular buildings). The Committee made 51 recommendations, about matters including training in endangered crafts and trades, a national grants scheme, archival programs and the establishment of an Australian Folklife Centre to protect Australia's folkloric heritage. To date, none of the Committee's recommendations has been carried out.

June Factor's study of children's folklore, *Captain Cook Chased a Chook* was published in 1988, and in 1989 Graham Seal's *The Hidden Culture: Folklore in Australian Society* pointed to the many forms of folklore throughout Australian society, extending the work done until then on bush music, dance and verse traditions and providing an overall interpretative framework. *The Oxford Companion to Australian Folklore* (1993), edited by Gwenda Beed Davey and Graham Seal, provided a wide-ranging survey of the folklore of the Australian community, both historical and contemporary, and of the various efforts made to record, preserve, study and disseminate those traditions.

As well as these and other books, a considerable body of folklore scholarship has also been published in journals such as *Meanjin*, *Overland*, the *Journal of Australian Studies and Australian Tradition*, established and edited for many years by folklorist and oral historian Wendy Lowenstein. Much other collected material and research has also been published in other places, including the internal newsletters and other publications of the various folklore organisations by, in addition to those already mentioned, collectors and scholars such as Shirley Andrews, Stan Arthur, Chris Buch, Bob Michell, Brian Crawford, Dave DeHugard, Brian Dunnett, Barbara Gibbons, Hazel Hall, Alex Hood, Percy Jones, Don Laycock, A.L. Lloyd, Arthur Lumsden, John Manifold, John Marshall, Barry McDonald, Steve Gadd, Ken McGoldrick, Roger Montgomery, Peter Parkhill, Lloyd Robson, Mark Rummery, Cathy Rummery, Bob Rummery, Jill Stubington, Ian Turner, Edgar Waters, Kel Watkins, Jeff Way, Geoff Wills and Alexander Vennard ('Bill Bowyang'), Bill Beatty, Bill Wannan, Thérése Radic, Patsy Adam Smith, Graeme Smith, Keith McKenry, Chris Woodland, Brad Tate, Bob Rummery, Jeff Corfield, Kel Watkins, Chris Sullivan, Mark Gregory, Jeff Willis, Alan Musgrove, Barry McDonald, Dave De Santi, Peter Ellis, Kevin Bradley and Rob Willis – a long but by no means comprehensive list.

It is important to note that most of this work has been, and continues to be, done by individuals and groups within the community rather than by institutions. It is a characteristic of Australian folklore that the great bulk of fieldwork, especially that carried out in rural and regional areas, has not been undertaken by universities or government cultural bodies. There have been some exceptions, including the work of academic anthropologists such as Jeremy Beckett, Kingsley Palmer and Karl Neuenfeldt, who have collected folklore, and a number of individuals already mentioned who have been involved in folklore studies at a number of universities. Otherwise it has been left to private enthusiasts to form their own organisations, such as those mentioned above and the more recent Victorian Folklife Association, to further collecting, preservation and related activities. Other organisations connected with the folk revival, notably the various state and territory Folk Federations, have generally been oriented more towards the performance aspects of folklore, though these did maintain the Australian Folk Trust from its establishment in 1977 to its demise in 1995. The Trust was committed to folklore collection and research, a role since carried on by the Folk Alliance Australia. In 2001 the Australian Folklore Network (AFN) was formed to promote communication between the various organisations and individuals involved in the diverse folklore field.

Despite the development of this considerable body of fieldwork and scholarship over the last fifty years, other than the Graduate Diploma in Australian Folklife established in the National Centre for Australian Studies, Monash University, by Gwenda Beed Davey in the late 1990s and its later continuation as a distance course at Curtin University of Technology from 2000, it is still not possible to take a comprehensive course of study in Australian folklore and folklife. A distance education unit at the University of New England has been taught by John Ryan for some years, as have occasional units of study offered at various institutions by staff with an interest in the field, including study of Greek folklore at Melbourne and La Trobe universities.

Weaving through these collecting and scholarly activities since the 1960s has been the development of folk festivals. This is a significant social movement in itself that deserves more discussion than can be given here. Part of the significance of the folk festivals, and the broader 'folk revival' of which they are a part, are the opportunities they have provided for the performance, display, learning and general sharing of folk traditions.

While these traditions are often thereby necessarily divorced from their environing contexts, they would not otherwise be brought to the attention of the substantial numbers of Australians who attend. Such events provide valuable opportunities for cross-cultural sharing and increased intercultural understanding. The revival of such art and craft traditions also clearly gives those involved in these activities constructive purpose and considerable pleasure.

It emerges from this account that a very great deal of the collection and study of Australian folklore has been — and continues to be — accomplished outside formal educational and cultural conservation facilities. As of 2003, Australia remains one of the few countries in the world without a formal course of undergraduate study in its own folk traditions. Australia's future folklorists may well need to learn how to study the traditions of their own communities in another country. *See also Old Bush Songs, Australian Folklore Association, Australian Folklore Society, Victorian Folklife Association, Folk Lore Society of Victoria, Victorian Folk Dance and Song Society, Folk Federations, Folk Festivals, Folk Revival, BIBLIOGRAPHY.*

A TO Z

A

ABBREVIATIONS
The not unique but marked tendency in Australian folk speech to shorten words and add an 'ie' or 'o' suffix, as in 'rellie' (a relative), 'pressie' (a present), 'Paddo' (Paddington, NSW), 'Rotto' (Rottnest Island, WA), 'Robbo' (Robert) and so on. Often referred to as the 'affectionate diminutive'. Long non-Anglo names, especially those of public figures, are frequently shortened, such as the Victorian politician Pandazopoulos ('Panda') and the footballer Dipierdomenico ('Dipper' – or 'The Dipper'). *See also Folk Speech*

ABORIGINAL FOLKLORE *See Indigenous Folklore*

'ACROSS THE WESTERN PLAINS'
Also titled 'The Jolly, Jolly Grog', a popular nineteenth century bush folk song on the savage after-effects of binge drinking, including the hangover ('I'm sick in the head and I haven't been to bed') and the loss of the singer's 'plunder' in 'a shanty made of tin'. The afflicted one is eventually forced to return to 'some hard yakka'. Probably derived from a sea song usually known as 'Across the Western Ocean'. *See also Bush, The; Bush Ballad; Grog; Pastoral Industry Folklore*

AEROPLANE JELLY

Some radio and television advertising jingles have provided so much public enjoyment that they have passed into folklore, and in true folkloric tradition, continue to be passed on from generation to generation by word of mouth, or what folklorists call oral transmission. 'Aeroplane Jelly' is one of the most notable of these commercials, and its words (as recalled by this author) are as follows:

I like Aeroplane Jelly,
Aeroplane Jelly for me.
I like it for dinner,
I like it for tea,
A little each day
Is a good recipe.
The quality's high
As the name will imply
You think that you're flying
Right up to the sky.
I like Aeroplane Jelly,
Aeroplane Jelly for me.

It is hard to know whether the catchy tune or the flying food concept was more responsible for the popularity of this old radio commercial, which first appeared in Australia in 1930, written by one of the partners in the manufacture of Aeroplane Jelly, Albert Francis Lenertz. However, its durability is legendary. 'Aeroplane Jelly' may still be sung by Australians in a variety of places and contexts, from the nursery to the pub to the football changing room. After some years of absence, Aeroplane Jelly is now back on the supermarket shelves. Another jingle to achieve folkloric status is the advertisement for Flick pest control:

How can you be sure
There are no white ants in the floor?
Borers in the door
Silverfish galore?
Get a Flick man,
That's your answer,
Give 'em one Flick,
And they're gone.

A similar early radio singing commercial which has passed into folk tradition is 'We're happy little Vegemites' (*see Vegemite*). *See also Folk Humour; Foodways*

AGRICULTURAL SHOWS

Along with picnic race days and local dances, these were often the earliest public social events observed in country areas after European settlement of Australia. Derived from British agricultural societies' show days, hiring fairs and an amalgam of other rural fetes and festivals, agricultural shows quickly became an established aspect of the Australian calendar, and in some capital cities have attained the prefix 'Royal'.

Smaller 'shows' are held at various times throughout the year in suburbs and country towns, according to the cycles and dictates of the seasons, of travelling 'show folk', and local custom. Organised and prepared for long before they begin, these events involve many folkloric elements, including exhibitions of rural, occupational and domestic skills, arts, crafts and sideshows, and the general conviviality of a festival gathering. *See also Bush, The; Customs; Field Days*

AH FOO, JIMMY

Said to have been a Chinese publican at the Longreach Hotel in Queensland in the 1880s, 'Jimmy' features in a number of yarns that depict him as a clever, cheerful type who cleverly overcharges the shearers for their drinks and outwits their attempts to ban Chinese cooks from the hotel during the anti-Chinese shearers' strike. In one such yarn Jimmy is approached by shearers and asked to sack his Chinese cook. When the deputation returns to see if their suggestion has been acted on, Jimmy tells them that he has sacked the cook and from now on will do all the cooking himself. *See also Folk Humour; Yarns*

'ALBURY RAM, THE'

This folk song, also known as 'The Ram of Dalby', is an Australian version of a British song usually known as 'The Derby Ram'. It tells a tall story of 'the finest sheep that ever was fed on hay': its wool was said to be so thick it grew up to the sky and a man who climbed on top of it in September 'never came down 'til June'. The song usually ends with a verse strongly suggesting that the teller of these tales is 'a lying son-of-a-bitch'. 'The Derby Ram' was also performed in a play titled *Van Diemen's*

Land, first performed in London in 1830. *See also Bush Ballad; Folk Songs; Pastoral Industry Folklore*

ALKIMOS GHOSTS

Wrecked about ten kilometres north of Mindarie Keys in Western Australia in 1963, the *Alkimos* boasts a number of ghostly and unlucky traditions. Although there was no loss of life during the grounding of the ship, she had been plagued by bad luck and bad navigation ever since her launching in World War II. West Australian folklore has it that the wreck continues to be haunted by a ghost known as 'Henry'. Just who Henry may have been in life and why he lingers does not seem to be known. People have reported hearing groans from one of the cabins or a dog barking in the engine room, seeing lights aboard the ship and even being held down by a ghostly presence. In keeping with such stories, the *Alkimos* is widely believed to be an evil object, bringing bad luck to those who go aboard it or even near it. *See also Ghost Lore*

ANNUAL HIGHLAND GATHERING

Since New Year's Day of 1869 the Scots of New South Wales have held annual highland games on 1 January, at first in Redfern and now in Penrith (both in New South Wales). Known as the Annual Highland Gathering, the games trace their descent to a tradition established in Scotland in the eleventh century. Today the games include traditional sports and competitive events such as 'Tossing the Caber' and 'Tug-o-War', as well as performances by pipers and dancers, the consumption of Scottish foods, and exhibitions of handcrafts. *See also Customs; Folk Sports; Maclean Highland Gathering*

'ANOTHER FALL OF RAIN'

A late nineteenth to early twentieth century bush ballad, usually sung to the tune of 'The Little Log Cabin in the Lane', which celebrates the difficulties of the shearers' life. After a hard season in which 'some had got the century [i.e. one hundred sheep shorn in a day] that never saw it before', now 'all hands are waiting for the rain', which means that they will be temporarily laid off with pay. Thought to be based on a poem by John Neilson, father of the noted lyric poet John Shaw Neilson (1872–1942). *See also Bush, The; Bush Ballad; Folk Songs; Pastoral Industry Folklore; Shearers*

ANTS

Widely believed to be predictors of weather. In some areas their upward movement is considered a sign of rain, in others their downward motion. There are many variations in weatherlore on the basic theme, with various types and colours of ant said to signal changes. *See also Folk Belief, Weatherlore*

ANZAC

Acronym of Australian and New Zealand Army Corps. First came into use in World War I after Australian and New Zealand troops landed at Gallipoli on 25 April 1915. The term 'Anzacs' is nearly synonymous with the more general 'diggers', though the Anzac tradition is more of an institution than a folk custom, as evidenced by the fact that use of the word 'ANZAC' itself is regulated by federal government legislation. The term is also used in various folkloric forms including 'Anzac biscuits' or, latterly, 'cookies', an oatmeal-based biscuit dating from World War I, and 'Anzac Cottage' or 'Anzac House' for commemorative buildings erected in various parts of Australia. *See also Anzac Biscuits; Anzac Day; Digger; Gallipoli*

ANZAC BISCUITS

The original army biscuit, also known as an Anzac wafer or tile, was developed by Arnott's Biscuits Limited during World War I, essentially as a long-lasting bread substitute for troops on active service. Many soldiers commented unfavourably on their hardness, some preferring to grind them up for porridge (add water and sugar, cook, serve with generous dollop of jam). Meanwhile, the wives, mothers and girlfriends of Australian soldiers, concerned about the nutritional value of army rations, sent food parcels to the fighting men. Due to the long transport times by sea, any such foodstuffs had to remain edible for at least two months unrefrigerated. Australian women came up with a biscuit based on a Scottish recipe using rolled oats and similar ingredients that did not readily spoil. At first called Soldiers' Biscuits, they were renamed Anzac Biscuits after the landing on Gallipoli. Throughout the war, women's groups such as the CWA (Country Women's Association), church groups and schools volunteered much time to making Anzac biscuits and packing them in used, airtight tins, such as Billy Tea tins, to keep them crisp while in transit. During World War II, with refrigeration, the biscuits were to some extent replaced in food parcels by other foodstuffs such as fruit cake. However, homemade Anzac biscuits are still baked today, and around Anzac Day are sometimes made and sold by charitable organisations to raise funds for war veterans. *See also* ANZAC; *Anzac Day*

ANZAC DAY

Annual national public holiday on 25 April, commemorating the landing of Australian and New Zealand troops at Gallipoli in 1915. While the day is a formal commemoration of nationhood and military sacrifice, as well as a reunion of old comrades, it has also generated many folkloric activities, including reunions and gambling at 'two-up'. *See also* ANZAC; *Digger; Gallipoli; Two-Up*

APRIL FOOL'S DAY

Celebrated on 1 April, this is a venerable European custom that has persisted in Australia. A successful prank played before midday makes the victim (or victims) an 'April fool'. Sgt-Major T. Murphy of the 1st Battalion AIF recorded in his diary in 1916 that the buglers played an April Fool's Day joke (unfortunately not specified) on the officers aboard his troopship (A.G. Stephens, 1917 p. 329). In recent years the mass media have been the main pranksters in this country, as the custom shows signs of decline in the wider community. *See also Customs; Folk Humour*

AUSTRALIA DAY

An official holiday held on 26 January and usually observed with leisure time and family-oriented activities. Traditionally it marks the end of the summer holiday period. This has become a somewhat controversial date in more recent times: 26 January is the date when Captain Arthur Phillip landed in Sydney Cove and took possession of the east coast of Australia for the British Crown, it is known to many Aboriginal people as 'Invasion Day'.

AUSTRALIAN CHILDREN'S FOLKLORE COLLECTION

This is possibly the world's largest collection of playground games, rhymes, chants, counting-out routines, insults, superstitions and jokes. Housed in the Melbourne Museum, the ACFC was established by June Factor and Gwenda Davey in 1979 at the Institute of Early Childhood Development (now part of the University of Melbourne). The archive has more than 10,000 card files (many now computerised) and also includes photographs, audio and video tapes, toys (mostly home-made), research reports and published papers, adult recollections of childhood play, and the results of a major research project in adult Aboriginal play recollections. A newsletter, *Play and Folklore*, has been published twice a year since the collection's inception.

A highlight of the ACFC is the Dorothy Howard Collection. Dr Howard, a pioneer in the intensive study of Australian playground games, travelled widely in Australia as an American Fulbright Scholar in 1954–1955, during which period she documented her researches with detailed notes and photographs. She gave her entire body of Australian work to the ACFC in the late 1970s and early 1980s. Another distinct collection within the ACFC is the Debney Meadows project carried out by Heather Russell in 1984, and published as *Play and Friendships in a Multicultural Playground*. This project includes fifty interviews with children from different cultural backgrounds talking about their friendship networks and play activities.

As well as children's own playlore, or the folklore *of* children, the Australian Children's Folklore Collection also holds a considerable body of folklore *for* and *about* children, notably field recordings carried out for the Multicultural Cassette Series, published in 1979. These recordings include songs, stories, baby games, lullabies and rhymes told to children by adults in Arabic, English, Greek, Italian, Macedonian, Serbian and Croatian, Spanish and Turkish, among other languages spoken in Australia. In addition to transcriptions of 'old wives' tales' about birth and pregnancy, there is a video compilation of folklore for children in English, Turkish and Vietnamese. The ACFC also includes material collected during projects undertaken at the Children's Museum of Victoria and the Royal Children's Hospital (Melbourne) and during regional studies in Moe (Victoria) and Burnie (Tasmania). *See also Children's Folklore*

AUSTRALIAN FOLKLORE
A journal of scholarly folklore studies, book reviews and notes, *Australian Folklore* was established by the Western Australian Folklore Archive in 1987. Since 1992 it has been published annually by the Australian Folklore Association. *See also Australian Folklore Association; Western Australian Folklore Archive*

AUSTRALIAN FOLKLORE

The term 'Australian folklore' is frequently used to refer to English-language folk traditions, most of which are derived from successive generations of British migrants. However, there are large bodies of folklore belonging to other languages and cultures in Australia. Pre-eminent among these is the folklore of the indigenous peoples (as separate from their spiritual beliefs and practices), both in their original languages and, since European settlement, increasingly in Aboriginal English. As well, there has been interaction between settler and Aboriginal traditions, as in the case of beliefs about the bunyip (*see Bunyip*), and in language, food, medicine and other areas. Migrants from non-British countries have also brought many of their festivals, customs and traditions with them, such as the popular Greek *rebetika* music, to name one. These traditions are maintained within the language and culture group (often more so than in the originating country), and have also sometimes interacted with the established traditions of earlier settlers, especially in relation to foodways, language and some of the more public celebrations, such as patron saints' processions and 'Chinese New Year'. It is reasonable to suppose that this process will increase over time. It must be noted, however, that such interaction may not always be positive: an example is the question in some communities over the appropriateness of British-derived folk customs such as Christmas carolling, and the focus of Australia's calendar, both official and folk, on the Christian calendar. *See also INTRODUCTION, Chinese Folklore in Australia, German Influences on Australian Folklore, Greek Folklore in Australia, Indigenous Folklore, Irish Influences on Australian Folklore, Italian Folklore in Australia, Rebetika*

AUSTRALIAN FOLKLORE ASSOCIATION, THE (INCORPORATED)

Formed in 1988 to promote the collection, preservation and study of folklore in Australia; to foster discussion and the dissemination of related information, and to promote understanding and appreciation of the important social and cultural roles of folklore. The association organises conferences and publishes the journal *Australian Folklore*. *See also Australian Folklore*

AUSTRALIAN FOLKLORE NETWORK (AFN)

A coalition of individual collectors, performers, academics and organisations with an interest in Australian folklore. The AFN, coordinated through the Australian Folklore Research Unit at Curtin University of Technology, maintains a National Register of Folklore Collections, coordinates research and fieldwork projects and holds an annual forum at the National Folk Festival in Canberra. The network publishes an e-newsletter every few months that informs its members of relevant events, projects and publications throughout Australia and internationally. The aims of the network and its affiliates are to promote folklore studies more broadly in education and through the community, and to pursue the establishment of a national folklore centre. *See also* CHRONICLE, *Folk Revival*

AUSTRALIAN FOLKLORE RESEARCH UNIT

The Australian Folklore Research Unit (AFRU) was established at Curtin University of Technology in March 2002. The unit initiates, facilitates and conducts research, fieldwork, publications, teaching and events designed to further the study of Australian folklore and folklife. The unit developed from folklore activities undertaken at Curtin University of Technology since the 1980s, including the development of Australia's only state folklore collection, the Western Australian Folklore Archive; the teaching of folklore units and research and publication in Australian and international folklore studies, including the foundation of the journal *Australian Folklore* in 1987 and the establishment of Black Swan Press in 1992 to publish research in folklore and related fields. AFRU aims to extend the work done so far and has established the Australian Folklore Network to facilitate communication and interaction between the many groups and individuals involved in the collection, preservation, study and dissemination of Australian folklore in all its many varieties. The unit also maintains the online resource base 'Folklore Australia'.

AUSTRALIAN FOLKLORE SOCIETY, THE

Established in 1979 to represent the views of collectors of Australian folklore, the Society began publishing its journal in 1984 under the editorship of Ron Edwards, of Kuranda, Queensland. *See also Folk Revival*

AUSTRALIAN INSTITUTE OF ABORIGINAL AND TORRES STRAIT ISLANDER STUDIES (AIATSIS)

Established by Act of Parliament in 1964 to increase specialist knowledge and understanding of indigenous societies. Situated in

Canberra, this scholarly government body funds and conducts fieldwork and research, publications and productions and holds the country's most extensive collection of indigenous cultural and historical materials. *See also Indigenous Folklore*

'AUSTRALIA'S ON THE WALLABY'

Widely sung bush song about itinerant bush life and the difficulty of making a living by occasional work, colloquially referred to as being 'on the wallaby', or 'on the wallaby track'. The verses are full of iconic Australian allusions, as is the chorus:

> *Australia's on the wallaby*
> *Just listen to the cooee;*
> *The kangaroo he rolls his swag*
> *And the emu shoulders bluey [a swag]*
> *The boomerangs are whizzing round*
> *The dingo scratches gravel,*
> *The possum, bear and bandicoot*
> *Are all upon the travel.*

Probably originating from the 1890s, this lyric may have been the basis for Henry Lawson's well-known poem 'Freedom on the Wallaby', which is often sung to the same tune and contains the often-quoted lines:

> *They needn't say the fault is ours*
> *If blood should stain the wattle.*

See also Bush Ballad; Folklore of Struggle; Folk Song; Labor Lore; Lawson, Henry, Work Lore

AUTOGRAPH BOOKS

While often thought of as a Victorian custom, keeping autograph books is still surprisingly common among girls and young women. Some examples of autograph book entries show both traditional and contemporary characteristics, together with the element of a sometimes mildly saucy flavour, as in this example from 1921:

> *Cats like mice,*
> *Mice like cheese,*

Lads like lassies and
Lassies like a squeeze.

Variations on the rhyme beginning 'Roses are red/Violets are blue...' are also popular. *See also Children's Folklore; Folk Humour*

B

BACK YARD

The quarter-acre block with a free-standing house is often described as the 'Great Australian Dream' in terms of the Australian lifestyle, and although apartment living is growing in popularity in major cities, the suburban house on its own block of land, complete with 'back yard', is still the principal form of housing. Unlike many American suburban residences without fences, the Australian housing block is almost always fenced, particularly the back yard. This practice gives householders options for individual forms of expression ranging from collections of junk to formal gardens, and for activities such as barbecues, games, keeping pets and growing vegetables.

These opportunities for individuality have made the Australian back yard a cherished icon, celebrated in films such as *The Castle* and songs such as 'I made a hundred in the backyard with Mum', which refers to cricket, one of Australia's national sports. The Australian back yard is likely to contain some kind of shed, itself another icon. The shed is usually male territory, and may range from a rough spider-infested construction used for keeping a few garden tools, particularly the lawn-mower, to an elaborate workshop for hobbies such as woodworking. It is now less common than in previous generations for back yards or sheds to be used for keeping fowls (known as 'chooks', an old English regional term now regarded by most Australians as their own), although the crowing rooster may still be an occasional source of neighbourhood disputes in the suburbs. Immigrants from Europe can be easily identified in the suburbs through vegetables, grape vines and fruit trees grown in their front yards, an unknown practice among many older Australians, who maintain the front garden for flowers, shrubs and lawns: in other words, 'for show'. A Greek-Australian of this author's acquaintance once described the Australian way of life as 'mowing bloody lawns'. *See also Crafts; Making Do*

BAGMAN'S GAZETTE

Rumour and gossip network among itinerant bush workers. Sometimes said to be an actual publication. *See also Bagman's Union; Bush Telegraph*

BAGMAN'S UNION

Mythical organisation of itinerant workers or swagmen. Sometimes 'swagman's union'. *See also Bagman's Gazette; Swagman*

BANANA-BENDERS

Folk speech, or nickname, for residents of Queensland, probably c. mid-twentieth century. Also Banana-lander, Banana-skin in older usages. *See also Folk Speech, Regional Rivalries*

B&S BALLS

Bachelors' and Spinsters' Balls. Of uncertain origin, though usually said to be an Irish custom, the B&S Ball is an occasion for young, usually unmarried adults to let their hair down with drinking, dancing and courting. More recently, dress has often become a mixture of the formal and the casual, and there is more than a hint of parodying the 'proper' balls of socialites and the wealthy. Previously a regular feature of rural social life, B&S balls have in recent years become more widely known and have also been mounted in cities, largely as a result of commercial interests, especially the alcohol industry. *See also Customs; Weddings; Dance*

'BANKS OF THE CONDAMINE, THE'

Also known as 'The Banks of the Riverine'. In this 1860s folk song a woman pleads with her true love to let her go shearing with him along the Condamine River (Qld). He refuses, saying the work is fit only for men and that ' your delicate constitution is not equal unto mine'. There is also a version in which the man is a horse-breaker. Thought to be based on an earlier British song called 'The Banks of the Nile', itself seemingly derived from an eighteenth-century song known as 'High Germany'. *See also Bush Ballad; Old Bush Songs; Pastoral Industry Folklore*

BARBECUES, BBQ

Usually known colloquially as a 'barbie', the open air grilling (or charring) of sausages, chops and steak is central to modern Australian leisure. The barbecue fireplace itself, which may well be home-made, resonates with the ethos of pioneering and the bush and is well suited to the outdoor lifestyle possible in much of Australia for most of the year. Traditionally, the man of the household does the cooking while the woman prepares side dishes and desserts. The 'barbie' in the modern sense of the practice is not an indigenous Australian custom but one imported in the 1950s from the United States of America, which in turn had borrowed it from South America. Many other cultures have outdoor 'cooking methods and accompanying cuisines, but the 'barbie' persists as an icon of Australianness, and as an occasion for folkloric interaction and expression of many kinds, such as drinking, gossiping and children's games. *See also Customs, Folk Speech, Foodways*

BARCOO DOG

Primarily a noise-making device for herding sheep, the Barcoo dog may also be used as a percussion instrument in bush music. Constructed of fencing wire shaped into a handle with a u-shaped prong between which are strung small metal snippets or bottle lids. When shaken, these make quite a noise. Barcoo dogs – the name is a pun on 'dog' rather than a marker of origin or provenance – may also be made of shanghai- (or ging) shaped sticks of wood. *See also Bush Music; Crafts; Musical Instruments*

BARLEES, BARLEY

Form of children's truce term widespread in Australia, used when a child wishes to temporarily halt a game or activity or concedes defeat. Such terms are also part of the lore of children in other countries, though have been little researched in Australia. *See also Children's Folklore, Folk Speech*

BARLOW, BILLY

Hero of a nineteenth-century emigration ballad who brings a thousand pound inheritance to Australia but finds the local merchants, Aborigines, bushrangers, the drought and other bush calamities too hard to bear. He ends up back in Sydney begging for work. Originally composed by Benjamin Griffin and first performed in 1843, the song is an Australian extension of a character popular in British broadside ballads. There were several local sequels. Versions of the song were also sung in the United States. *See also 'Colonial Experience'; Migration Lore*

BAR MITZVAH, BAT MITZVAH

The *Bar Mitzvah* is an important rite of passage for Jewish males around the age of thirteen, when the boy becomes an adult in terms of the Jewish religion. The occasion may be marked by a ceremony in the synagogue when the boy may present readings and recitations from the

Torah. It may also be marked by a celebratory dinner held by the family. The *Bat Mitzvah*, when girls of twelve or thirteen are similarly held to have reached adulthood within the Jewish religion, has become a prominent celebration only in recent years. The rituals associated with the *Bat Mitzvah* vary between communities, and may be held for individual girls or groups. As with the *Bar Mitzvah*, the *Bat Mitzvah* involves proceedings both within the synagogue and in family celebration. *See also Customs, Religious Lore*

BARRACKING

The Australian version of boisterously supporting one's own sporting team or hero, or (less often today) denigrating the other side. Barracking can be a form of verbal art, wit or abuse, and has been brought to its finest development in football, especially in the popular codes of Australian Rules and Rugby League and, to a lesser extent, in cricket and boxing. Said to derive from the 1870s–80s term to 'poke borak', meaning to verbally abuse by shouting and jeering (though some lexicographers dispute this), barracking is a much-loved Australian sporting custom. The content varies from game to game and supporter to supporter, but a few selected football examples recorded in 1917 give the flavour: 'Yer couldn't pass the sugar before the tea gets cold'; and little man to big man: 'Garn, you're overgrown; you forgot to get yurself pruned this year.' Big man replies: 'Get away, yer little sawed off. Pity yer mother didn't put some superphosphates in yer grub when you was young; mighter made yer grow a bit.'

Since the 1970s, the negative aspect of barracking has been joined by the practice of 'sledging', in which individual players – especially in cricket – are insulted in various ways, sometimes racially, by opposing players and members of the crowd. *See also Customs; Folk Speech; Larrikin; Sports Lore*

BASTARD

A widely used term in Australian folk speech with a subtle range of meanings ranging from the vehemently insulting 'a right bastard' to the affectionately humorous 'old bastard'. *See also Bastard from the Bush, The; Folk Speech*

BASTARD FROM THE BUSH, THE

Earthy folk parody of a poem by Henry Lawson titled 'The Captain of the Push'. The bastard gets the better of a bloodthirsty group, or 'push', of larrikins and so, as in many folk works of this type, demonstrates the superiority of the bush male over the city male. The parody is said to have been penned by Lawson himself and may even have been written before 'The Captain of the Push'. *See also Bastard, Bawdry, Larrikin; Lawson, Henry, Recitation*

BASTARDISATION

Initiation rites which incorporate cruel or degrading elements have come to be known collectively as 'bastardisation'; they appear to occur particularly, though not exclusively, in the military forces. A series of scandals in the year 2000 (and previously) had so concerned the Australian military authorities, and the general public, that early in 2001 every member of the forces was compelled to watch a specially produced videotape outlining the forces' expectations about correct behaviour between its members. Bastardisation occurs in civilian workplaces, boarding schools and other institutions as well as in the military and police, and some incidents have involved injury or even death to victims. It is not unrelated to the victimisation of whistleblowers or to sexual, political or racial harassment of one kind or another, and may be considered a particularly cruel form of bullying which is, needless to say, contrary to Australian law. *See also Customs; Initiation Customs; Work Lore*

BATTLER

Individual who, despite having few material advantages, struggles against overwhelming odds with stoic humour. Probably coming into use c. the 1890s, the battler is portrayed implicitly in much earlier folklore of the bush, in which people battled elements such as fire, flood, drought, poverty, the banks and other authorities, often with little hope of success. In more recent times the concept has become a powerful icon of popular nationalism in the phrase 'the little Aussie battler'.

'Battler' is a term of approval often used by politicians to apply to Australians, whether rural or urban, who are 'doing it hard' and who may be considered in Bernard Shaw's terms as 'the deserving poor'. The opposite of battler is 'bludger', a term of disapproval often used by politicians and opinionated talkback radio commentators ('shock jocks') for the 'undeserving poor' who avoid work at all costs. Both terms may also be used by the general public in a less pontificatory way, a bludger being any person who does not contribute their fair share to the task on hand. 'Bludger', like 'bastard', may be used with affection or even approval in some circumstances, as among friends. See also Bludger; Folk Speech; National Icons

BAWDRY

Crudity, vulgarity and straightforward obscenity are features of all folk traditions. Australian bawdry includes the common stock of English-language song, verse, joke and story of the Rugby football variety, together with our own unique contributions such as 'The Hairy Old Bushman', a recitation of extreme obscenity and racism. Reprographic and electronic forms of folklore such as anonymous faxes and emails also tend towards the bawdy, usually in the form of humorous treatments of ethnic stereotypes, gender relations, homophobia, politics, work, religion and topical issues. While bawdry is usually associated with males, especially in all-male or predominantly male groups, women also have bawdy traditions, some indications of which were provided by Nancy Keesing in her book Lily on the Dustbin: Slang of Australian Women and Their Families (1982). Australian folk speech is often regarded by outside observers, commentators and visitors as especially scatological and crude. See also Bastard from the Bush; The; Folk Humour; Folk Speech; Women's Folklore

BAZAARS

Like fetes and markets, bazaars are a form of folk commerce. They are usually held to raise funds for a worthy cause such as a church, school, hospital or Scouts' organisation, and are usually run by volunteers. Bazaars will typically include stalls selling home-made foods such as cakes and jam, second-hand books, miscellaneous 'white elephants' and discarded household items and ornaments, on the basis that one man's poison is another man's meat. Bazaars may include competitions, lucky dips, raffles and traditional games of skill such as the coconut shy. Today's coconut shy may include politicians' faces instead of coconuts. Organisers of larger events may hire commercial amusements such as inflatable castles or shooting galleries. The charitable or community purposes of bazaars make them different from garage sales, car boot sales or trash and treasure sales, which are usually individual money-raising efforts. *See also Community Fairs; Customs, Markets*

BEACH LORE

Surf, sea, sun and sand are the focus of a great deal of Australian leisure activity. As with other facets of Australian life, these pastimes have their share of folklore. Traditional cures for jellyfish or bluebottle stings are various, ranging from wet sand to vinegar to ammonia or 'blue', a proprietary form of washing bleach. Remedies for sunburn include cold tea. Beach activities, apart from swimming and sunbaking, include folk sports such as cricket, football, volleyball, building sand castles, beachcombing, picnics and many other family pastimes. One folk group that makes extensive use of the beach is surfers or 'surfies', who have their own considerable bodies of folk speech, custom and belief. Although institutionalised, the surf lifesaving operations are based on the folkloric notion of volunteer service to the community. The surf carnival, with its attendant competitive events, remains an icon of Australian life, together with the 'bronzed Aussie' figure of the surf lifesaver himself, in recent years augmented by a greater number of female lifesavers. *See also Customs; Family Folklore; Folk Sports; Hughie; National Icons*

BELL-RINGING

There are two main forms of bell-ringing. The first is church bell-ringing involving the ringing of peals on bells hung in church towers. While this has been a widespread activity in Britain since at least the early seventeenth century, there are very few bells suitably hung in Australia for this custom to be popular. Secular carillons include that in Canberra's Lake Burley Griffin. Perth in Western Australia has a similar structure (known popularly as 'The Cockroach') in which to hang – and play – the bells of London's St Martin's-in-the-Field church, which were transported to Perth for safekeeping during the Blitz.

Handbell-ringing, a European custom of some age, usually involves six players playing a full three octaves on a set of thirty-seven bells. This, again, is not a widespread custom in Australia, though there are some practitioners, including a longstanding group at Brookhampton in Western Australia. The Brookhampton Bellringers were established in 1904 when a set of English-made bells was brought to Brookhampton

Hamlet. As late as 1994 some group members were descendants of the original players. *See also Customs; Folk Music*

BENDIGO EASTER FAIR

An annual custom beginning the Saturday before Easter. Originating as a charity event in 1871, the fair now runs for twelve days of carnival, displays, exhibitions, competitions and associated diversions. The fair culminates in a Gala Procession (the largest of three) that features a 91.5 metre Chinese dragon, *Sun Loong*, the longest in the world and a reflection of the extensive Chinese presence on the Victorian goldfields. The awakening of the dragon on Easter Sunday is a highlight of the celebration. *See also Chinese Folklore in Australia; Customs*

BIG BURRAWONG

The mythical sheep station on which the mythical Crooked Mick worked. According to legend, Burrawong (in some versions Burramugga) is the largest sheep station in the world and lies on the eastern boundary of the mythical Speewah. Everything on Big Burrawong is huge, including the sheep, the waterholes and the shearers, not to mention the yarns. It takes a giant crane to lift the soup pot for the shearers' meals, the table salt is held in a thousand-gallon shaker and the blancmanges are so large that three rouseabouts were smothered to death when one fell on them. *See also Crooked Mick; Pastoral Industry Folklore; Shearers; Speewah; Work Lore, Yarns*

'BILL BOWYANG' *See Bowyangs*

BILL THE BULLOCKY *See 'Nine Miles from Gundagai'*

BILLY

The billy, a usually blackened metal receptacle for cooking, and carrying and brewing tea, is a staple of bush folklore. It appears in numerous folk songs and poems as the essential accoutrement of the swaggie, overlander and any other of the itinerant workers celebrated in song, verse and yarn. There is even a song dedicated to 'My Old Black Billy'. *See also Bush, The; Bush Ballad; Foodways; Swagman*

'BILLYGOAT OVERLAND, THE'

Comic bush song about droving a mob of goats overland, usually sung to the tune of 'The Lincolnshire Poacher'. *See also Folk Humour; Folk Songs*

BINDIEYE, JACKY

Legendary Aboriginal character (also Jacky Bindi-i), usually a stockman, sometimes a station rouseabout, sometimes a layabout, who appears in a number of bush yarns common in the north of Australia. In these stories Jacky's exaggerated stupidity usually has the effect of undercutting the assumed superiority of white authority figures, including the boss, policemen and magistrates.

On one occasion Jacky and the boss need to cross a flooded river but the only boat is on the far bank. The boss tells Jacky to swim across and bring the boat back. Jacky protests, saying that there may be crocodiles in the river. The boss tells him he need not worry as crocodiles never touch blackfellas. Jacky replies that the crocodiles might be colour-blind and that it would better to wait until the flood subsided. On another such occasion Jacky is on a distant part of the property minding a mob of sheep, and dependent on the weekly provisions delivered to him by the boss. One week the boss forgets to bring Jacky's rations. Jacky, not too happy, tells the boss that he has only a bone left from last week's rations and that it will be another week before any more meat comes. The boss laughs and tells him not to worry, saying 'The nearer the bone the sweeter the meat'. When the boss returns the next week the sheep are in a terrible condition as Jacky has kept them where there is no grass to eat. The boss turns on Jacky and angrily asks him what he thinks he is doing. Jacky just laughs and says, 'The nearer the ground, the sweeter the grass.'

Jacky Bindieye's other main activity is stealing sheep, for which he is frequently brought before the courts. At one of his hearings the judge gives Jacky three years in prison and asks him if he had anything to say. 'Yes,' says Jacky angrily. 'You're bloody free with other people's time.' In another court appearance, this time for being drunk and disorderly, the magistrate fines Jacky and gives him twenty days in prison. 'I'll tell you what I'll do, boss', says Jacky. 'I'll toss you – forty days or nothing.' This form of humorous passive resistance is found in the traditions of many other occupied or colonised groups. *See also Folk Heroes; Folk Humour, Folklore of Struggle; Indigenous Folklore; Yarns*

BIRDIE

Nickname given to General William Birdwood (1865–1951, later Sir and then Baron Birdwood of Anzac and Totnes), by Australian and New Zealand diggers at Gallipoli. Birdwood became the centre of a cycle of yarns in which he appears as a 'digger with stripes', a leader who recognises and accepts those egalitarian qualities that the men of the First Australian Imperial Force valued highly. Birdwood's acknowledgement of, and acquiescence in the values of the digger, is held up for admiration in these narratives. One often-repeated example is the story of Birdwood chatting to English officers in London's Strand when a digger walks by without saluting, as usual. 'Why didn't you pull him up?' asks one of the English officers, aghast at this casual insubordination. 'Look here,' said Birdie, 'if you want to be told off in the Strand, I don't!' *See also Anzac; Digger; Folk Humour; Work Lore; Yarns*

BIRDSVILLE RACES

The hot, dry and dusty Birdsville Races have been run since 1882. Originally a small Queensland bush horse race meeting, in recent years the event has grown from a few hundred people to 6000–7000, assisted by satellite television broadcasts and general tourism promotion. The dates of the races have changed over the years. In 2001 the event was held in August–September. *See also Customs; Folk Sports; Picnic Races*

BIRTHDAYS

The annual celebration of birthdays is a persistent and vibrant custom in Australia, as in many other places in the world. The occasion is marked by the giving of gifts and birthday cards and a general well-wishing for the individual's happiness. A birthday party is usually characterised by a birthday cake topped by the appropriate number of burning candles, which are blown out by the individual, ideally in one breath to ensure luck. Traditionally, the person whose birthday it is also makes a wish as the candles are blown out, and makes the first cut in the cake. Adult birthday parties may include speeches and toasts, and particular attention is generally given to multiples of ten, such as 30th, 40th, 50th, 60th celebrations.

In Australia the most elaborate birthday celebration is likely to be the twenty-first birthday. Although legal adulthood in Australia now occurs at eighteen years, the twenty-first birthday is still the one most celebrated by family and friends, when the 'key to the door' may be ceremoniously presented (even if the birthday person has had it since childhood). The twenty-first may be celebrated at home, in the local hall or in an expensive catering establishment, and may feature music, dancing and food, including a large birthday cake. No similarly elaborate birthday celebrations are likely to take place until an individual reaches a grand old age such as ninety or one hundred, and a one hundredth birthday will usually be marked by a letter (previously a telegram) of congratulations from Queen Elizabeth. In recent years a fortieth birthday has frequently come to be imaginatively celebrated – among friends rather than family as a rueful or comic farewell to youth. It may feature humorous or unusual presents, or a fine meal in a restaurant, or a fancy dress party in a private house.

It is interesting that one of the most popular, and most international, practices at birthday celebrations, the singing of 'Happy Birthday', highlights the process whereby a song by a known author has passed into folk tradition. The National Library of Australia holds a 1989 copy of the sheet music of the song 'Happy Birthday' by Mildred and Patty Hill, copyrighted in 1935. In fact, the Hill sisters wrote the song in 1893.

Relatively recent additions to birthday customs may include, on the day itself, the hanging of a banner or large sign announcing the person's name and age in very visible locations, such as pedestrian or vehicular bridges across motorways. Also new is the adolescent birthday custom of holding an informal motor rally, usually in the bush; often these are related to eighteenth, and thus coming-of-age, birthdays.

In Chinese tradition, calculation of a child's age takes the nine-month gestation period into account, thus a child is already almost one when born. A complicating factor is that at Chinese New Year, or Spring Festival, another year is added to every child's age, as this occasion is considered to be everyone's birthday. So, if a child is born close to Chinese New Year he or she may be considered to be two years old, even though only a few weeks or months of age. Hard-boiled eggs, dyed red, may be given to guests at Chinese birthday parties – they signify good luck, health and prosperity.

Children's birthdays are often celebrated at a party, and these parties can take many forms (and cost varying amounts of money). Usually the birthday child's friends are invited and are expected to bring a present. In turn, they will expect to be sent home with, at the very least, a bag of lollies (sweets or candy) and a piece of birthday cake. The cake may be professionally made, perhaps in the shape of a doll or a railway engine.

Parents who can afford it may hire a clown, magician or snake handler, playground equipment or even a discotheque set-up as additional entertainment. Traditional foods provided at children's birthdays include fairy bread (thin bread and butter with multicoloured sprinkles, usually called 'hundreds and thousands') and chocolate crackles made with Rice Bubbles, cocoa, coconut and copha. In recent years many parents have chosen to have children's birthday parties away from home: at a cinema, park or fast food restaurant such as McDonald's. *See also Customs; Horses' Birthday; Naming Days*

BLACK ALICE

Aboriginal heroine of two eponymous nineteenth-century bush ballads. In one she is an earthy good-time girl with 'a boy in Camooweal, and one in Goondiwindi'. The other, composed by G. H. Gibson and published in 1881, is usually titled 'Sam Holt' (a parody of 'Ben Bolt', an English popular song of the 1840s) or 'A Ballad of Queensland'. In this song Alice is the sentimentalised love object of a white settler. *See also Bush Ballad; Folk Songs; Old Bush Songs; Racist Folklore*

BLACK FRIDAY

In Christian countries, 'Black Friday' is any Friday that falls on the thirteenth of the month. Friday is generally considered an unlucky day in Christian countries because Christ was traditionally believed to have been crucified on Good Friday. The Romans believed that thirteen was an unlucky number, a superstition reinforced by the fact that there were thirteen present at the Last Supper: Christ and the twelve apostles. While this is generally given as the explanation for the origin of Black Friday, research by folklorists for the *Dictionary of English Folklore* have failed to locate any references to Black Friday before the early twentieth century. However, the belief has certainly become firmly established since then.

Black Fridays, because they fall on the traditionally unlucky thirteenth day of the month, are believed to be especially unlucky. According to research published in the *British Medical Journal* in 1993, a study of accidents on a section of the M25 found that there were 52% more accidents on Friday the thirteenth. In Australia, 'Black Friday' is a term used for any Friday of disaster, such as the devastating bushfires of Friday, 13 January 1939. Fridays are generally thought to be bad days to undertake new ventures, journeys or voyages, to move house or to start a new job. Being born on a Friday, or courting on a Friday, may also be considered unlucky. *See also Customs; Folk Belief; Religious Folklore*

BLACK LADY OF MOUNT VICTORIA, THE

A ghost usually said to be that of Caroline James, murdered in Little Hartley in 1842, is reputedly often seen on the steep incline to 'Second Bridge' on Mount Victoria (NSW). The woman, dressed in black, is followed by a hearse drawn by four black horses. There have been numerous reports of this apparition, at least one of which includes a curse. The 'Black Lady of Mount Victoria' was celebrated by Lawson in his 'The Ghost at the Second Bridge':

> *She'll cross the moonlit road in haste*
> *And vanish down the track;*
> *Her long black hair hangs to her waist*
> *And she is dressed in black;*
> *Her face is white, a dull dead white –*
> *Her eyes are opened wide –*
> *She never looks to left or right,*
> *Or turns to either side.*

See also Ghost Lore; Lawson, Henry

BLACK MARY

Aboriginal accomplice and lover of New England (NSW) bushranger Frederick Ward, known as 'Thunderbolt'. In Thunderbolt folklore Mary Ann Ward (maiden name Bugg or Briggs, 1834–1867/or c. 1905) takes the role of the loyal helper, assisting the bushranger in his escape from Cockatoo Island and helping him avoid subsequent recapture, often while impersonating a man. Her death is the subject of conjecture, with one story having her dying of tuberculosis (from which Ward also suffered) in 1867 and another claiming she lived until 1905, producing thirteen children from two marriages. There is also a related, if fading, tradition that Thunderbolt had a 'half-caste' female accomplice called 'Yellow Long', or 'Lee You Long'. This may have been one of Mary Ann's aliases. Female accomplices were extremely rare in bushranging history, and when present, were inevitably made much of by the press and, later, romantically inclined writers. *See also Bushrangers; Folk Heroes and Heroines; Kelly, Kate; Thunderbolt*

BLACK STUMP, THE

Mythical spot where civilisation ends and the outback begins, as in 'this side of the black stump'. The expression 'past the black stump' means an isolated location that is a very great distance away. A 'Black Stump' appears in Rolf Boldrewood's *Robbery Under Arms* (1888), but the term does not appear to have been in use with its current meaning before the early twentieth century. *See also Bush, The; Folk Speech*

BLESSING OF THE FLEECE

This custom appears to have been introduced into rural areas of New South Wales and Queensland during the 1990s. It is essentially a modern harvest thanksgiving custom, usually held in a woolshed or other appropriate wool industry location, presided over by a (usually Protestant) minister of religion. A sheep is shorn, then the fleece is laid out and blessed while the congregation sings appropriate hymns and religious songs, such as 'Bringing in the Sheaves'. *See also Customs, Pastoral Industry Folklore; Lore, Religious Lore*

BLESSING OF THE FLEET

The custom of blessing fishing fleets is widespread in Europe, with extant traditions in Britain, Greece, Italy and elsewhere. In Australia this is often, though not exclusively, associated with Italian and Greek fishing communities. Probably the best known local observance is that which was revived among Italians in Ulladulla (NSW) at Easter 1956. There are also a number of other blessing of the fleet customs observed around the country, though not always at Easter. While some of these are highly public spectacles, attracting thousands of sightseers and tourists, the impetus behind the custom is firmly traditional, often involving more particular folk customs, such as the celebration of a saint, as in the Fremantle Blessing of the Fleet in November and the Geraldton Blessing of the Fleet (both WA), as well as similar events in Sydney, Port Pirie (SA) and elsewhere. These customs are often related to the commemoration of a village or regional saint in the country of origin. *See also Customs; Italian Folklore in Australia; Religious Folklore*

BLOKE

General term for a male. Like much Australian folk speech of the nineteenth century-derived from British usage and has a variety of meanings, both positive and less so. 'The Bloke' was also a term used widely in the bush for the employer or 'boss'. C. J. Dennis's creation of *The Songs of a Sentimental Bloke* (1914) focused much of the folklore of 'the bloke' as a typical, knockabout Australian male. A later, post-1960s generic term for a similar folk figure, but often with a negative emphasis on his uncouthness, is 'ocker'. *See also Folk Speech, Larrikin*

BLOODY

So frequently, widely and inventively employed from colonial times that it has earned the title 'The Great Australian Adjective', and was celebrated in a poem of this title by W.T. Goodge. C. J. Dennis also wrote a well-known poem on the same subject, and there are a number of folk variations on this theme dating from World War II (1939–45) in which the adjective is extensively deployed for humorous effect. In a World War II version usually known as 'Bloody Darwin' a long list of complaints is made about the lack of recreational facilities in that city, finishing with the verse:

> Best bloody place is bloody bed,
> With bloody ice on your bloody head,
> Then they think you're bloody dead,
> In bloody, bloody Darwin.

As well, 'the Great Australian Adjective' is widely heard in folk expressions of every kind. *See also Folk Speech*

BLOOMSDAY

An increasingly popular event, held on 16 June, celebrating the literary achievements of Irish writer James Joyce, author of *Ulysses*, *Portrait of the Artist as a Young Man* and *Finnegan's Wake*, among other works. In *Ulysses*, Joyce fictionally celebrated his first outing with the real-life Nora Barnacle, an event that took place on 16 June 1904. In the novel, Joyce is represented by the main character, Stephan Dedalus, Nora is Molly Bloom and her husband is Leopold Bloom, after whom the day is named. *See also Customs*

BLUDGER

One who avoids responsibility, especially in relation to work, and who lives off the efforts of others; derived from English slang and in use at least as early as the mid-nineteenth century for one who lived off the earnings of a prostitute. Widely used as a term of abuse, as in 'dole-bludger'. *See also Battler; Folk Speech; Insult and Invective*

BLUE

A word with various folk meanings. A red-haired male will often be nicknamed 'Blue', while 'a blue' is a fight. Someone or something considered to be notably 'Australian' may also be referred to as 'true blue', and to 'make a blue' is to make a mistake. More generally, it also denotes something sexually off-colour, as in 'blue joke', 'blue movie' or 'blue language'; or sadness, as in 'feeling blue'. *See also Folk Speech*

BLUE LADY OF NEW NORCIA, THE

Apparition said to fly around the clock tower of the Western Australian monastery town of New Norcia at midnight. Sometimes said to be either the ghost of a nun who taught at one of the schools, or of a young pupil. *See also Folk Tales; Ghosts*

BLUEY *See Swagman*

BOB THE SWAGMAN

Swagman hero of a popular nineteenth-century ballad 'The Old Bark Hut', who is obliged by reduced circumstances to live in rough and ready accommodation – 'I'm forced to go on rations in the old bark hut.' *See also Bush, The; Bush Ballad, Swagman*

BOCCE

Italian version of lawn bowls that has become increasingly popular in Australia since the 1990s. *See also Customs, Games, Italian Folklore in Australia*

BONFIRE NIGHT *See Cracker Night*

BOOMERANG

Probably from the Dharuk language in the Sydney region. A boomerang is a curved wooden implement used in some areas of Australia by Aboriginal people for hunting or fighting. Although it does not always 'return to sender', this is the popular view

of the boomerang, and has led to the widespread use of the word in Australian-English folk speech. For example, a person might be cautioned against spreading gossip or scuttlebutt 'as it might boomerang' (rebound on the sender). The boomerang is one of Australia's best-known icons and a symbol of 'Australianness'. *See also Folk Speech, National Icons*

BORROLOOLA LIBRARY, THE

The Northern Territory town of Borroloola, 60 kilometres inland on the south-west of the Gulf of Carpentaria, is famous for a library of 3000 leather-bound volumes that, according to the most common version of the legend, were donated to the town by American philanthropist Andrew Carnegie around the end of the nineteenth century. Cornelius Power, a policeman stationed at Borroloola, wrote letters appealing for books, and the then Governor-General of Australia, Lord Hopetoun, is said to have been instrumental in having the Carnegie Foundation fund a library. The Carnegie name was displayed in the library as benefactor, though there is no evidence that Andrew Carnegie did in fact donate the books. However it came into existence, the Borroloola Library was the largest and most comprehensive body of learning in the Northern Territory and many claimed to have gained much from its riches. The town's reputation as a place of learning generated a famous Sunday debating session in the tradition of Sydney's Domain and London's Speaker's Corner. The library was still intact in the 1930s, according to author and journalist Ernestine Hill in *The Great Australian Loneliness*, but by the 1950s had succumbed to the ravages of white ants. Although the Borroloola Library certainly existed, it has generated an expanding body of lore that has added to the already rich folk traditions of the Northern Territory. *See also Yarns*

'BOTANY BAY'

Theatrical parody of an earlier transportation ballad usually called 'Farewell to Judges and Juries', 'Botany Bay' features the well-known chorus 'Singing toora-li-oora-li-addity', etc. The song was part of the musical comedy *Little Jack Shepherd*, performed in London in 1885 and in Melbourne the following year. A good example of a 'fakesong' – or one deliberately composed in a traditional idiom – that has become a folk song. *See also Convict Lore, 'Farewell to Judges and Juries', Folklorism, Transportation Ballads*

'BOUND FOR SOUTH AUSTRALIA'

Nineteenth-century seaman's worksong in which the singer claims that 'In South Australia I was born ... South Australia, round Cape Horn' and in which the sailors are 'Bound for South Australia'. A shanty for capstan or halyard, related to a similar song known as 'The Codfish Shanty'. *See also Folk Songs; Maritime Lore; Work Lore*

BOWYANGS

Lengths of cord or hide, or a narrow strap used in the nineteenth and early twentieth century to tie the trousers of a working man up at the knee, preventing the cuffs from dragging. The journalist and writer Alexander Vindex Vennard took the pseudonym 'Bill Bowyang' to edit a series of famous bush songs between 1933 and 1940. *See also Bush Ballads; Old Bush Songs; Pastoral Industry Folklore; Work Lore*

BRADMAN, DON

Known in folk speech as 'The Don', Sir Donald Bradman (1908–2001) was knighted by Queen Elizabeth II in 1949 for his services to cricket, by which time he had acquired legendary status in Australia and other cricketing nations around the world. Bradman's achievements as a batsman in first-class cricket are still unsurpassed, and include 117 centuries (one hundred runs). Donald Bradman was born in Cootamundra in country New South Wales, showed his cricketing talent while still a schoolboy in 1926, and continued his notable fast scoring throughout his sporting career. A popular song of the 1930s, 'Our Don Bradman (well I ask you, is he any good?)' is still known, though fading, in the twenty-first century.

Rivalry between England and Australia focused on Bradman's successes during the 1930s. During 1932 and 1933, the years of what Australians still refer to as 'the infamous' bodyline series, the England team, under captain Douglas Jardine, succeeded in reducing Bradman's scores by sending down balls aimed at the batsman's body, a practice which was eventually stopped. Bradman played his last tour of England in 1948 and, by supreme irony, was bowled for a duck (zero score) by Englishman Eric Hollies.

Sir Donald Bradman is frequently nominated as one of Australia's major sporting icons, and on his death in February 2001 at the age of 92 was lauded by media worldwide. To some conservative commentators, including Australian Prime Minister John Howard, Bradman symbolised all that was best in a past and more gentlemanly era. A boulevard in Adelaide, in Bradman's later home state of South Australia, was renamed after him, and a major outrage arose when a sex shop in that street incorporated the new street name in its title. *See also Folk Speech; Folk Sports; Nicknames; Sport Folklore*

BRADY, MATTHEW

An English transportee (1799–1826) who escaped from Tasmania's Port Macquarie prison in 1824 and conducted a reign of bushranging terror in the colony. Treated in convict folklore as great hero, Brady ridiculed the reward offers made for him by offering a reward of his own for anyone who would capture the colony's Governor. Captured at last, Brady was tried and hanged in April 1826. *See also Bushrangers*

BRASS BANDS

Brass bands received considerable publicity towards the end of the twentieth century from the British film *Brassed Off*, but they have a much older place in Australian folk and popular music, and from origins that are not only British. In the middle of the nineteenth century German street bands were a popular form of entertainment, although the term 'German band' was often used generically and its members were not necessarily German. The Tanunda Brass Band was formed among South Australia's German immigrant community in 1860, and still exists today. The Victorian goldfields balladeer Charles Thatcher published his satirical song 'Buying Land' in 1865, and describes the ways 'new chums' were enticed to buy 'an entire swamp' by attractions such as champagne and 'a noisy German band'. Brass bands usually have a connection with a place or occupation, a classic example being the Thompson's Foundry Brass Band from Castlemaine, Victoria. Today's brass bands are more likely to be associated with a municipality. The 'Big Bands' beloved of music schools around Australia are mainly brass, although their repertoire (mostly jazz and swing) is somewhat distinct from that of more traditional brass bands. *See also Folk Music*

BRICKFIELDER

Originally a term used to mean a cool southerly wind in the Sydney region, but later used elsewhere, especially in Western Australia, to mean a hot, dusty breeze. *See also Cockeye Bob; Folk Speech; Fremantle Doctor; Southerly Buster*

BRING A PLATE

The egalitarian custom of contributing some food to the communal table when invited to another's home, or to a community social event, is a long-standing one in Australia. It has, reputedly, been the cause of much confusion and embarrassment for visitors unfamiliar with local usage, who have arrived at their hosts' house carrying an empty plate. *See also Customs*

BRINK (BRINKS), BLUEY

Pestiferous drunk who, in a nineteenth-century bush ballad, annoys Jimmy the barman so much that he substitutes sulphuric acid for Bluey's usual poison. Bluey is delighted with the kick delivered by the new drink, declaring, 'It will make me the ringer of Stephenson's shed' and 'It gives me great courage to shear and to fight.' But, when he returns to the bar for more, he also wonders aloud, 'Why does that stuff set my whiskers alight?' *See also Bush Ballad; Folk Humour'*

'BRISBANE LADIES'

Famous overlanding ballad also called 'Augathella Station' or 'The Queensland Drovers', with the rousing chorus:

> We'll rant and we'll roar like true Queensland natives (or drovers),
> We'll rant and we'll roar as onwards we push
> Until we return to the old cattle station (or Augathella Station)
> For it's flaming dry going in the old Queensland bush.

Probably based on a similar sailors' song. *See also Bush, The; Bush Ballads; Folk Songs, Pastoral Industry Folkore*

BUCKLEY'S CHANCE

Famous colloquial saying meaning no chance at all. Various derivations are extant but the most common is that the term comes from the experiences of William Buckley (1780–1856), an escaped convict who lived among indigenous people for 32 years, from 1803, in southern Victoria. Another version arises from the Melbourne store 'Buckley and Nunn', and the saying that went 'You have two chances, Buckley's and Nunn'. Often rendered simply as 'You've got Buckley's.' *See also Folk Speech*

BUCKS' NIGHT

Also known as a 'stag night/party', this is a traditional male celebration of the groom's last night of freedom before chaining himself down to married life, domesticity and responsibility. A night of alcoholic excess and horseplay, it is often marked with symbols of loss of freedom, such as the groom's mates making him wear a ball and chain, or in some other way detaining him. Occasionally these rituals result in something more serious than a hangover, as in the case of the unfortunate gentleman whose drunken mates, so the story goes, chained him aboard the midnight flyer from Sydney to Brisbane. He was unable to be back in time for the wedding, which had to be postponed. *See also Customs, Weddings*

BULLAMAKANKA

Fictional place far away from civilisation, as in the phrase 'out past Bullamakanka'. Uncertain origin, possibly originating from pidgin. Other phrases with similar meaning include 'the never-never', 'oodnagalahbi', 'the donga', 'the mulga', 'the sticks', 'back o' Bourke', 'out to buggery', 'the back of beyond' and 'out past the black stump'. *See also Black Stump, The; Folk Speech*

BULLOCKIES

Bullock-drivers, notorious for their toughness and ability to swear, an achievement celebrated in literature and folklore in such songs and verse as 'Five (Nine) Miles from Gundagai', 'Holy Dan' and 'Bullocky-o', among others. *See also Bullockies' Ball, Bullocky-o!, Pastoral Industry Folklore*

'BULLOCKIES' BALL'

Title of a bush song about a celebration that gets hilariously and inevitably out of hand as alcohol takes its toll. The chorus gives the flavour:

> Oh, my hearties, that was a party,
> Help yourself, free, gratis all.
> Lots of prog [food] and buckets of grog
> To swig away at the bullockies' ball.

There are variants involving Larrikins ('Fanny Flukem's Ball'), all similar to, and probably based on, the Irish 'Finnegan's Wake'. *See also Bullockies; Bullocky-o!; Bush; Bush Ballads; Folk Humour; The; Irish Influences in Australian Folklore; Pastoral Industry Folklore*

'BULLOCKY-O!'

Bush song celebrating the life and occupation of the bullocky: 'I'm the king of the bullock drivers, don't you know? Bullocky-o!' goes the chorus. *See also Bullockies; Bullockies' Ball; Bush, The; Bush Ballads; Pastoral Industry Lore*

BUNYIP

Creature of Aboriginal mythology, usually said to be hairy, though sometimes feathered, and to live in billabongs and waterholes, from where it will attack unwary passing humans. Although based on an indigenous belief, the Bunyip has merged with other water-monster traditions brought into Australia, such as the northern English 'Jenny or Ginny Greenteeth'. *See also Folk Belief; Indigenous Folklore; Legendary Animals; Yarama; Yowie*

BURNS NIGHT

Held on 25 January to commemorate the birth of Scotland's national poet, Robert Burns (1759–1796), this is an evening of feasting, drinking, poetry and music celebrated by the Scots and their guests throughout the world. The foods consumed are traditional and peculiar to Scotland, the most important being the haggis. Many toasts are drunk in Scottish whisky and the ceremony proceeds with the recitation of poems and the singing of songs composed by Burns. Music is provided by Scots bagpipes. *See also Annual Highland Gathering; Customs; Maclean Highland Gathering; Tenterfield Highland Gathering*

BUSH, THE

Impossible to avoid in any consideration of Australian folklore, the bush looms large as a symbol of Australian identity and myth. A great deal of Anglo-Celtic folklore is related to and/or derived from the real or imagined experiences of pioneers, overlanders, free selectors, itinerant bush workers, bushranging and the like (though, interestingly, not of the explorers). The song 'The Old Bark Hut' presents a comic view of the bush worker's experiences:

> *Ten pounds of flour, ten pounds of beef,*
> *Some sugar and some tay;*
> *That's all they give a hungry man*
> *Until the seventh day:*
> *If you don't be mighty sparing*
> *You'll go with a hungry gut,*
> *That's one of the great misfortunes*
> *In the old bark hut.*

To many Australians, 'the bush' is anywhere in Australia outside the major coastal cities, probably including regional towns and cities but not as far as 'the outback', which is truly remote. The bush has major iconic status in Australian life, as befits a country with just over 200 years of written history since first European settlement/invasion, and one which is still largely a primary producer. The argument about the relative merits of city vs. country life is a long-standing one, and notably featured in a debate between two prominent writers, Henry Lawson (city) and A B. ('Banjo') Paterson (country) in the *Bulletin* magazine in the later years of the nineteenth century.

In 1958 Russel Ward published *The Australian Legend*, an influential book which argued that the roots of Australian identity and nationalism are to be found in the bush, and particularly in the itinerant pastoral worker who valued independence, self-reliance, mateship and 'a fair go', values which have been internalised (or mythologised) in the Australian national character. Paterson's poem 'The Man from Snowy River', first published in 1895, is still publicised as a true symbol of Australianness, and featured in film and on television. Australians' beliefs and mythologies about the bush are two-sided, however. Particularly in earlier generations, the bush was a place to be feared, and children and adults 'lost in the bush' became the subjects of both writings and paintings. Some of these have acquired iconic status, such as the painting by William Strutt (1825–1915) entitled *Found! Mr Duncan, Roderick, Bella and David*. Conversely, Australians in large numbers flock to Uluru (Ayer's Rock) in Central Australia as a kind of secular pilgrimage to the heart of the outback.

Bush lore is strongly masculine, celebrating the 'bushman', tends to ignore – and occasionally derogate – indigenous peoples, and focuses on action at the expense of emotion. In popular nationalism the bush is also the location of the characteristically or uniquely 'Australian', a view that has impelled most folklore collection and study, from 'Banjo' Paterson's *Old Bush Songs* (from 1905), the post-World War II retrieval of bush traditions by individuals associated with the Bush Music movement, to Bill Wannan's many influential collections, beginning with *The Australian* in 1954. While the bush – and its many meanings – have in recent years been out of favour with most intellectuals, publishers and politicians, it persists in popular consciousness as the mythic site of the values, attitudes and experiences of Anglo-Celtic Australia. *See also Australian Legend; The; Bush Band; Bush Music; Old Bush Songs; Pastoral Industry Lore*

BUSH BALLAD

A term used fairly loosely to describe bush poems and folk songs. The bush ballad, usually in its recited form, is still among the most frequently encountered types of folklore in contemporary Australia. As well as having a continuing folkloric existence, the bush ballad is perhaps the most representative form of popular Australian literature, its most noted exponents including A. B. ('Banjo') Paterson and Henry Lawson. There has, and continues to be, a strong interaction between the oral bush ballad and its literary form. *See also Bush, The; Folk Songs; Lawson, Henry; Old Bush Songs; Paterson, A.B. ('Banjo')*

BUSH BAND

A musical ensemble that may consist of the following instruments in any number or combination: fiddle, accordion, concertina, guitar, banjo (four or five-string), tin whistle, bush bass (made from a tea-chest with a broomstick neck on which a string or cord is stretched), lagerphone (a broomstick with slat of wood nailed across the top and covered in bottle-tops; played by banging it on the floor and scraping a saw-toothed stick across the bottle tops, preferably – but not necessarily – in time), and perhaps bones or spoons for percussion. Sometimes a piano may be included. While many of these instruments are known to have been popular in the bush, the defining items of bush bass and lagerphone appear to have been adopted only since the revival of Australian folk music in the 1950s, an era in which skiffle bands, often featuring a tea-chest bass and a (usually American) folksong repertoire, became briefly popular. There may be some traditional precedent for the bush band in the form of the 'ship's foo-foo band', a skiffle-like ensemble of improvised instruments evolved by sailors obliged to make their own entertainment in the pre-electronic era. Since the 1960s there has been an increasing use of mandolins and, more recently, modernised versions of 'citterns' (derived from medieval stringed instruments of this name) and bouzoukis, especially among Irish-influenced musicians, as well as electronic combinations involving bass, drums and electric guitars. *See also Bush, The; Bush Ballad; Bush Music; Folklorism; Folk Revival*

BUSH CARPENTER

A term that may be used either to praise or to deride an untrained craftsman or his work as 'bush carpentry'. When derisory, it is usually in reference to rough and ready workmanship; when used in praise, it is for the skill and resourcefulness shown by the untrained artisan in making anything from a shed to a fence, dog kennel or letter box. The ability to 'do it yourself' (DIY) is much valued in Australian folklife, in both city and country, and is an ability which has arisen out of the Australian experience, both on the land and on the suburban quarter-acre block. *See also Folk Speech; Making Do*

BUSH DANCE

As used in the twenty-first century, the term 'bush dance' can refer both to an event and to the type of dancing which takes place at such an event. 'A Bush Dance' is likely to be more informal than 'A Woolshed Ball' or 'A Colonial Ball', and the latter is likely to involve dancers dressing in colonial costumes. The term 'bush dance' came into use in Australia with the folk revival of the 1950s, in which both researchers ('collectors') and musicians rediscovered and popularised nineteenth-century dances, dance music and songs such as 'Click Go the Shears' and 'Botany Bay'. Both songs and tunes were used at bush dances, and folk clubs and folk festivals taught the dance routines. The use of the term bush dance is somewhat of a misnomer, as nineteenth-century social dance was as popular in the cities and towns as in 'the bush', although the term 'bush dance' was not used in colonial days. As used today, the term 'bush dance' probably reflects Australian folk beliefs that the bush is the source of all good things ('the Australian Legend'). Australian nationalism and a fear of American domination provided a key impetus to the 1950s folk revival, and its supporters followed the legend and looked to the bush for the source of the elusive Australian identity.

Bush dances are still common in Australia, although less so than in the 1950s, 60s and 70s, and may be organised by a folk club, school or community organisation. The format has not changed a great deal, and is likely to feature a bush band. Much of the bush band's instrumentation features an invented rather than an authentic tradition. The guitar, lagerphone (made with beer bottle tops loosely nailed onto a broom handle) and the bush bass (tea chest) were not used for dances in Australian colonial days, the fiddle and piano being more common accompaniments. Bush dances are likely to include quadrilles, reels, schottisches, waltzes and polkas – the dances represent both British country traditions and popular European dances. *See also Bush Bands, Bush Music, Bush, The; Dance, Musical Instruments*

BUSH LAWYER

A bush lawyer is a self-styled expert, 'one who knows', and who lets others around him know that he knows. The bush lawyer will argue in the best courtroom tradition for his knowledge or interpretation of events, which may range from how to run a chook raffle in a pub to what is really going on in Australian politics or the United Nations. His expertise is usually entirely self-defined, and he may have no formal training in any of the areas of life which he 'knows' about. He is also likely to be an expert at talking over the top of his opponents. *See also Bush, The; Folk Speech*

BUSH MUSIC

Form of music played by a bush band. Includes typically upbeat bush ballads such as 'The Lachlan Tigers', 'On the Road to Gundagai', 'Click Go the Shears', and bush dance tunes drawn from a varied repertoire of English country dance music, Irish jigs and reels, waltzes, polkas, schottisches and varsoviennas, usually from nineteenth-century European popular music sources. Traditionally, such music was played at rural social occasions and dances by whatever musicians were available, often an accordionist, perhaps a concertina-player, a fiddler and a pianist. The 1950s development of the bush band was largely a formalisation of this approach (usually without the piano) and since the 1960s electric instruments and sometimes drums have been increasingly used to play bush music. Perhaps the best-known exponents of this approach are 'The Bushwhackers'.

While the term 'bush music' is used mostly to identify the essentially Anglo-Celtic music described above, folk music-making in rural and regional communities is much more diverse and includes other styles, including country and western music, blues (especially among indigenous performers), old-time music (nineteenth and early twentieth-century popular music), musical repertoires derived from non-British immigrant groups, including Germans, Italians, Yugoslavs, Polynesians and more recent influences such as reggae, rock and hip-hop. *See also Barcoo Dog, Bush, The; Bush Band, Bush Dance, Folk Revival*

BUSH MUSIC CLUB, THE

Formed in Sydney in 1952 to encourage the collection, research and performance of traditional bush music, song, dance, yarns and recitations. The club holds an extensive archive of materials, publishes *Mulga Wire* (originally *Singabout*) and organises festivals, concerts, dances and social occasions. *See also Bush, The*

'BUSH OF AUSTRALIA, THE'

Nineteenth-century emigration ballad, also known as 'The Pommy's Lament', in which the migrant has many unhappy experiences, loses his thousand pounds and returns to England to work breaking stones on the roads – an unhappy fate which, however, he prefers to the hard life in Australia. *See also Bush, The; Migration Lore*

BUSH TELEGRAPH

A network of bush people where news circulates by word of mouth. Also known as 'the mulga wire'. This interesting term does not apply only to the bush, but refers to the ways knowledge or rumour can spread informally through a given population. The 'news' being spread is usually passed from person to person without going into written or electronic form. There is an element of the mysterious about the bush telegraph, particularly in view of the rapidity with which news can spread, and its wide coverage of different locations. *See also Bagman's Gazette, Folk Speech*

BUSH TUCKER

Bush tucker refers to a wide variety of native plants and animals regularly eaten by Australia's indigenous people, and becoming increasingly popular in the mainstream population. Meats such as kangaroo, emu and crocodile are available in most Australian cities and export of these products is growing. Wattle seed, Kakadu and Illawarra plums, quandongs and bunya nuts are a few of the other native plant foods slowly moving into Australians' regular diet.

The appropriation and commercial exploitation of native foods in Australia is a matter of concern to Aboriginal people in terms of cultural ownership and remuneration. These matters are discussed extensively in a 1998 report on Australian indigenous cultural and intellectual property rights, prepared by Aboriginal lawyer Terri Janke and published as *Our Culture: Our Future*. Many indigenous plants in Australia also have proven or potentially significant therapeutic value and financial potential, such as the Western Australian Smokebush (*genus conospermum*) which may have significance in the treatment of AIDS. *See also Folklore; Folk Speech; Foodways*

BUSHMAN'S FAREWELL

A minor but persistent form of song/recitation in which the speaker curses a particular part of the country on his departure. Frank the Poet's famous 'Farewell to Van Diemen's Land', probably composed in 1849, is an early example and may have been the model on which subsequent versions were based. The most frequently encountered version of Frank the Poet's piece went:

> *Land of Lags and Kangaroo,*
> *Of 'possum and the scarce Emu,*
> *The farmer's pride but the prisoner's Hell*
> *Land of B...s fare-thee-well.*

The 'B...s' in the final line is sometimes interpreted a 'bastards', though is more likely to have been 'buggers', as other collected examples are generally explicit about the reference to sodomy. Versions of the 'Bushman's Farewell' have been collected from most states. The conclusion of a well-known Queensland version provides the general flavour:

> *To stray in thee, O land of mutton,*
> *I would not give a single button,*
> *But bid thee now a long farewell,*
> *Thou scorching, sunburnt land of hell.*

See also Folk Poetry, Folk Speech, Recitations

BUSHRANGERS

Criminals or escaped convicts who, from the earliest years of settlement, ranged the bush either alone or in gangs, robbing travellers and homesteads to survive. A small number of these men – and an even smaller number of their female accomplices – became folk heroes of the outlaw type descended in English-language tradition from the fictional Robin Hood. Accordingly, the traditions surrounding these figures, both historical (such as Jack Donohoe) and legendary (such as The Wild Colonial Boy), present their protagonists as the enemies of the rich, the police and the government, and as the friends of convicts and the poor. Bushrangers, well known and obscure, who are celebrated in folklore include, in addition to the above, Matthew Brady, Martin Cash, Fred Lowry, Jack Power, Jack Lefroy, the Clarke brothers, 'Thunderbolt', 'Mad Dog' Morgan, 'Captain Moonlight', Ben Hall, Frank Gardiner, John Gilbert, John Burke, John Vane, John O'Meally, 'Moondyne Joe', Steve Hart, Joe Byrne and Dan Kelly. A number of Aboriginal figures were also accorded outlaw hero status by their own people, including 'Pigeon' (Jandamurra), Yagan and Pemulwuy. The bushranger of folklore embodies many of the most powerful notions of national identity, outstandingly in the figure of Ned Kelly. *See also Black, Mary; Brady, Matthew; Bush, The; Cash, Martin; Donohoe, Jack; Folk Heroes; Gardiner, Frank; Hall, Ben; Jandamurra; Kelly, Ned; 'Mad Dog' Morgan, Daniel; Pemulwuy; Thunderbolt; The Wild Colonial Boy; Yagan*

BUTCHERS' WINDOW SIGNWRITING

A seasonal occupational custom that dates from at least the early years of this century is the late winter painting of butchers' shop windows with advertisements for 'New Season's Spring Lamb'. These colourful signs are often decorated with Australian wildflowers, wattle being a special, though seasonally inappropriate, favourite (wattle blooms mostly in autumn and winter). Around mid-December these decorations are replaced with 'Season's Greetings' in readiness for the Christmas trade in pork, ham and turkey. Usually these Christmas decorations display the remnants of the European Christmas tradition in their use of snow, red berries and green holly as decorative motifs. As a documenter of this folk custom, Vane Lindsay, describes it in his *Aussieosities* (1988): 'The best of these graphic expressions are comparable with English "fairground" popular art and, as such, become significant elements of an indigenous Australian form.' Slogans such as 'try a little tenderness', 'we can meat all prices' and 'our meat is not deer' (complete with painting of deer, antlers, etc) are usually painted in red, white and blue colours and changed regularly. These gentle witticisms link with a common belief or observation that butchers are often, like 'Banjo' Paterson's barber in 'The Man from Ironbark', 'humorists of note'. Although the number of independent butcher shops is declining with the spread of supermarkets, the slogans persist. The careful and some say, artistic, arrangement of meats in butchers' windows is also part of butchers' traditional pride in their craft. *See also Customs; Folk Art; Work Lore*

BYRNE, JOE (JOSEPH)
Member of the Kelly gang of bushrangers who features frequently in Kelly folklore, usually as 'brave Joe Byrne'. Killed at Glenrowan, June, 1880. *See also Bushrangers; Folk Heroes; Kelly, Ned*

C

CABBAGE PATCH, THE

Derogatory New South Wales name for Victoria, thought to be no bigger than a vegetable garden compared with the larger colony/state. Those who reside there were 'cabbage-patchers'. Rarely heard today. *See also Folk Speech; Regional Rivalries*

CASH, MARTIN

Van Diemen's Land bushranger celebrated in song and story, Martin Cash (c. 1808–1877) was born in Ireland, transported to New South Wales in 1828 and then to Tasmania. He escaped and led a band of bushrangers in the early 1840s. He was caught and sentenced to hang for the murder of a policeman but his sentence was commuted to life imprisonment and he was eventually released as a 'model prisoner', spending the last twenty years of his life as a farmer. His ballad, said to have been widely circulated among the convict population during the 1840s and later, treats him as a hero:

> He was the bravest man that you could choose
> From Sydney men or Cockatoos [ex-inmates of Sydney harbour's
> notorious Cockatoo Island prison]
> And a gallant son of Erin,
> Where the sprig of shamrock grows.

See also *Brady, Matthew; Bushrangers; Folk Heroes*

'CATALPA, THE'

Ballad fancifully recounting the events of April 1876 when six Fenians, Irish political prisoners, were spirited away from Fremantle Prison in Western Australia aboard an American whaleship, *The Catalpa*. Sung to various tunes, the most frequently heard of which is a variant of the Irish 'Rosin the Beau (or Bow)'. This song has a rousing chorus:

> Come all you screw warders and gaolers,
> remember Perth Regatta Day,

take care of the rest of your Fenians,
or the Yankees will steal them away

– which probably explains why this ballad of the incident has lasted in tradition while others have not. *See also Convict Lore; Irish Influences on Australian Folklore*

CAT'S CRADLE

Elaborate figures made with the hands and a loop of string something over a metre in length include the 'cat's cradle' and the 'parachute', 'Eiffel Tower', 'cup and saucer', 'cat's whiskers' etc. They are popular games with children, mainly girls, of primary school age. String figures, or string games, involve a great deal of skill and sometimes require a second person to complete the pattern.

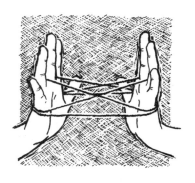

They are of great interest because of their occurrence in many different locations and among many different peoples, including Inuit (Eskimo), Australian Aboriginal, many Asian, African and European peoples. Adults as well as children may perform the routines, which can be extremely elaborate, even involving moving elements. *See also Children's Folklore, Games*

CAZALY

Roy Cazaly (1893–1963) was an outstanding player of Australian Rules Football in the 1920s and 1930s who contributed his name to a still-current Australian folk saying and rallying cry 'Up there, Cazaly!', which has been used in a variety of contexts, including among Australian soldiers in World War II. Cazaly was noted for his high leaps during football games, and played and coached in a number of football teams, including St Kilda and South Melbourne. The song 'Up there Cazaly' by Michael Brady is widely known, not only among football supporters. *See also Folk Heroes; Folk Speech, Sports Lore*

CHAIN LETTERS

By their nature an international form of folklore, chain letters have been circulating the world's postal systems since at least World War I. The most common and probably the oldest is that which promises good luck and fortune to the person who sends on the letter to a number of recipients and dire consequences up to and including death for those who do not – 'Do not break the chain' is the usual warning. Often in these letters there will be a reference to a religious figure, usually 'St Jude', which can cause serious concern to those who receive them. In recent years a number of chain letter parodies have evolved, including 'The Fertiliser Letter', which deals humorously with the deposition of human faeces on people's front lawns, and another, usually titled 'Chain Letter for Women' or 'A Chain Letter With A Difference' in which recipients are asked to bundle up their husbands and post them on. Eventually, says the letter, 'you will receive 16,874 men and some of them are bound to be a hell of a lot better than the one you already have'. Even more recent developments of this genre include chain faxes and emails. *See also E-lore, Folk Belief*

CHAMBERLAIN, AZARIA

The infant Azaria Chamberlain disappeared from her family's tent in an Ayers Rock (Uluru) camping ground in August 1980. The ensuing legal events involving Azaria's parents Lindy and Michael Chamberlain became the subject of intense national controversy. Speculation about the guilt of the dingo vs. the guilt of the child's mother generated a large body of folklore, notably 'dingo jokes' ('What's worse than a bull in a china shop? A dingo in a tent'), a variety of the 'sick' joke, but also photocopy-lore and rumours about witchcraft and Satanism based on ancient folk beliefs. *See also Belief; Dingo; Dingo Jokes; Folk Humour; Jokes; Satanism*

CHANUKAH (OR HANUKKAH)

Beginning on the 25th day of the Jewish month of *Kislev* (usually December), the 'Festival of Lights' lasts for eight days and celebrates a 2000-year old victory of the Jews in Palestine. Sacred candles are lit in the home, gifts are exchanged, special food (potato latkes, fruit pudding) is consumed and parties are held for children, in which a special spinning top called a dreidel is used in a game of chance involving sweets or nuts. *See also Customs, Religious Lore*

CHARTERS TOWERS COUGAR, THE *See Legendary Animals*

'CHERRYWOOD GUN, THE'

Rumoured to be the title of a folksong about the Eureka Stockade, though the song has not yet come to light. *See also Eureka Stockade, The; Folk Songs*

CHILDREN'S FOLKLORE

Children's folklore is one of the oldest continuous folk traditions in human society. Although some changes may have taken place in them, many children's games go back as far as recorded history. Many of the more than eighty games depicted in Flemish artist Pieter Brueghel's famous painting *Children's Games* (1560), including marbles, mud pies, dressing up and chasey, are still played today.

Children's folklore can be looked at along two main dimensions, folklore *for* children and folklore *of* children. The games mentioned above are children's own lore, folklore *of* children, and they are passed on from one generation of children (usually while aged between seven and twelve years) to the next, mainly in the primary school playground. A large responsibility of primary school teachers is to understand, encourage and protect this wonderful body of children's culture, and not to ban some games (such as marbles) because they allegedly 'cause fights' nor, conversely, to over-enthusiastically paint hopscotch grids in the playground. Children like to draw their own, changing the size of the grids according to the age of the players.

In Australia, the Melbourne Museum in Victoria is home to what may be the world's largest collection of children's playground lore, the Australian Children's Folklore Collection (ACFC), founded by June Factor and Gwenda Davey in 1979. The collection includes more than 12,000 games, rhymes, jokes, taunts, counting-out rituals, handclapping chants and other types of children's lore. One jumping game is done to the rhyme:

> The cat's got the measles,
> The measles, the measles;
> The cat's got the measles,
> The measles got the CAT!

Many items in the ACFC can be considered international: string games, for example, occur among widely differing cultures, including the Inuit (Eskimo), Australian Aboriginal and many Asian and European cultures. It is interesting to speculate whether generations of white Australian children might have learned some of their string games from Australian Aboriginal children and adults.

While a great deal of children's lore has remained the same through generations (or centuries), a few types have gone out of fashion, such as hoops, whipping tops and girls' singing/circle games such as 'Green Gravel' and 'In and Out the Window', which were popular in some Australian primary schools until pre-World War I. There are even fewer new games, and the most notable new game (post 1950) is 'Elastics', which is discussed in a separate entry.

Folklore *for* children is equally ancient. One of the first books produced in English by the fifteenth-century printer William Caxton was *Aesop's Fables,* and eighteenth-century books of nursery rhymes included *Tommy Thumb's Pretty Song Book* (1744) and *Gammer Gurton's Garland* (c. 1784). One rhyme printed in Gammer Gurton was 'I love sixpence, a jolly jolly sixpence', which was revived as a popular song during World War II. The modern version (below) is similar to the eighteenth-century rhyme:

> *I've got sixpence,*
> *A jolly jolly sixpence,*
> *I've got sixpence*
> *To last me all my life;*
> *I've got tuppence to lend*
> *And tuppence to spend*
> *And tuppence to send home to my wife.*

Nursery rhymes are undoubtedly directed at young children (*see Nursery Rhymes*), but fables, folk tales and fairy tales such as 'Cinderella' or 'Snow White' were originally stories for adults, to entertain, to teach moral lessons, or to provide social criticism, and the children's versions which we know today have been considerably simplified and 'cleaned up' for the young. Numerous writers have researched original versions of folk tales. One of the best-known is Jack Zipes, particularly for his pioneering book *Breaking the Magic Spell: Radical Theories of Folk and Fairy Tales* (1979).

Folklore *for* children is folklore devised and transmitted by adults for children's amusement and instruction. Besides nursery rhymes and folk tales, there are many other types of this lore, such as tickling, bouncing and finger (and toe) games, including

> *This little pig went to market,*
> *This little pig stayed at home;*
> *This little pig had roast beef,*
> *This little pig had none.*
> *And this little pig went wee wee wee;*
> *Wee wee all the way home.*

Other types include customs and rituals such as those involving Father Christmas and the Tooth Fairy; paper dolls and drawings such as stick figures; warnings (such as 'If the wind changes while you're making that face...'), reprimands and evasions. The last three types are included in the collections of 'family sayings' published by Gwenda Davey in *Snug as a Bug* (1990) and *Duck Under the Table* (1991). A well known 'family saying' is the mysterious 'Wigwam for a goose's bridle', said by adults to curious children who ask once too often 'What are you making?' These sayings seem to exist in many different languages, and many show considerable wit and sharp humour. In response to a child's question 'What's for dinner?', a Greek-Australian mother might reply 'my liver and kidneys', an Anglo-Australian 'bread and scrape' (or 'duck under the table'), and a Croatian-Australian 'cakes with honey'. Family sayings have many different functions, apart from amusement and verbal 'showing off'. Functions include evasion, e.g. 'How old are you, Gran?' 'As old as my tongue and as young as my teeth'; maintaining adult privacy, e.g. 'little pigs have big ears'; reducing tensions 'what do you think this is – bush week?' and training in table manners 'all joints on the table will be carved'.

There is an additional type of children's folklore which is worth considering, namely folklore *about* children. This is sometimes expressed in proverbs or homilies such as 'spare the rod and spoil the child' or 'children should be seen and not heard'. There are folk beliefs about children, sometimes called 'old wives' tales', such as 'if you tickle the baby's feet you'll make it stutter', and customs to predict the sex of an unborn baby by dangling a wedding ring on a string over the mother's abdomen to see if the ring turns left or right, or swings in a circle or like a pendulum. There are other folk beliefs about children expressed as common clichés, such as 'children are cruel', 'babies don't feel pain' and 'children don't feel the cold'. Like all aspects of children's folklore, these beliefs are worthy of study, as many are simply excuses for inertia or irresponsibility. *See Australian Children's Folklore Collection; Cat's Cradle; Counting Out; Elastics; Games; Handclapping Games; Hopscotch; Marbles; Nursery Rhymes; Skipping/Skippy. See also* INTRODUCTION

CHINESE FOLKLORE IN AUSTRALIA

Chinese immigrants first came to Australia early in the nineteenth century, but began arriving in large numbers on the eastern goldfields, mainly from south China, during the 1850s. After the goldrushes, the Chinese who remained were often found market gardening on the outskirts of larger cities, or in urban 'Chinatowns', although there were also large Chinese communities in places such as Darwin and Broome, as well as a small presence in many country towns. Much Chinese folklore is associated with the Chinese lunar calendar, involving periodic customs such as the Mid-Autumn Moon festival and rites of passage similar to those found in most cultural groups. As befits a society with such a lengthy history, there is an enormous body of Chinese tradition associated with folk tales of gods, heroes, warriors and magicians, outlaws and other folk heroes, many of whom are also celebrated in ballad and verse, proverbs and large repertoires of traditional wisdom. Chinese folk belief is also extensive, involving the Chinese calendar and one or more of the various religious systems common in China. 'Chinese New Year' (the Spring Festival) is the most familiar Chinese folk custom to most other Australians, though there is also strong Chinese influence in such events as the Bendigo Easter Fair and Broome's *Shinju Matsuri*. Chinese herbal medicine has also spread beyond the Chinese community in recent years, as has dragon boat racing. *See also Bendigo Easter Fair, Children's Folklore, Chinese New Year, Double Ninth Festival, Dragon Boat Festival, Feast of the Hungry Ghosts, Fo Dan, Mid-Autumn Moon Festival, Quing Ming, Shinju Matsuri*

CHINESE NEW YEAR

Late January/early February. The Spring Festival (*Xin Nian/Tet*), marking the start of the first lunar month of the Chinese calendar, is celebrated by Chinese throughout the world, regardless of the country in which they reside. The kitchen god of the house is traditionally consulted one week before the New Year. The god then reports to heaven on the activities of the house. While the god is away, the home must be cleaned, debts paid and the rooms decorated with flowers. Fireworks mark the return of the kitchen god from his heavenly reporting on New Year's Eve. New clothes, symbolic of the end of the bad aspects of the past year, are worn, and relatives and friends are visited with gifts of food and drink. Greetings are traditionally 'May you prosper', or variants of this well-wishing. Red (for luck) paper parcels of money and new clothes are given to children, to as yet unmarried couples and to friends on the first day of the New Year. Street processions, including dances of dragons and sometimes lions, are a universal feature of this festival, and are accompanied by the music of drums and gongs. Dragon boats may be raced at this time of the year, as they are in many Australian cities; the Lion Dance, the Dragon Dance and Fan dance are other popular features of this celebration.

It is the custom to prepare large family meals at this time, though increasingly these are provided by Chinese restaurants. 'Mooncakes' (usually rice, sesame seeds and kumquat) are a Chinese New Year delicacy. The home and its surrounds may be specially decorated with lanterns and various religious offerings to mark the first full moon of the New Year. This Lantern Festival (*Teng Chieh*) heralds the end of the New Year celebrations and the official start of Spring. Like many folk customs, Chinese New Year is increasingly commercialised, though the event remains an important family and Chinese-Australian community observation. *See also Chinese Folklore in Australia; Customs, Folk Sports*

CHOOK RAFFLE
The raffling of a chicken as a traditional method of community fundraising. While chickens are no longer the luxury food item they once were, the term 'chook raffle' is still often used to describe any kind of grassroots fundraising. The phrase comes from more rugged days in Australian pubs such as the period of six o'clock closing, or the 'six o'clock swill'. The 'swill' referred to the practice of drinkers lining up several glasses of beer in order to have drunk their fill before the legal closing time of six o'clock. With reform of Australian licensing laws, the swill ended in the 1960s. Until licensing reform, features of life in the public bar (men only) might include bottles of oysters or mussels sold at the bar (for nourishment), shady characters offering stolen goods which had 'fallen off the back of a truck', Salvation Army men and women

selling copies of *The War Cry*, radio broadcasts of horse races and the practice of illegal betting, vendors of lobsters or crayfish (to take home to pacify the wife), and chook raffles. The organiser of the chook raffle might sell tickets for a live chicken in a hessian bag, its feet sticking out for easy carrying. It was by no means unknown for the organiser of the chook raffle to disappear, ticket money, chook and all, so that the phrase 'chook raffle' has passed into Australian folk tradition to signify a wide range of suspect or dodgy activities in business, commerce and politics. In the contemporary era, when chicken is no longer a rare treat, a common raffle or lucky ticket draw in pubs and clubs offers a prize of a 'meat tray', which may include a half side of lamb, neatly cut up and arranged in the best butcher's tradition. *See also Customs, Folk Speech, Grog, Lamington Drive*

CHRISTENING

While christening a baby by officially naming it and receiving it into the body of the church is an aspect of the formal observance of the Christian religion, there is usually a social event to follow. Typically this takes the form of snacks, tea and coffee and sometimes alcohol, provided in the home by the christened child's parents for the godparents, grandparents, in-laws and close family friends.

Godparents are a particularly important element of Greek Orthodox christening customs. The child cannot be christened fewer than forty days after its birth, and is named after the father's parents. The Best Man and Matron of Honour at the parents' wedding are frequently chosen as the godparents, or wedding sponsors, of the children. This *koumbaros* relationship is one that is generally maintained throughout the lives of all involved. The child and the christening party return to the church three times to properly incorporate the newly christened baby into the church.

'Banjo' Paterson's poem 'A Bush Christening' (1895) is set in 'the outer Barcoo where the churches are few' and describes with much comedy the christening of an unwilling ten-year-old boy by an outback 'whisky priest'. *See also Customs, Family Folklore, Religious Lore*

CHRISTMAS

25 December is celebrated each year in the Christian Church as the day of Christ's birth, and special church services are held, sometimes at midnight on Christmas Eve (24 December). Christmas is a joyous

occasion, and these church services, which may also be attended by persons who otherwise are not church-goers, may include traditional carols.

The meaning of Christmas includes religious, commercial and social or folk elements. The giving of Christmas presents, much promoted by shops and business enterprises, is relatively new in the English-speaking world, dating, together with Christmas trees and Christmas cards, largely from the nineteenth century. Commerce is linked to Christmas not only through sales but through the appearance of Father Christmas 'in person' in most big stores in Australia. Some stores, such as Myer's in Melbourne and David Jones in other capital cities, also devote considerable time, artistry and money to special Christmas window displays, often featuring fairy tale or mythological themes. A visit to the city to look at 'Myer's windows' is now part of Christmas traditions for many Australian children and families.

The social and folkloric elements of Christmas observance are much older than today's commercially influenced customs, and festivities and family gatherings at this time of year (in the northern hemisphere, the winter solstice) are at least as old as the ancient Roman festival of Saturnalia, held in mid-December in honour of the god Saturn. Saturnalia was a time of 'goodwill to all men', still an important aspect of Christmas religious and folk customs.

In Australia, Christmas is the time for annual holidays from school and work, and for family gatherings. It is interesting that some Australian folk sayings about Christmas do not seem to be confirmed in practice. Australians often say that Christmas is too hot for a traditional dinner, that a picnic by the beach is preferable, and that family reunions at Christmas time 'can be hell'. Yet in 1985, 1987 and 1990, the Saulwick Polls surveyed a thousand Australians in each year about their attitudes towards, and activities at, Christmas time. The results showed that more than 90% of people spent Christmas with their family, and that these gatherings were 'pleasant, relaxed, peaceful and good for family relations'. More than 80% had a special meal in the middle of the day, and for more than 60%, the meal was a 'substantial hot meal', including plum pudding. Apart from regular church-goers, most Australians do not go to church on Christmas Day, and see Christmas mainly as a time for family reunion. Christmas traditionally extends to Twelfth night or Epiphany Eve, 6 January, when the Christmas decorations should be taken down. This is also the time in Italian tradition when the old witch *la befana* visits good children with presents. See also *Curling; Customs; Family Folklore; Father Christmas; Religious Lore; Folklorism*

CHRISTMAS IN JULY

An occasional social gathering such as a dinner party when a group of friends or workmates combine for a traditional Christmas dinner such as roast turkey and plum pudding in the Australian winter, usually in July. The meal will generally be held in the house of one member of the group, and may be a cooperative one, with all participants preparing some of the fare. The rationale (if one is needed) is that the Australian Christmas in December is too hot for traditional European Christmas fare. The fact remains that most Australians do still observe a traditional Christmas in December. Perhaps Christmas festivities are so enjoyable that once a year is not enough.

This custom is of recent origin – probably the early 1970s – and was at first observed by British migrants and Anglophiles. It has widened in popularity and become an occasion for celebrating northern hemisphere Christmas customs in Australia, with holiday cottages, hotels and restaurants offering 'Christmas in July' accommodation specials during this usually slow period of the tourist season. The folk traditions of Christmas are usually fully replicated but the religious associations are generally absent, except incidentally through the occasional singing of traditional carols. See also *Christmas; Customs; Folklorism; Migration Lore*

CLAYTON'S

A term derived from the 1980s advertising of a non-alcoholic beverage, in which the slogan was: 'Clayton's – the drink you have when you're not having a drink'. In popular parlance 'Clayton's' now means something that is unsatisfying, or an unsatisfactory substitute, particularly with the implication that something essential is missing – or has been withheld – from the experience, event or item, thus: 'That was a Clayton's game'; 'This is Clayton's legislation.' See also *Folk Speech*

'CLICK GO THE SHEARS'

Famous shearing song to the tune of 'Ring the Bell, Watchman' (composed by Henry Clay Work in 1865) and making extensive use of shearer's occupational terms such as 'board' (area in woolshed where sheep are shorn), 'blow' (a single stroke of the shears) and 'ringer' (fastest shearer in the shed), among others. Probably late nineteenth to early twentieth century. A similar set of words was sung to a different tune in a version collected by John Meredith from Jack Luscombe, Ryde (NSW) in 1953 and titled 'Click, Click, That's How the Shears Go'. *See also Bush, The; Bush Ballad; Pastoral Industry Folklore; Shearers; Work Lore*

COATHANGER, THE

Folk name for Sydney Harbour Bridge, probably derived from journalese and rarely used by 'Sydneysiders'. *See also Folk Speech*

COCKATOOS

Often associated with weatherlore in which these birds, often of the black variety, flying in a particular direction are said to be signs of rain. Cockatoos are also noted in bush tradition for their toughness as meat. *See also Weatherlore; Foodways; Folk Belief*

COCKEYE BOB

Northern Territory and northern West Australian term for a small whirlwind. Also 'cockeyed Bob'. *See also Brickfielder; Eco-Lore; Fremantle Doctor; Southerly Buster*

'COCKIES OF BUNGAREE, THE'

Humorous bush song, dating from at least the 1890s, detailing the rigours of working for one of the notoriously miserly and hard-driving 'cocky' farmers of Victoria's Bungaree region, near Ballarat. The chorus runs:

We used to go to bed, you know, a little bit after dark
The room we used to sleep in was just like Noah's Ark
There was mice and cats and dog and rats, pigs and poultry
I'll never forget the time we had down in Bungaree.

The cocky works his labourer cutting chaff from before dawn to long after dusk – 'I hate the bloody nightwork they do on Bungaree', he finally declares, exasperated and exhausted. *See also Bush, The; Bush Ballad; Cocky; Free Selector; Pastoral Industry Folklore*

COCKY

An abbreviation of 'cockatoo farmer', meaning a small farmer or selector who, like the cockatoo, scratches out a living from the earth. The term occurs in various combinations, including 'cocky farmer', 'cow cocky' and, for golden syrup, 'cocky's joy'. In folklore, cockies are notoriously hard-bitten, miserly and hard men to work for, as in the well-known ballad 'The Cockies of Bungaree' and the similar 'The Stringybark Cockatoo'. In Bungaree:

> The nights they are so hard, they'll break your heart in two,
> If you ever work for Cocky Burke, you very soon will know.

'The Inglewood (or 'New England) Cocky' is another of a number of related traditions, in which the cocky's family are raised 'on pumpkin and bear' (alternatively, 'beer'). *See also Bush, The; 'Cockies of Bungaree, The'; Cow Cocky; Folk Speech; Free Selector*

'COLONIAL EXPERIENCE'

A 'new chum' song in which the recently arrived migrant at Sydney Cove finds the climate, conditions and work in Australia so hard that 'Instead of roaming foreign parts/I wish I'd studied the Fine Arts'. *See also Barlow, Billy; Migration Lore; New Chum*

COLOURS

The lore of colour is ancient, extensive and culture-specific. In Christian tradition, for example, black is the colour of mourning, while in many parts of India white is associated with death. The symbolism of colour in Australia includes the Christian notion that white symbolises purity and virginity (hence the white bride's dress of the traditional wedding). A traditional rhyme provides some idea of the extent of colour lore in relation to marriage:

> Married in white you have chosen all right.
> Married in blue your love will be true.
> Married in pink your fortunes will sink.
> Married in green you are ashamed to be seen.
> Married in grey you will go far away.

Since the eighteenth century, green has been considered unlucky, at first as a clothing colour, but eventually the belief spread to include any green object. The colour was also associated with death, as in the saying 'wear green and you will soon wear black'. In clothing, blue is associated with baby boys and pink with baby girls.

In Chinese and Chinese diaspora traditions, red is generally considered to be the colour of health, wealth, happiness and luck, and features strongly in Chinese-Australian culture. In Anglo-Australian tradition red is the colour of danger or of heightened significance, as in the phrase 'a red-letter day'. Red is, of course, also associated with blood, and there is a considerable body of ancient lore in most cultures relating to blood, including menstrual blood, folk notions of 'blood' as a marker of race and/or of breeding or lack of it, and the Christian religious significance of Christ's blood. *See also Chinese Influences on Australian Folklore; Folk Belief; Religious Lore; Weddings*

COMING OF AGE

The attainment of legal, religious or customary adulthood is observed by most cultural groups. In Anglo-Celtic Australia the most familiar form has long been the 'Twenty-First Birthday'. This took the form of a large, often extravagant party, paid for and organised by the subject's parents on his or her reaching what used to be the legal adult age of twenty-one. The usual birthday party trappings of cakes, foods, drinks and presents were often accompanied by a silver 'key to the house', symbolic of the person having now attained the right of free entry and exit without the need for parental consent. Such traditions, nowadays largely irrelevant when children may leave home in early adolescence and single-parent families are common, are nevertheless strongly adhered to in many quarters. Interestingly, it is often the children themselves who insist on the 'Twenty-First', even though the legal age of adulthood in Australia is now eighteen. The practice of the 'Twenty-First' is now moving towards the eighteenth birthday, but it is not uncommon for both to be celebrated in similar flamboyant and enthusiastic style.

Other cultural groups observe adulthood in different ways. Best-known perhaps is the Jewish 'Bar-Mitzvah', the religious and cultural coming of age of Jewish males. While this is officially ceremonialised in the synagogue, it is also an occasion of great rejoicing and conviviality among family and friends.

Most ethnic and religious groups observe coming-of-age with some form of festive activity. *See also Bar/Bat Mitzvah; Birthdays, Customs*

COMING OUT (1)

This phrase has two widely different meanings in Australia. It can refer to homosexuals publicly announcing their sexual orientation, or it can refer to young women making their entry into society and the adult world via a debutante ball. For most of the twentieth and earlier centuries, homosexual people risked legal sanctions such as imprisonment and social punishment ranging from ostracism to injury or death if their sexuality became widely known. 'Poofter bashing' was a not uncommon pastime among some young men, and some resulting deaths have been widely publicised. The years of Gay Liberation in the latter part of the twentieth century have led in Australia to wider tolerance. Some individuals, including well-known public figures, have 'come out' and made their sexuality known to the public. In Sydney, the popular Gay and Lesbian Mardi Gras is the most dramatic expression of coming out, when homosexual men and women from all round Australia and some overseas countries celebrate their sexuality and their 'gay pride' with considerable humour and satire. 'Coming out' (from 'coming out of the closet') is essentially a voluntary act, in contrast to 'outing', an objectionable practice whereby some zealots (straight and gay) publicly name people they believe to be homosexual against their will or without their consent. *See also Customs; Gay and Lesbian Mardi Gras*

COMING OUT (2)

The second and older meaning of the phrase is less commonly used nowadays, possibly because it has been overtaken by the meaning described above. Today, the folk saying is that Julie is 'doing her Deb' rather than 'making her debut' or 'coming out'. Debutante Balls still take place in Australia, particularly in country areas, and they may be an important social event in the community. The focus of the Deb Ball is on young girls, around sixteen years of age, who wear elaborate long white dresses and are presented to a notable person in the district, such as the Mayor or Shire President. Together with their partners, who usually wear (mostly hired) formal attire, the Debs parade through the hall and perform some demonstration dances before the audience joins in the dancing. 'Doing your Deb' signifies that a young woman has entered the adult world, and in times gone by, could now be considered for marriage. Like the twenty-first birthday, the individual may have well and truly entered the adult world somewhat earlier, but nostalgia and the love of ritual and of a grand celebration keep the Debutante Balls going. *See also Customs, Deb Balls*

COMMUNITY FAIRS

These local events take a variety of forms. The traditional one is that of the village or church fete, which was usually aimed at fundraising for the church or some aspect of local community life, perhaps a sporting team or the purchase of play equipment for a park. The fete was, and still often is, characterised by games, sports, competitions such as talent quests, lucky dips, 'white elephant stalls' or 'jumble sales' at which all sorts of junk and knick-knacks might be purchased, displays of local skills and trades, exhibitions and sale of local produce and arts and crafts, cake stalls with mothers volunteering specially baked cakes, a barbecue or 'sausage sizzle' (traditionally organised and staffed mainly by males), and just about any other form of human activity that might conceivably bring in some money for the cause. All contributions to, organisation of and labour for the fete was by volunteers.

While fetes have by no means disappeared, they have been increasingly supplanted in urban and suburban areas by 'community fairs'. Although these are similar in organisation and aim to the fete, they generally aim to be more inclusive of the broader community and are not in aid of one particular cause. Consequently, the community fair attracts a host of self-help and community groups, including Parents' and Citizens'/Teachers' groups, church groups, Scouts, Guides, Brownies; charity, heritage and environmental organisations; as well as small-scale private entrepreneurs and local and state government bodies such as the police, fire brigade, ambulance or urban planners, who have – or would like to have – a close relationship with community activities. These and similar groups are generally intent on raising funds for themselves, rather than for some central or common project or need.

A community fair may be held only once a year, as distinct from a community market, which may take place once a month. Markets are likely to feature locally grown produce and locally made crafts, and are held as simple money-raising ventures by the vendors. A community fair is likely to have a greater emphasis on entertainment, and may include hired attractions such as a merry-go-round, jumping inflatables and even more death-defying enticements. The fair may be run by a community organisation such as Rotary or Lions in order to raise funds for local worthy causes. *See also Bazaars; Customs; Markets*

'CONVICT MAID, THE'
Nineteenth-century broadside ballad of a young woman who stole from her master to please her lover and is transported to Botany Bay. In common with most broadside ballads, which were commercially produced songs rather than folk songs (though many became folk songs), the song has a moralising ending:

> Oh, could I but once more be free,
> I'd ne'er 'gain a captive be;
> But I would seek some honest trade,
> And ne'er become a convict maid.

See also Convict Lore; Transportation Ballads; Women's Folklore

CONVICT LORE
Source and subject of our earliest settler folklore. Ballads of transportation, such as 'Judges and Juries', 'Van Diemen's Land' and many others were composed in Britain from the considerable broadside ballad trade and shipped to Australia with convicts and migrants. Locally composed ballads and traditions soon sprang up, especially concerning convict bushrangers such as Jack Donohoe and the bushrangers of Van Diemen's Land, such as Martin Cash and Matthew Brady. 'Frank the Poet' is also credited with the composition of many songs and poems reflecting the convict view of life, such as 'Moreton Bay' (a song paraphrased by Ned Kelly in his notorious 'Jerilderie Letter'):

> One Sunday morning, as I went walking,
> By Brisbane waters I chanced to stray;
> I heard a convict his fate bewailing
> As on the sunny river banks he lay:
> 'I am a native of Erin's island,
> Though banished now from my native shore,
> They tore me from my aged parents,
> And from the maiden that I do adore.

As well as such ballads, the lore and legendry of convictism, replete with brutal overseers, wrongs and injustices, heroic and villainous convicts, along with many elements of convict folk speech, persisted in Australian tradition long after the end of transportation. See also Bushrangers;

Folk Speech; Frank the Poet; Kelly, Ned; Logan, Captain; Ring, The; Transportation Ballads

COO-EE

Call used in the bush to locate lost persons or communicate position over long distances. Beginning at mid-pitch on the first syllable, the second syllable ends an octave higher. Almost certainly derived from indigenous Dharuk (NSW) usage. *See also Bush, The; Folk Speech; Indigenous Folklore*

COOK, CAPTAIN JAMES

Captain James Cook (1728–79), 'discoverer' of Australia, features in a number of Aboriginal traditions in which Cook, his men and especially his sailing ship *Endeavour* feature as the returning ghosts of the dead or are interpreted in some other supernatural way. In some areas of the Northern Territory, Captain Cook has become conflated with Ned Kelly. In children's lore Captain Cook lives on in the rhyme:

> *Captain Cook chased a chook*
> *All around Australia*
> *Lost his pants in the middle of France*
> *And found them in Tasmania.*

In rhyming slang, to 'take or have a look' is to 'take a Captain Cook'. Captain Cook also features in Inuit tradition, a consequence of his navigation to what is now Canada. *See also Children's Lore; Indigenous Folklore*

COOKS

Cooks are known in rhyming slang as 'babbling brooks', often abbreviated to 'babbler'. The cook is an important figure of fun and target of insults in the folklore of bush workers, especially shearers, and also in the traditions of the Australian foot soldier, the digger. There are many yarns, songs and poems that feature cooks, usually as hard-bitten individuals seemingly determined to poison those they feed. One of the best-known anecdotes is that of the shearer or digger who, suffering from a worse-than-usual dose of cooking, says loudly that the 'cook is a bastard'. The boss or commanding officer overhears this complaint but cannot tell who uttered it. Annoyed, he calls out to the diners, 'Who called the cook a bastard?' Immediately echoes back the response: 'Who called the bastard a cook!' From this image arises another colloquialism for cook: 'bait-layer', a reference to the laying of poisoned baits to kill unwanted pests. *See also Bush, The; Folk Speech*

CORN DOLLIES
Rural folk craft involving the weaving and tying of corn or wheat stalks or leaves into a variety of shapes and designs, ranging from the simple to the extremely complex. Common in Britain, this tradition of making and giving 'favours', as they are often called, migrated to Australia, where it is still carried out in some wheat-growing communities – around Koorda in Western Australia, for example. In common with many other folk crafts, corn dolly-making has been revived in recent times, and the range, variety and complexity of the traditional designs has been extended considerably. *See also Crafts, Leather Plaiting; Quilting*

CORNSTALKS
Traditional name for residents of New South Wales. Probably early nineteenth century and heard infrequently now. *See also Folk Speech; Regional Rivalries*

CORRIGAN, TOMMY
Sometimes said to have been Australia's greatest jockey, Corrigan was killed in an accident at Caulfield racecourse in August 1894. His death was the subject of song and poetry, including a widely known Melbourne broadside usually titled 'The Death of Tommy Corrigan'. *See also Disasters; Folk Heroes; Sports Lore; Turf Lore*

CORROBOREE
From the Dharuk language 'garaabara', meaning a ceremony involving the decoration of the body with coloured pigments, dance, music and song. A corroboree may be religious and relate to ritual and mythological aspects of Aboriginal belief (some corroborees take place at full moon, some only at night) or may be an informal, festive get-together. Whether ceremonial or informal, the senses of meeting and communality are central to corroboree. The term has also been used in Australian English to refer to a party, as in 'the shearers are having a corroboree tonight'. *See also Customs, Folk Speech, Indigenous Folklore*

COSSIE

A colloquial term, mostly used in New South Wales, for a swimming costume, also known in Australia as togs, swimmers or bathers. Cossie is a good example of regional variation in Australian folk speech, a phenomenon which today receives more attention from linguistics experts than in previous years. Some other commonly quoted examples concern the names of popular foodstuffs, such as large fruit buns (Boston Buns, Berlin Buns etc) or processed meat sausage (Strasburg, Devon, German Sausage, Polony etc). *See also Folk Speech*

COUNTING OUT

There are a large number of rhymes and rituals used by primary school children to decide who will be 'it' or 'he' in a game about to be played. Some rhymes are extremely complex, such as the one described by the Brisbane researchers Lindsay and Palmer:

> *Eenee meenee macka racka,*
> *Rar ri dominacka,*
> *Chickalacka lollapoppa,*
> *Hom Pom Push.*
> *Out goes one! Out goes two!*
> *Out goes another one*
> *And that is you!*

Counting out rhymes, like much children's folklore, are a part of our British heritage, and the same or similar rhymes are found in all English-speaking countries (as well as similar versions in other languages). Adults have been fascinated for many generations by the magical nonsense language used in rhymes such as 'Eetle ottle, black bottle' and 'Inky pinky ponky'. According to prominent English researchers Iona and Peter Opie, theories have been put forward that children's counting out rhymes are survivals of 'ancient Welsh language' and 'witches' incantations'. However, these theories are no more proven than other adult speculations such as those about the political origins of nursery rhymes.

Many counting out rhymes involve simple pointing to the body or the feet, but some have more elaborate movements. 'One potato, two potato' has been around for generations, and involves all players holding out their fists. On each number, the child doing the counting hits the fists of the others in succession, and the fist hit on the word 'More!' is put behind the player's back. The last fist left standing means that that player is 'it'.

> One potato, two potato
> Three potato, four,
> Five potato, six potato,
> Seven potato MORE.

See also Australian Children's Folklore Collection; Children's Folklore; Games

COUNTRY MUSIC

To borrow a line from the famous film *The Blues Brothers*, there is country *and* western music, although in Australia today, this music is less commonly referred to as 'country and western' and more often as simply 'country'. In her long entry on country music in *The Oxford Companion to Australian Folklore* (1993), Monika Allen discusses perceived differences between folk and country music, and despite some controversy, few would dispute that in Australia, folk music finds its major roots in the United Kingdom and Ireland whereas country music, stylistically at least, has been heavily influenced by the United States.

Country music centres on the annual Tamworth (NSW) Festival held in January over the Australia Day weekend, and country music stars such as Slim Dusty and, in his day, Tex Morton, are Australia's most prolific and loved recording stars. The overlap between country and folk music centres on themes connected with the bush, and the bush ballad has an honoured place in country music circles. Country music is extremely popular among Aboriginal people, and has produced many Aboriginal performers and composers such as the late Dougie Young. His song 'The land where the crow flies backwards, and the pelican builds her nest' is regarded as a classic by many country and folk music enthusiasts. *See also Bush Ballads; Bush Music; Folk Songs; Indigenous Folklore*

COUSIN JACKS

South Australian term for male miners of Cornish origin or descent. In yarns, Cousin Jacks are usually portrayed as stupid. *See also Cousin Jennies, Drongo, The; Kernewek Lowender*

COUSIN JENNIES
South Australian term for the wives of Cornish or Cornish-descended miners. *See also Cousin Jacks*

COW COCKY
A cocky farmer who runs a dairy farm. *See also Cocky*

CRACKER NIGHT
A general term for evenings when fireworks are exploded in local communities. Cracker Night has been associated with various dates in Australian tradition, including the now-defunct Empire Day (24 May) and the largely defunct Guy Fawkes Night (5 November). Guy Fawkes' Night is, however, still celebrated with a bonfire in Moe, Victoria. Many parts of Australia have banned or restricted the use of fireworks for other than big 'official' events such as New Year's Eve. The only time at which it is legal for the public to explode fireworks in the Northern Territory is on the evening of 30 June. This 'Cracker Night' celebrates the Territory's attainment of self-government in 1978. *See also Customs, Empire Day, Guy Fawkes' Night*

CRAFTS
Handcrafts of many kinds have an honoured place in Australian folklore. They are mostly learned within families, although formal classes in many crafts do exist. Folk crafts such as knitting and crochet are almost always learned from a member of the older generation, such as a mother or grandmother, and many women can recall their first lessons at grandma's knee. Embroidery of many kinds is a popular pastime, usually among women, although some of what are traditionally called 'women's crafts' may also be practised by sailors during long hours at sea, and by some other men. Jennifer Isaacs, a leading writer on the subject, has documented Australian women's handcrafts in books such as *The Gentle Arts* (1987). Handcrafts may provide interesting examples of the cross-over between folk art and high art, as in the world-renowned Victorian Tapestry Workshop in Melbourne, whose products can be seen in prestigious locations such as Parliament House and the National Library in Canberra, and at Melbourne Airport.

What might be considered men's handcrafts are elaborately documented in Ron Edwards' numerous books on bush crafts, which feature leather plaiting and a large number of uses for wood and fencing wire. These crafts are not only practised in the bush, and the suburban home on the quarter-acre block will frequently include home-made objects such as letter-boxes and sheds, made with varying degrees of skill. Woodwork is a popular craft, mostly though not exclusively among men, and like tapestry, has crossed over into art of the highest order. The Australian experience, in both pioneering days and in contemporary times, has required a considerable amount of improvisation, 'do it yourself' (DIY) or 'making do'. In the best folkloric tradition, most of these skills are learned directly from other people, both family members and others. Australians do not take classes in how to paint a fence, make a dog kennel or sew on a button. *See also Crochet; Embroidery; Knitting; Leather Plaiting; Making Do*

CROCHET

Using a single crochet hook rather than knitting needles, this largely women's craft may involve making similar objects as are made by knitting in wool, cotton, linen or other fibres. Crochet has links with tatting and lace-making. The techniques are different, but all three skills may be used to make borders for handkerchiefs, decorative table mats or larger objects such as bedspreads. Whole garments such as women's jumpers, dresses and skirts may also be crocheted, and a common product is the crocheted 'Afghan', a rug made from small crocheted squares, often using left-over wool. Like the 'Wagga rug', made in earlier generations from chaff bags and unwanted clothing or fabric, the Afghan represents both thrift and skill, and a woman's desire to create something colourful and useful for her home. Crochet is almost certainly learned within the family, or from friends. *See also Crafts; Women's Folklore*

CROOKED MICK

Legendary occupational hero of Australian shearers and other outback workers. Mick can shear more sheep, cut more trees and do anything faster than anyone else. He is usually said to reside in a mythical, faraway place called 'the Speewah', where everything grows in unnaturally large proportions; or the pumpkins are so big they can be used as houses, the trees are so tall they have to be hinged to let in the sunlight, the sheep are so large they cannot be shorn without climbing up a ladder, and so on. Mick's various anecdotes and antics were collected together by folklorist Bill Wannan in his book *Crooked Mick of the Speewah*, published in 1966. *See also Bush, The; Big Burrawong; Folk Humour; Pastoral Industry Folklore, Speewah; Yarns*

CROSSING THE LINE

While not strictly an Australian custom, this ritual used to take place when passenger ships crossed the equator and was experienced in some form by most migrants to Australia until the 1970s. In 1865 Elizabeth Anketell, *en route* to Victoria, described the custom as it was in those days, including the practice of 'shaving' those who had not previously crossed the equator:

> ... *the victim is placed on a stool [and] is held by 2 men blackened all over to represent Negroes. Neptune and his wife dressed up in a most hideous manner sit in [?] a large brush dipped in pitch and tar is put all over the face and into the mouth. If possible they put dirty oil in the first boys mouth; he is then rolled into a tank of see [sic] water and nearly smothered by the 2 negroes [sic], coming out half suffocated like a drowned rat ... [I had to] actually shake hands and kiss Mrs Neptune* ... (quoted in J. Anketell 1998, p. 8)

By the 1950s and 1960s this event had been made more user-friendly and institutionalised as an item of shipboard entertainment and a diversion from the monotony of the voyage. King Neptune still presided, of course, though the 'shaving' was now purely symbolic and first-timers crossing the line – mostly assisted passage immigrants – were simply dunked in the ship's swimming pool. *See also Customs, Migration Lore, Maritime Lore*

CROWEATERS

Folk name for residents of South Australia, said to derive from the need of early settlers to eat crows when supplies of mutton ran out. Mid–late nineteenth century. *See also Folk Speech, Regional Rivalries*

CUPPA

The cup of tea or 'cuppa' is a staple and much-loved part of the Australian diet. Indian tea is the most popular, although a wide variety of China and other teas are available, and herbal teas such as peppermint, rose hip and camomile have grown in popularity in recent years. Australian women in particular love their cup of tea, and 'a cup of tea, a BEX and a good lie-down' (immortalised in a theatrical production), is a comic summary of a female ideal of rest. Since large-scale immigration after 1945 brought changes to the Australian diet, good coffee has become another staple. The coffee shop, the espresso machine and the cappuccino are popular and widespread, often under Italian management. In some cases the great Australian 'cuppa' has been recognised in eating places which advertise 'cuppacinos', although probably not in Italian bistros. It is hard to know whether the 'cuppacino' is presented tongue-in-cheek or whether it is yet another of the common spelling and grammatical errors (like the dreaded wandering apostrophe) which enliven public life and discourse in Australia. *See also Folk Speech; Foodways*

CURLEW

In the Hunter Valley region of New South Wales, and elsewhere, the cry of this bird is sometimes said to be an omen of impending death. *See also Folk Belief*

CURLING

Cornish miners in South Australia have a strong Christmas carol singing or 'curling' tradition, and are known to have carried out this custom at least as early as 1865. *See also Christmas; Cousin Jennies; Customs; Uncle Jacks, Kernewek Lowender,*

CURRENCY

A term used in colonial days to describe non-Aboriginal persons born in the colonies of Australia, especially New South Wales, as in 'currency lad' and 'currency lass', and occasionally heard in convict songs and transportation ballads. *See also Folk Speech*

CURTIN'S COWBOYS

Folk name used variously for a mounted unit that patrolled north-west Australia during World War II and, in Queensland, for the Civilian Construction Corps, dubbed 'Curtin's Comic Cowboys'. John Curtin was Australia's Prime Minister for much of World War II. *See also Folk Speech*

CUSTOMS

The practices referred to by folklorists as 'customs' are an extremely large sector of folklore. They are usually divided into three groups: life cycle customs, also known as rites of passage, which concentrate on the passage of the individual through the various stages of life, from birth, through christening, birthdays, coming of age, marriage, anniversaries and death; occasional customs carried out at appropriate moments, such as housewarmings and completion customs like topping out a newly completed building; and calendar or periodic customs that are observed on a particular day or period of a calendar. Customs are usually associated strongly with belief, either of a formal religious kind, or of a folk or 'superstitious' kind, or with a secular belief in the appropriateness of observing a particular set of activities at a particular time and place. Relatively little research has been undertaken into Australian folk customs, though a good number are, often for the first time in print, included in this guide. *See also April Fools' Day; Blessing of the Fleece; Blessing of the Fleet; Christmas; Easter; Funerals; Harvest Customs; New Year's Day; St Valentine's Day; Weddings*

CUTTING DOWN TALL POPPIES
A widespread folk speech term describing the Australian tendency to undercut and criticise individuals who are elevated above the everyday by reason of wit, ability or luck. *See also Folk Speech*

CYPRUS BRIG, THE
Name of a ship taken over by convicts in the ballad titled 'Seizure of the Cyprus Brig', thought to have been composed by 'Frank the Poet'. The events related in the song occurred on a voyage to Tasmania's Port Macquarie penal station in August 1829, during which the vessel was seized by convicts in Recherche Bay. *See also Convicts, Frank the Poet*

D

DAD AND DAVE

Probably an original literary invention of Australian author 'Steele Rudd' (Arthur Hoey Davis, 1868–1935), Dad and his gormless son Dave first appeared in the *Bulletin* magazine in 1895. Four years later the sketches appeared in book form under the title *On Our Selection*, followed by various new editions and sequels. The books were best-sellers and appear to have inspired the numerous humorous folk tales and jokes told about Dad and Dave. These concentrate on portraying Dad, Dave and the family as country hicks, as in this brief example:

> *Mum: Dave's gone and broke his leg, Dad!*
> *Dad: D'yer think we ought to shoot 'im?*

Dad and Dave yarns portray Dave as a harmless simpleton, very much in the tradition of the widely distributed 'numb skull' folk stories. In one typical exchange, Dave is leaving home to join the army. Mum, worried about her son in the big city, prevails on Dad to give him a fatherly lecture about the perils of drink, gambling and women. Dave is anxiously and honestly at pains to let Dad know that he never has any truck with such things. Dad returns to Mum and says: 'You needn't worry. I don't think the army will take him anyway, the boy's a half-wit!'. *See also Drongo, The; Folk Humour, Folklorism; Folk Tales*

DAMPER

Unleavened bread baked in the ashes of a campfire. Damper was the typical 'tucker' of the bushman and features frequently in bush tradition. Derived from a British dialect term for a small bite to eat. *See also Foodways, Johnny Cakes*

DANCE

Social dancing, or ballroom dancing, has been a popular pastime in Australia since the arrival of the First Fleet; also dancing is also an important part of traditional Aboriginal culture, for both ritual and entertainment purposes. As stable communities were established in

Australia in post-colonial days, the local hall followed the pub and the police station as an important centre of community life, and halls were 'made for dancing'. Apart from the Methodist Church which banned dancing on church property until the late 1940s, many churches ran local dances in their own halls. In colonial days, dancing was so popular (and many a tough shearer was an expert) that until halls were built, dances were held in woolsheds, out of doors and even in small private houses. Contrary to beliefs about Australia being isolated by 'the tyranny of distance', the latest 'hit' dances from Europe such as the waltz, polka and mazurka reached Australia very quickly, and would be taught 'hot off the boat' by dancing schools such as Mr Wivell's Academy and Assembly Hall in Melbourne's Fitzroy, described by Shirley Andrews in her definitive book *Take Your Partners: Traditional Dancing in Australia* (1979). Sheet music for pianos was also an important means of spreading the latest hits.

Social dancing is an area where folk culture and commercial popular culture mix happily. Mr Wivell's Academy was undoubtedly a commercial venture, but many popular dances in the nineteenth century came from folk tradition, whether English country dances and Scottish reels, quadrilles or European waltzes and mazurkas. In the twentieth and twenty-first centuries, dancing (such as disco) has been influenced by American customs and media, although Old-Time and New Vogue ballroom dancing still takes place, and Latin American dances such as salsa and tango are growing in popularity. Some traditional set dances such as the Lancers may still be performed in Old-Time dances today.

Traditional dances from Australia's many immigrant groups flourish in Australia. Children's classes are held, often as part of the program at 'Greek school', for example, and folk dance is an important part of cultural maintenance in ethnic communities. Some groups mount highly skilled adult dance troupes which make frequent public performances. Most community festivities are likely to include some dance displays, whether Irish, Scottish, Greek or German, and these attractive performances have no doubt helped make 'multiculturalism' a well-accepted part of Australian life. *See also Bush Dance; Musical Instruments*

DARCY, LES

James Leslie Darcy (1895–1917) was an outstanding pugilist commemorated in song and story for his strength and perseverance. He was widely believed to have been murdered in the USA by Americans jealous of his skills and fearful of his impact on American boxing, as the best known of his ballads has it:

> He gave up hope, when he got that dope,
> Way down in Tennessee.

In fact, Darcy died of blood poisoning arising from an injury received in the ring before he left Australia. Darcy was much more than a sporting celebrity, though, and up to and during World War I took on the character of a national hero, celebrated in tradition with an intriguing mixture of pride, grief and affection. *See also Folk Heroes, National Icons*

DARWIN BEER CAN REGATTA
Held in Darwin one Sunday in July or August, depending on the neap tide. Since 1974 this light-hearted race of boats constructed of empty beer cans has been carried out at Mindil Beach. Associated events may include a thong-throwing competition and a bathing beauty contest, among other irreverent events. It is usually said that this custom is a true reflection of the feisty spirit of Darwin. *See also Customs, Folk Sports*

DAWN SERVICE, THE
Now part of the Anzac Day observance on 25 April, the Dawn Service evolved in various places during the 1920s from spontaneous, grassroots observances as a non-religious, non-military recognition of the dawn landings at Gallipoli in 1915. Originally a simple gathering of silent participants in a returned diggers' ceremony of toasting dead comrades and wreath-laying, the dawn service has gradually acquired some trappings of military and religious observance, including the playing of 'The Last Post', the firing of a single rifle-shot and the recitation of Lawrence Binyon's well-known poem 'Lest We Forget'. For many, the Dawn Service is the most important and moving aspect of Anzac Day, perhaps because its simplicity echoes the dislike of formality that Australians often think of as essential to the Australian ethos. There are claims that the Dawn Service originated in Albany (WA), others that it originated in Queensland.

The Dawn Service may also be preceded by another custom related to the dawn landings at Gallipoli. This is usually held in ex-service clubs before dawn and involves the eating of a small meal and the drinking of a tot of alcohol, replicating the last meal of the Anzacs before they boarded the boats that would take them to the beaches. *See also* ANZAC, *Customs*, *Digger*, *Gallipoli*

DEAD HORSE TREASURE, THE

A lost treasure tradition. Brock's Creek (NT), about 160 kilometres south-west of Darwin, is where a group of prospectors made a rich gold strike in 1880. Swearing off the grog, they worked hard to get as much of the gold into the saddle-packs of one of their horses before the wet season and lack of food overcame them. At the end of a week or so they had the horses saddled with a fortune and ready to go. They decided to have 'a drink' to celebrate their good fortune. The one became 'a few' and then too many. Their drunken merrymaking frightened the horses away, including the one laden with the gold. Despite months of desperate searching, the horse was never found. It is said that prospectors in the Northern Territory still look closely at any bones they find in the hope that they may stumble again across the 'Dead Horse Treasure'. *See also Lost Treasures, Yarns*

DEB BALLS

The Debutante Ball, usually known colloquially as 'the deb ball' or 'doing your deb', has a long history in Australia. Originally a British upper-class event designed to launch young women into society, these were often highly formal and socially significant affairs. While the custom has declined in popularity in our less formal age, the Deb Ball is still kept up seriously in many country towns and, according to reports, is making something of a comeback in suburban areas as well. Nowadays the class elements that were originally integral to the Debutante Ball have been largely lost, and the affair has become a kind of rite of passage for young women from a variety of social groups.

Considerable expense is involved in the preparations for the sixteen to seventeen year-old girls who take part in this custom. Elaborate ball gowns are made for the (usually) evening event and the girls are partnered by young men in formal wear. Dances and processions, often of considerable difficulty, are carefully rehearsed for the big night, the peak of which is the 'presentation' of each girl to a person of note who has been invited as guest of honour to officially acknowledge the 'coming out' of the young women. *See also Bush Dance, Coming Out (2), Customs, Dance, Women's Folklore*

DIGGER

A term with two important meanings in Australian folklore:
1. Someone who dug for gold during the mid-nineteenth century goldrushes, from c. 1840s.
2. From 1917 a volunteer Australian or New Zealand foot soldier of non-commissioned rank. Later extended to non-commissioned ranks in all Australian and New Zealand military defence forces. Often abbreviated to 'dig'. *See also ANZAC; Birdie; Gallipoli; Goldrush Lore; War Lore*

DINGO

The wild Australian dog is widely considered an icon of national identity, admired for its ability to live off the land. This characteristic is celebrated in the folk simile 'a dingo's breakfast', said to be 'a piss and a good look round'. But the dingo also has an ambivalent folkloric presence. In folk speech the term 'low dingo' is an insult, and from 1980, with the disappearance of Azaria Chamberlain, the nation developed a form of 'sick' joke known as 'the dingo joke'. The dingo jokes, and much related humour, generally expressed the national preoccupation, anxiety and differing viewpoints about whether a dingo had or had not taken baby Azaria from an Alice Springs camping ground. *See also Chamberlain, Azaria; Dingo Jokes; National Icons*

DINGO JOKES

Riddle jokes, mostly of the 'sick' type, widespread throughout Australia during the Azaria Chamberlain disappearance in 1980 and its lengthy aftermath. Some dingo jokes reflected popular scepticism of 'the dingo did it' theory, such as 'What runs round Ayers Rock on its back legs with its front legs in the air?' 'A dingo doing a victory lap'. Others were of the 'sick' joke variety: 'What kind of droppings have pink booties?' 'A dingo's'; 'What were the two dingoes arguing about outside the tent?' 'Eat in or take away' and 'Did you hear where they've found Azaria Chamberlain?' 'In a meat pie in New York'. *See also Chamberlain, Azaria; Dingo; Folk Humour*

DINKI-DI

Title of a well-known folk song and also an item of folk speech. From the chorus of a famous digger song of World War I, known as 'Horseferry Road'. Versions of the song were sung in World War II, when a chorus was added: 'Dinki-di, Dinky-di, I am a digger and I won't tell a lie.' The term 'dinky-di' is used more generally to describe an Australian, 'a dinky-di Aussie', and also to describe something which is genuine or true. *See also Digger; Fair Dinkum; War Lore*

DINNER PARTY

The dinner party has a long history as a form of entertainment and social interaction. It was associated especially with the upper and middle classes of Britain, who transmitted the practice, along with its codes of manners and etiquette, and many others, to Australia during the nineteenth century. The proper conventions for such dinner parties involved an elaborate form of invitation and reply, seating arrangements according to precedence, the ladies rising after dessert, a certain etiquette for after-dinner small-talk and a whole array of social taboos. In *Australian Etiquette*, a guide to such matters published in 1885, dinner parties were described as mainly for the married and the middle-aged, though the presence of young, unmarried persons was often desirable.

The dinner party survives today. Mostly, though not entirely, shorn of its more elaborate conventions, it is still a custom associated with the more affluent sectors of society, or those who aspire to such a milieu. Young, unmarried people often hold dinner parties, with the custom being particularly prevalent amongst 'yuppies' (young, upwardly mobile professionals) during the 1980s. The dinner party is also an element of occupational life, especially in relation to climbing the promotions ladder. The more informal custom of having a group of friends around for a home-cooked meal is not usually referred to as a 'dinner party'. *See also Customs; Foodways*

DISASTERS

As in many other traditions, notable accidents, wrecks and other tragedies often generate folkloric reactions. These may be in the form of song, verse or stories, about the deaths of noted sporting or public figures, and even animals; and in customs such as commemorations and material forms such as home-made crosses and wreaths. The death of the Princess of Wales, and the September 11 attack on the World Trade Center in

New York City in 2001 and subsequent military action in Afghanistan, for example, generated a vast body of sick jokes, parodies and other lore transmitted broadly by electronic mail through the Internet, or on websites. *See also Darcy, Les; Granville Rail Disaster, The; Jokes; Kembla Grange Mine Disaster Commemoration; Phar Lap; Roadside Shrines, Robinson, Alec; Stone, Willy; Sunshine Rail Disaster, The; Urban Legends*

DIVING FOR THE CROSS

Custom associated especially with the Greek Orthodox observance of Epiphany in which young men dive for a cross thrown into the sea or inland water body. The diver who retrieves the cross is popularly believed to be blessed with good luck. *See also Customs; Folk Belief; Religious Lore*

DIWALI (DIVALI)

A Hindu festival lasting for five days from the first day of the month of *Kartik* (October–November) in the Hindu calendar. *Diwali,* or 'The Festival of Lights', is in some parts of India regarded as the New Year, and is celebrated accordingly with the closing of books, house cleaning, visiting, gift exchange, consumption of festival foods, fireworks and general preparations and well-wishing for a happy and prosperous year, including the purchase and wearing of new clothes. Its defining feature is the lighting of windows and other parts of the house with candles and lamps. It is celebrated as a holiday throughout India for five days, although there are numerous local variations on the festivities. *See also Customs; New Year's Day; Religious Folklore*

DOG ON THE TUCKERBOX, THE

A tourist stop near Gundagai, on the Hume Highway between Melbourne and Sydney, noted for a fine sculpture of a dog sitting on a tuckerbox which was created by the local artist Frank Rusconi and unveiled by the then Prime Minister, Joseph Lyons, in 1932. The poem 'Nine Miles from Gundagai' (and similar titles – sometimes five miles rather than nine) is one of Australia's most popular bush ballads. Often attributed to Jack Moses, there are a number of earlier versions dating from the nineteenth century. It is a subject of debate as to whether the dog was a loyal mate guarding his master's property or a wretched cur that spoilt the tucker by sitting (or worse) in the box, and various ballads canvas both possibilities. The Rusconi statue enshrines the dog's loyalty,

and this version is the most popular interpretation. *See also Dogs;*
National Icons

DOGS

Dogs feature extensively in Australian folklore. They are variously
valued as companions to swagmen and others, as protectors and saviours
and as workers of stock. The most famous folk dog is probably the one
that sat on – or more properly shat in – the tuckerbox at Gundagai in the
song variously titled 'Nine Miles from Gundagai' or 'Five Miles from
Gundagai'. However, there are many other dog traditions, such as 'The
Loaded Dog' of Henry Lawson's well-known short story and 'Red Dog of
the Pilbara', a north-west Australian tradition fictionalised in book form
by Louis de Bernieres in 2001. *See also Dingo, Dog on the Tuckerbox, The;*
Loaded Dog, The; 'Nine Miles from Gundagai', Red Dog

DONOHOE, JACK

The bushranger hero Jack Donohoe (or Donahoe, Donahue) was found
guilty of intent to commit an unspecified felony and transported to New
South Wales for life in 1824–5, he escaped from custody in 1827.
Donohoe was credited in ballads and by some witnesses with many
attributes of the outlaw hero: he was courteous to women, never robbed
'the poor' (in this case the convict and ex-convict population), was
heroically daring, and 'died game'. He enjoyed the sympathy and support
of convict society, many of whose members provided Donohoe and his
gang with food and shelter and information about trooper movements.
This assistance kept Donohoe alive until 1830, when he was killed in a
shoot-out with the trooper police near Sydney. John Meredith published
an in-depth study of the folklore of Donohoe in *The Wild Colonial Boy*
(1982). *See also Bushrangers; Folk Heroes; Wild Colonial Boy, The*

DOUBLE FIVE FESTIVAL *See Dragon Boat Festival*

DOUBLE NINTH FESTIVAL

This is held on the ninth day of the ninth moon of the Chinese calendar
(August–September). *Chung Chiu Chieh* is based on a Chinese legend in
which a hermit escaped a dreadful natural calamity by ascending a high
hill. Chinese people continue to mark this occasion by climbing to high
places for picnics in which cakes symbolising 'highness' are eaten, and by
kite-flying and other outdoor activities. May be observed especially by

Chinese with origins in Singapore, Hong Kong and mainland China. *See also Chinese Folklore in Australia; Customs; Foodways*

DOVER

Clasp-knife named since at least 1870 after a proprietary brand. Mentioned in the nineteenth-century song 'The Wallaby Brigade', about itinerant bush workers:

> *You've only to sport your Dover*
> *And knock a monkey* [sheep] *over,*
> *That's cheap mutton on the Wallaby Brigade.*

See also Bush, The; Folk Speech, Pastoral Industry Folklore

DOYLE, TOM

Historical character who, during the 1960s, was publican and mayor of the eastern goldfields town of Kanowna in Western Australia. Tom was an Irishman whose unusual interpretations of words and phrases unfamiliar to him provide the humour of the many yarns told about him in Western Australia. In one of these gaucheries, the newly married Tom takes his bride to Melbourne to honeymoon in a grand city hotel. The manager of the hotel asks the wealthy but unsophisticated Tom if he would like the bridal chamber. Tom replies that while his wife may require it, he will be happy to piss out the window as usual. Other Tom Doyle stories concentrate on his embarrassing public outbursts. He is a mixture of the numbskull and the frontier, or bush, hero, and very much a local 'character'. *See also Folk Humour; Local Lore; Yarns*

DRAGON BOAT FESTIVAL

One of the three most important festivals of the Chinese calendar, and traditionally held in late June, this now takes place at various times. Known in English as the 'Dragon Boat Festival', it goes under a variety of Chinese names, including *Shih Jen Chieh* (Poets' Festival) and *Hsa Chieh* (Summer Festival). Most of the names refer to the festival's relationship to the summer solstice and to ensuring rain for a good harvest.

Mainly a southern Chinese and generally South-East Asian Chinese festival celebrating the middle of summer, this falls on the fifth day of the fifth month (hence its folk name of the 'Double Five' festival) of the

Chinese lunar calendar. This month is believed to be a dangerous one, and its fifth day to be particularly so. To ward off such danger, everyone dresses up and takes a meal – usually *tsung tzu*, glutinous rice dumplings – down to the shores of the waterway that will carry the Dragon Boat race. Traditional music and singing are part of this festival; the Vietnamese customarily bake a special rice cake offering to Buddha on this day to ward off any possible ill-luck that may befall them at this dangerous period of the Chinese year. Traditionally, the Dragon Boat competition may end with the capsizing of boats and the occasional drowning of competitors.

The Dragon Boat Carnival in Sydney in April 1984 was the first such event held in Australia, and other cities have followed suit with enthusiasm. There are now many non-Chinese participants in Dragon Boat racing. *See also Chinese Folklore in Australia; Customs; Folk Costume; Folk Sports; Foodways; Religious Lore*

DRINKING GAMES
A form of folkloric amusement especially popular with youth. Drinking games may range from relatively sedate activities in which players try to keep a mildly complex rhythm going as they become increasingly inebriated, to straightforward skolling competitions such as 'Centurion', in which players try to drink a shot-glass of beer each minute for one hundred minutes. The last one left standing wins. Those who vomit, lose, and those who miss a turn must drink six shots before the next six-minute mark comes up. Other associated activities include folding paper money, cigarette packets or other items in ways that reveal humorous, obscene or otherwise surprising results, such as folding a five-dollar note to produce a picture of Queen Elizabeth II of Australia wearing spectacles. (This particular game has been rendered obsolete since the Queen was dropped from the five-dollar note in 2001.) No doubt similar diverting pastimes will develop around the new currency in due course. Many drinking games involve hand, arm and face gestures of varying complexity and inanity. *See also Customs; Games; Grog*

'DROMANA MOUNTAIN LION, THE' *See Legendary Animals*

DRONGO
The Drongo is the Australian numbskull, a heroically stupid figure, usually in a bush setting, who interprets literally whatever he is told.

When the boss tells him to 'hang a new gate', the Drongo takes the gate out to the nearest tree and hangs it in a noose. When asked to dig some turnips about the size of his head, the Drongo is found pulling up the entire turnip patch and trying his hat on them for size. The name 'Drongo' in this sense is said to derive from the name of an Australian racehorse famous for losing races. As well as a Northern Australian name for a bird, it is also RAAF slang for a recruit. *See also Dad and Dave; Folk Humour; Folk Tales; Folk Speech*

DROP BEARS

Mythical creatures of Australian tall-tale tradition that are said to drop from the trees onto unsuspecting dupes walking below. Often described as koalas with large heads and sharp teeth. *See also Folk Humour; Hoop Snakes; Legendary Animals*

'DROVER'S DREAM, THE'

Famous whimsical droving song in which a drover of sheep dreams of a fantastic procession of bush animals who have a bush dance, complete with orchestra, before his very eyes. The song, which also exists in other versions, ends when the drover's irate boss wakes him from slumber demanding to know 'where the hell are all the sheep!?', or colourful variants thereof. *See also Bush, The; Bush Ballads, Folk Humour, Pastoral Industry Folklore*

DUNN, JOHN

Bushranger and member of the Weddin Mountains (NSW) confederacy of the Frank Gardiner–Ben Hall gang. *See also Bushrangers; Gardiner, Frank; Gilbert, John; Hall, Ben; Vane, John*

DUNNY

A common term for a lavatory or toilet, usually, but not always, an outdoors one. The outdoor dunny is a popular subject of humour, probably (as Freud might say) to compensate for the anxiety produced by the spiders and snakes alleged to lurk there. 'The Redback [spider] on the toilet seat' was a popular Australian novelty/country music song for some years. The celebrated outback toilet or thunderbox is passing into history in both town and country as sewerage systems or individual septic tanks become widespread, but Australian folklore still enshrines a number of yarns about practical jokes played on persons sitting in the dunny, sometimes involving throwing stones, setting fires, sticks of dynamite, or pretending the 'dunny cart man' was about to remove the pan from under the sitter's backside. Most families have dunny legends; this writer's mother used to tell of the children chasing the dunny cart with rude cries, and the dunny man retorting 'Never you mind, there's some of yours in there.' A popular Australian novelty/country music song for some years, and a colourful 'bush curse' is 'may all your chooks turn into emus and kick down your dunny door'. *See also Folk Speech*

'DYING STOCKMAN, THE'

Song in which a stockman asks to be 'wrapped up in his stockwhip and blanket' and buried 'deep down below ... in the shade where the coolibahs grow'. Probably adapted by Horace Flower in the 1890s from any number of similar songs in English-language tradition, including 'The Dying Rake', 'The Dying Cowboy' (the well-known song 'The Streets of Laredo' is an American representation of this widespread theme), and the dying sailor of 'The Tarpaulin Jacket' and similar ballads. A version called 'The Dying Bagman' was quite widely sung in Australia during the Great Depression; there are many other occupational versions, such as 'The Dying Sleeper-cutter' and 'The Dying Aviator', including a number of bawdy parodies usually involving a dying harlot. *See also Bush, The; Bush Ballad; Bawdry; Folk Songs; Pastoral Industry Folklore*

E

EASTER

Easter is the holiest time in the Christian calendar, commemorating Christ's crucifixion and resurrection, and in the Christian churches it is a time for mourning followed by celebration. Like Christmas, Easter has three elements, and incorporates religious, commercial and folk practices. Easter is held at the time of the equinox; in the northern hemisphere it marks the beginning of spring and all the new life and growth which follow the northern winter. The celebration of spring is older than Christianity, and the word 'Easter' is often said to be derived from the name of a pre-Christian goddess of spring and fertility, Eostre. Easter is also close to the Jewish Passover, the celebration of the Jews' liberation from bondage in Egypt.

These varied and ancient themes of rebirth or renewal have all contributed to the place of Easter in secular folk culture as a time for holidays and rest from work. Unlike Christmas, Easter in Australia is less for large-scale family reunion than for individuals or families to 'recharge their batteries' and renew their energies, perhaps taking some extra days from annual leave and travelling to a holiday destination.

Other secular customs surrounding Easter have both folk and commercial elements. Eggs, like rabbits, are ancient, pre-Christian symbols of birth and fertility, although chocolate eggs and Easter Bunnies are commercial products of fairly recent origin. It is interesting to note that in Australia in the late twentieth century, calls were heard for Australia's feral scourge, the rabbit, to be replaced with an endangered native animal, the bilby, and chocolate 'Easter Bilbies' are now seen in Australian shops. Easter customs in the Greek Orthodox religion include the preparation of hard-boiled eggs dyed red, which are cracked between individuals with the joyous statement that 'Christ is Risen!'. Ukrainian and some other immigrant communities in Australia paint and dye elaborate designs painted and dyed on boiled eggs. Eating hot cross buns at Easter time, an old English tradition, is very popular, and many Australian adults will recall at least part of the nursery rhyme:

Hot cross buns, hot cross buns,
One a penny, two a penny,
Hot cross buns.
If you have no daughters
Give them to your sons;
One a penny, two a penny,
Hot cross buns.

The Orthodox Church generally observes Easter one week after the Western church, with a similar combination of solemnity and celebration. Just before midnight on Orthodox Easter Eve members of the Greek Orthodox faith assemble in church, where a candle-lighting ceremony is carried out by the priest. It is considered good luck to receive the first light from the priest's candle, and to take a lighted candle back to the home, where a specially prepared resurrection meal of soup, red eggs and Easter bread is eaten by all the family. Fireworks, said to symbolise the earthquakes and lightning at Christ's resurrection, may also be a part of the celebration. Easter is especially important in Greek-Australian culture, and even those who do not observe the religious significance of the event frequently participate. *See also Customs; Religious Lore*

ECO-LORE

Ecological lore. There is a close relationship between many forms of folklore and the natural world. Local legends tell how rivers, caves, mountains or other natural features were created and/or named. Local speech is usually full of folk names for flowers, trees, animals and other natural features. Weatherlore and crop-planting techniques often depend upon the virtues traditionally associated with cycles of sun, moon and stars, while the behaviour of animals, plants and insects may also be considered significant in predicting the future. Foodways and folk medicines are especially closely related to the natural environment, while many traditional designs, motifs and forms may seek to reflect elements of nature, such as flowers, animals and landscape. *See also Crafts; Flowers; Folk Medicine; Foodways; Weatherlore*

EID-UL-ADHA

An Islamic Festival of Sacrifice in memory of the prophet Abraham whose faith was tested by God's instruction to kill his son Ishmael. It is traditional in late August for Muslim families to slaughter a sheep or cow according to Islamic law and to share the cooked meat with friends, relations and the poor. It is not uncommon for Muslims to dress in their best clothes and to offer prayers during this period. *See also Customs; Folk Costume; Foodways; Religious Folklore*

ELASTICS

Unlike many children's playground games whose origins are often lost in antiquity, Elastics has not been documented in either Australia, the UK or USA any earlier than the 1950s, and some folklorists suspect it may have originated in South-East Asia and travelled to the West as one of the more benign consequences of the Vietnam War. Elastics is almost exclusively a girls' game, and requires a loop of narrow elastic of about 4 metres (12 feet) which is sometimes supplied commercially (in fluorescent pink). Two players stretch the elastic tautly between them, and the players perform increasingly elaborate jumps and movements with the loop anchored at different heights (*anklies, kneesies, bumsies* etc). The aim of the game is to complete the sequence without becoming entangled in the elastic. Primary school girls from South-East Asia (Vietnam and Laos, for example) have been observed to be particularly skilled at 'high jump' where the elastic stretched at, say, necksies is caught with one foot. Rhymes may accompany the games, such as

England, Ireland, Scotland, Wales,
Inside, outside,
Monkeys' tails.

See also Australian Children's Folklore Collection, Children's Folklore

ELECTION NIGHT PARTY

These are frequently held for federal and state general elections throughout Australia. They have developed along with television coverage of 'election night' and usually take the form of an after-dinner party at someone's house. Participants may be asked to 'bring a plate', usually of 'nibbles' such as cheese and crackers, dips, etc, and it is understood that they will bring their own drinks. As the election results are televised and commented upon throughout the night, these are watched, discussed and argued about. Most election night parties end amicably, whatever the results, but it is not unknown for a combination of politics and alcohol to lead to unhappy consequences, some possibilities of which were explored in David Williamson's famous play (and later film) *Don's Party. See also Customs; Folklore; Foodways; Political Lore*

E-LORE

Sometimes called xerox lore or faxlore, as noted in the title of Graham Seal's 1996 book *The Bare Fax*. This contemporary form of folklore encompasses more than the photocopier or the fax machine, though; and email is the latest means of circulating jokes, drawings and other sardonic comments on modern life.

Anonymous wit, scuttlebutt or political commentary in written form is as old as writing itself. As well as writing on walls, typewritten or handwritten items circulated in communities well before the invention of the photocopier. This writer recalls as an adolescent schoolgirl the clandestine circulation at school of a tattered handwritten copy of *The Bride's Confession* (allegedly written by Lord Byron). Like the *Confession*, much E-lore is obscene or at least designed to titillate. It can also be sexist and racist, as in the Xeroxed copies of a (fake) *Aboriginal Employment Application Form* widely circulated in central Australia during the 1980s.

E-lore is a popular means of circulating jokes, often involving topical events, and with email, international transmission is easy. Within days of the death of John F Kennedy Jnr in his aeroplane crash in 1999, for example, numbers of (undoubtedly tasteless) 'disaster jokes' were flying around the world. The following are a few less painful examples to arrive in Melbourne:

> *How did JFK learn how to fly?*
> *Crash course.*
>
> *What do the Kennedys fear the most?*
> *Old age.*
>
> *What do Republicans say about JFK's political chances for President?*
> *All washed up.*

See also Faxlore; Graffiti; Folk Humour; Jokes

EMBROIDERY

One of the most ancient of handcrafts, usually done by women, but not always. Embroidery or 'needlework' is most truly a folk tradition, and the first steps are usually learned from a mother or grandmother. As with knitting and crochet, folk tradition and commerce work happily together, since embroidery cottons, wools and other threads, as well as pre-printed patterns, are produced by companies such as Semco. The Embroiderers' Guild of Australia holds exhibitions and much of its work is in the realm of fine art. With the exception of exhibition work, most needlework is done for the embroiderer's own family use, and sometimes for a young woman's glory box or trousseau. Many European women migrating to Australia brought elaborately embroidered bed linen and other household fabrics, once considered to be an essential part of a bride's dowry. Embroidery today is not as common a women's pastime as in previous generations, and many families cherish an embroidered 'sampler' done by a great-grandmother or an even earlier ancestor, perhaps at an age as young as six years. *See also Crafts; Women's Folklore*

'EMMAVILLE PANTHER, THE' (NSW) *See Legendary Animals*

EMPIRE DAY

No longer observed, Empire Day, or 24 May, was established in 1905 as a recognition of the ties to Britain of the various Empire countries, including Australia. Although an official observation of imperial patriotism, like most decreed holidays it provided an excuse for festivities of all kinds, including such sticky delights as holding your hands behind you while you tried to eat a bun or other cake off your shoulder. During the 1950s, despite its renaming as 'Commonwealth Day', the original purpose of Empire Day became almost totally submerged by the popular elements of fireworks and bonfires that had become an integral part of the observance, known in most parts of the country as 'Cracker Night'. *See also Cracker Night; Customs; Guy Fawkes' Night*

ENGAGEMENT/BETROTHAL

The formal announcement of a couple's intention to marry may be marked by the man presenting to his fiancée a ring, usually set with one or more diamonds. Sometimes gold rings may be exchanged, although both these customs are less common now than they were in previous generations, probably due to an increasing number of couples living together before or without marriage. Nevertheless, many cohabiting individuals refer to their partner as their 'fiancé or fiancée'. A formal engagement or betrothal may be celebrated with a party either at home or in a catered venue.

In Greek tradition, both parties may exchange rings on engagement and the fiancé presents the woman with a bowl of sugared almonds and the guests bring cakes and flowers. The trousseau, often of hand-made linen and lingerie, is usually displayed a week before the wedding to the bride-to-be's female friends and relatives. *See also Customs; Weddings*

ENGLISH INFLUENCES ON AUSTRALIAN FOLKLORE

At the 1996 Census 45.29% of the Australian population stated they were of English origin. Yet the English element in Australian culture is often a taken-for-granted aspect of everyday life. Whereas Irishness and, to a lesser though significant extent, Scottishness are frequently remarked and studied facets of Australia's multicultural population, the much larger impact of English culture is often overlooked or subsumed under such terms as 'British' and 'United Kingdom'. The fundamentally English foundations of modern Australia and the continuing connections of family, trade, education and migration have produced a culture that, while distinctive, owes a great deal to English influences, especially in areas such as folksong and verse, calendar and other customs, folk belief, children's folklore and folk tales. *See also Cousin Jacks; Cousin Jennies; Customs; Folk Tales; Morris Dancing*

ESSENFEST

Meaning 'eat festival', this is a Barossa German (SA) annual harvest festival of food and alcohol. It is one of the oldest Barossa customs and is usually considered to be the most authentic. It involves the wearing of traditional German costume, a Festival Queen, preparation of local delicacies, tours, picnics and games including *kegel*, a local version of skittles played in a purpose-built alley or *kegelbahn* in the Tanunda Showgrounds. *Essenfest* is held every second year, alternating since 1965 with the much more elaborate Barossa Vintage Festival. *See also Customs; Festivals; German Influences on Australian Folklore*

'EUABALONG BALL'

Probably descended from a nineteenth-century song by 'Vox Silvis' titled 'The Wooyeo Ball', 'Euabalong Ball' seems to be a light-hearted early twentieth-century version in which 'the lads of the Lachlan, the great and the small/Come bent on diversion from far and from near'. According to the song, 'There were shielahs in plenty, some two or three score/Some weaners, some two-tooths and some rather more.' *See also Folk Humour; Pastoral Industry Folklore*

EULO QUEEN, THE

Folk name of a famous female publican of the Eulo Hotel (or Hall). Eulo was a small Queensland opal-mining town about 70 kilometres west of Cunnamulla. The Eulo Queen (sometimes 'Belle'), whose name may or may not have been Isobel Gray, was known for her flamboyance and her alleged wealth, accumulated from the gifts of smitten admirers. She died in Eulo, by then little more than a ghost town, in 1925, reputedly in her nineties. *See also Bush, The; Folk Heroes*

'EUMERELLA SHORE, THE'

Also known as 'The Numerella Shore', this 1860s ballad of free selection and cattle duffing (stealing) is set in the Monaro (NSW) region, rather than the Eumerella River in Victoria. *See also Bush Ballad; Bushrangers*

EUREKA STOCKADE, THE

Insurrection by gold miners at Ballarat (Vic.) in December 1854. While this event has considerable historical significance and is celebrated in trade union and Australian Labor Party circles as well as in literature, art and film, it seems to have left peculiarly few traces in folksong, folk verse or custom. This apparent absence has long puzzled collectors of folksong and verse, though it is known that a considerable folk tale tradition exists among descendants of those who participated – on both sides – of this event. Further research and fieldwork may yet reveal a Eureka folk tradition to complement its literary and political mythologies. *See also Cherrywood Gun, The; Folklore of Struggle; Labor Lore; Southern Cross;The; Work Lore*

EVIL EYE, THE

A National Library of Australia oral history project, the Greek-Australian Oral History and Folklife Project (1997–1999) revealed that most of the thirty Greek-Australian women interviewed in Melbourne accepted the notion of 'the Evil Eye' as a malevolent force in the world, capable of causing distress, actual physical harm or death to any person, particularly those who are 'too happy' or 'too self-satisfied'. Some described rituals which they practised to counter the influence of the Evil Eye, such as making the shape of the Cross with oil in a bowl of water. The small sample interviewed for the project included women born in Australia and in Greece, and included women active in their professions in Australia. The Evil Eye is a potent folk belief among immigrants of many different ethnic origins living in Australia. *See also Folk Belief; Pointing the Bone; Satanism; Witchcraft*

F

FAIR DINKUM

That which is 'fair dinkum' is true or genuine, and this popular Australian phrase may be used in a variety of ways, to describe an honest or sincere person or set of ideas, or to query the truth or sincerity of an utterance: 'Are you fair dinkum?' or 'Is that fair dinkum?' Although still widely used, the term is probably less common than in previous generations. *See also Dinki-di; Folk Speech*

FAIR GO

Folk speech term that reflects the Australian notion of fair play and the egalitarian ideal that everyone should be treated fairly and equally and have the opportunity to better themselves. The practical application of this notion in today's society remains debatable. Along with anti-authoritarianism, mateship and the bush, the fair go is a central element of Australian cultural identity, and is found throughout Australian folk expression. 'Fair go, mate' and 'Fair crack of the whip' are examples of the common usage of this concept. In his *Dictionary of Australian Colloquialisms* (1996), G.A. Wilkes notes 'fair go' as the call used in the game two-up to indicate that the coins may now be spun, but it is not known whether the particular use (in two-up) or the general use of the term came first. *See also Bush, The; Folk Speech; National Icons; Two-Up*

FAIRY TALES

Seventeenth-century European writers took traditional folktales and reworked them – usually sanitising them in the process – for educated, middle-class, urban readers. These 'fairy tales' as they came to be called, have been enormously popular ever since, especially in printed and animated or filmed forms. Although these forms of fairy tale may differ from the original folk tales, versions derived from them are frequently recounted by adults to children, and in this way stories of 'Cinderella', 'Sleeping Beauty', 'Beauty and the Beast', 'Red Riding Hood', 'Hansel and Gretel' or 'Jack and the Beanstalk' have passed back into oral folk tradition. There is evidence that such tales were told among transported convicts and also among the nineteenth-century middle classes. *See also Children's Folklore; Family Folklore; Folk Tales*

FAMILY FOLKLORE

The family is a major site of folk tradition and of primary importance in the transmission of many traditions. Family folklore may consist of any or all of: stories about family members (alive or dead), and family events and places; songs, including nursery stories, rhymes, lullabies and dandling songs; foodways; medicines and treatments for ills; arts and crafts such as knitting, needlework, quilting, handcrafts, gardening and any number of other domestic skills; beliefs, including prejudices and superstitions; customs relating to birthdays, anniversaries and other rites of passage, reunions and picnics. Sayings, family names and etymologies are also among the many genres of family folklore. There is also a rich vein of family vulgarity which has been little documented to date, including jokes about toilets and farting. *See also Birthdays; Christening; Family Reunions; Father's Day; Funerals; Mother's Day; Weddings*

FAMILY REUNIONS

In a country where family members may live great distances apart in different towns or states, it is a popular pastime for them to get together for a 'reunion'. Family reunions may take a variety of forms, and may be both regular and occasional. They may also vary in size, from the immediate family (a couple, their sons and daughters and, if these are adult, their own partners and children) to the extended family (grandparents, aunts and uncles, great-grandchildren) or to a real 'gathering of the clan' such as 'all members of the McCorquodale family'.

Regular family reunions are mostly calendar-related, and occasional gatherings are likely to centre around rites of passage such as weddings, christenings, bar mitzvahs or other special occasions, such as golden Weddings or grandma's ninetieth birthday. Depending on the size of the gathering, family reunions may be held in a family home or in a restaurant or catered venue. The main activity at the gathering is likely to be eating (and drinking), although large reunions may include music, dancing and speeches. *See also Christmas; Customs; Family Folklore; Mothers' Day*

FANCY DRESS

Dressing up in fancy costumes has been a popular pastime in Australia for many generations, although there have been changes over the years. Young children's fancy dress parties or parades (say in a local hall), which were popular in the inter-war years, have been largely replaced with private fancy dress birthday parties and special days at school, perhaps to raise money for the school or for charity. Primary school children may come to school dressed as fairies, dragons, Batman and other favourites, and secondary schools might shed uniform for one day in favour of ordinary clothes. These 'mufti days' or 'casual days' also take place in offices and other business establishments.

Fancy dress balls were once a popular community event, but today it seems likely that the only costume balls remaining are high society (charity) or arts costume balls or the Colonial Balls organised by folk enthusiasts. In the 1980s and 1990s it became popular among twenty or thirty-somethings to organise private dinner parties with a theme which required fancy dress, such as a 1920s or 1970s party. An extension of this enthusiasm was the Agatha Christie-type 'Murder Party', with dinner party guests given a role to play which required costume. Murder Parties had some help from commerce with elaborate kits available for purchase, but the folk pastime of 'dressing up' was or is a major feature of the night's entertainment.

Dressing up to attend sporting events is increasingly popular in Australia in the twenty-first century. It may include face painting and clothing (especially large hats) in a favoured team's colours, or a variety of unrelated costumes. Father Christmas clones are especially popular towards Christmas time. Horse races, particularly the Melbourne Cup in November each year are great occasions for fancy dress, which may range from haute couture and designer fashions to bizarre costumes such as crocodiles, kangaroos and spacemen. The ultimate fancy dress occasion in Australia may be the Gay and Lesbian Mardi Gras held in Sydney each February, which features outrageous costumes and topical impersonations such as the mass cloning of actor Joanna Lumley as Patsy (*Absolutely Fabulous*), Government Minister Amanda Vanstone or would-be politician Pauline Hanson. Historical re-enactments such as the discovery of gold (all over Australia) or Captain Arthur Phillip landing at Botany Bay are also popular occasions for dressing up. *See also Customs; Folk Costume*

'FAREWELL TO JUDGES AND JURIES'

Transportation broadside ballad of the early nineteenth century on which the late nineteenth century (and much better known) stage parody, 'Bound for Botany Bay' was based. Also known as 'Adieu to Judges and Juries, and 'Newry Transport'. *See also 'Botany Bay'*; *Convict Lore*; *Transportation Ballads*

FATHER CHRISTMAS

The popular image of Father Christmas (also known as Santa Claus) derives from both folk traditions and commercial advertising, the latter mainly in the USA. The jolly man with white whiskers and a red suit is largely a post-nineteenth century creation, popularised in the twentieth century by elaborate advertisements for Coca Cola in magazines such as *The National Geographic*. Of older ancestry were religious or folkloric figures such as Saint Nicholas in Holland and elsewhere in Europe; La Befana in parts of Italy, who brought presents for well-behaved children; and 'Good King Wenceslaus' in Central Europe, who distributed goods to poor people, such as the 'flesh...wine...and pine logs' mentioned in the Christmas carol about the King of the same name. Saint Nicholas is often accompanied by one or two 'Black Peters', who may punish bad children by carrying them away in a sack. While Saint Nicholas celebrations are still held at Christmas among Dutch communities in this country (such as at Moe in Victoria), it is debatable whether the frightening black figure of *Zwarte Pieter* is a tradition worth maintaining in contemporary Australia.

The date when Father Christmas delivers his presents has changed over some generations. In the nineteenth century, Boxing Day (26 December) was the day for giving or exchanging 'Christmas boxes' or presents, but today children hang up a stocking (or more likely a pillow-slip) on Christmas Eve (24 December), with the expectation that Christmas morning (25 December) will reveal Father Christmas's visit and his gifts. Commerce has a strong stake in Father Christmas, with retail sales usually skyrocketing at Christmas time, and many large retail stores such as Myer's in Melbourne providing a traditional Santa for children to visit, to tell their hopes for Christmas presents, and receive a gift, usually for a fee paid by the parents. Today, post offices in Greenland and Iceland (being close to the North Pole) are inundated at Christmas time with letters from children addressed to Father Christmas. These letters not only ask for presents, but sometimes resemble prayers in their requests for less material gifts such as family health and happiness. *See also Christmas; Customs; Family Folklore; Zwarte Pieter*

FATHER'S DAY
Invented in America in 1910 (where it is observed in June), Father's Day has spread throughout the Western world and is observed in much the same fashion as Mother's Day within many families. Father's Day did not become established until 1956 in Australia, where it is celebrated on the first Sunday in September. By the early 1990s Father's Day was third in popularity behind Christmas and Mother's Day for the purchase of greeting cards in this country (*Women's Weekly*, September 1993, p. 163) and, impelled by retailers, it is also widely observed by the giving of gifts. Although a commercial custom, having no basis in folk tradition, the willingness of many to take part and use the day as an expression of family unity and affection (real or contrived) suggests that it has become part of the modern folk calendar. *See also Customs; Folklorism; Mother's Day*

FAXLORE
Humorous drawings, mock memoranda, fake official forms, satirical letters and similar items usually related to occupational life, transmitted via facsimile machine on sheets of A4 paper. A collection of such lore, *The Bare Fax*, was published by Graham Seal in 1996. *See also E-lore; Folk Humour; Work Lore*

FEAST OF ST JOSEPH
Held on 19 March, a Catholic commemoration of Joseph, husband of Mary and legal father of Jesus. In Italian tradition the feast is that of San Guiseppe and involves almsgiving, the consumption of special foods and, in Sicily, riding on donkeys through the village by villagers representing Joseph, Mary and Jesus. *See also Customs; Fiesta; Italian Folklore in Australia; Festivals; Religious Lore; Village Saints' Processions*

FEAST OF THE HUNGRY GHOSTS, THE
Going under a variety of traditional Chinese and local names, depending on the areas in which it is observed, this festival for the propitiation of the ghosts of dead ancestors is comparable in some ways to Halloween. The feast falls on the fifteenth day of the seventh moon, usually around August on the Gregorian calendar. At this time the gates of hell are said

to be opened, for the only time in the year, allowing the spirits of the dead to wander the earth for thirty days. To ensure that these ghosts or spirits remain friendly, it is believed necessary to offer prayers, food and money, especially on the first, fifteenth and thirtieth days of the seventh moon. As well, the keepers of the dead must be offered propitiation. The deities are thought to be further propitiated by entertainment, so this festival is typically accompanied by song, drama, dance and other art forms. *See also Chinese Folklore in Australia, Customs, Religious Lore*

FEAST OF THE SEVEN SISTERS

Less poetically known as the Seventh Evening (*Ch'i Hsi*), this Chinese feast falls on the seventh day of the seventh moon, usually around early August. It is a festival particularly associated with women, and emphasises domestic skills. Prayers are traditionally said at 11pm, when women, wearing their best clothes, offer fruit, meat, cakes and vegetables in memory of the legendary Weaving Maiden, who is allowed by the Sun-God on this one night of the year to meet her husband, the Cowherd. This festival is especially popular among Malaysian Chinese. *See also Chinese Folklore in Australia, Customs, Religious Lore*

FEDERSCHLEISSEN

'Featherstripping', a German custom practised in the Barossa Valley (SA) German community from the 1840s to the 1930s. These were evening gatherings during which women plucked feathers from geese or other fowl or stripped the quills from already plucked feathers. The down was used as stuffing for bedding. The activity was usually associated with a forthcoming wedding and had a strongly social flavour, with cake and coffee being consumed, gossip exchanged and songs sung. *See also Customs; German Influences on Australian Folklore; Sewing Bee; Women's Folklore*

FEMALE FACTORY, THE

Name for the Parramatta (NSW) and Hobart (Tas.) institutions where females were imprisoned and put to work in the early years of the colony. Occasionally used in convict song and verse. *See also Convict Lore; Transportation Ballads;, Women's Folklore*

FESTABEND AND SCHUTZENFEST

The *Schutzenfest*, or shooting festival, is a German tradition that has been observed by South Australia's German community since at least 1854, when it was recorded as being celebrated in Adelaide.It has not been celebrated continually, as it was discontinued during World War I and not revived until after 1945. Hahndorf, Lobethal and other country towns with German populations kept this custom active. The festival is a series of shooting competitions that take place on the second Saturday of January, accompanied by singing, dancing, eating and drinking from morning to midnight. Since the revival of *Schutzenfest* in 1964, this event has been preceded on the Friday before by the *Festabend*, also an occasion for traditional German dancing, singing and conviviality. *See also Customs*, Essenfest, Federschleissen, *German Influences in Australian Folklore*

FESTE

A general term for Italian festivals celebrating village saints. These occur throughout Australia at different times, wherever there are significant numbers of Italians from a particular village or region, or where a number can come together. Italians may travel extensive distances to attend such events. Some examples of *feste* in Australia are the Festival of Our Lady of Terzito, Hawthorn (Vic.), observed principally by families from the Isle of Salina, Italy; the Festival of San Rocco held in Mt Hawthorn and Leederville areas in Western Australia; and a number of such events that have become clustered around 'Blessing of the Fleet' observances, including those in Ulladulla (NSW), Fremantle (WA) and elsewhere.

Maltese celebrations deriving from various originating Maltese villages are similar to Italian celebrations of village saints. These are held in centres of Maltese population, most notably Melbourne and Sydney. The most popular Maltese festa is the Feast of Our Lady on 8 September, which commemorates the defeat of the Turks in 1856. *See also Customs, Essenfest, Festabend, Fiesta, Italian Influences in Australian Folklore, Maltese Folklore in Australia, Fiesta, Religious Folklore, Schutzenfest, St Patrick's Day*

FESTIVALS

Australia's multicultural society has a number of festivals or special events associated with particular ethnic communities, and these might be generically described as 'festas', although the term 'festival' is more commonly used. Some are politico-religious events, such as St Patrick's Day (17 March), and others such as Melbourne's *Glendi* and *Antipodes* festivals, organised by Greek community associations, are more overtly cultural in nature. All festas, however, are likely to include singing and dancing. Some festas embody both folk and commercial elements, such as the Italian Lygon Street Festa held in Melbourne's popular restaurant and coffee shop precinct in Carlton, close to Melbourne University. In Lygon Street the Festa activities feature food, food-related activities such as a waiters' race, and perhaps older traditions such as flag throwing and waving.

Festas in Australia may be associated with a particular region, such as the German-settled Barossa Valley in South Australia, which hosts a number of festas, including an *Essenfest* (food), *Schutzenfest* (shooting) and an *Oompah Festival* (brass bands). These popular festivals, together with the region's noted wines, German-style buildings and much promoted (though not necessarily historically accurate) *Gemutlichkeit,* or fun-loving atmosphere, have made the Barossa region one of Australia's most popular tourist destinations.

Festas vary in the extent to which they are oriented towards putting on a show for outsiders, as opposed or being essentially for the ethnic group itself. The Barunga Festival, held near Katherine in the Northern Territory, is essentially one of the latter. Organised by the Jawoyn people, it is attended by Aboriginal people from all over the Territory, who demonstrate their traditional performances and skills, mainly to each other.

By contrast, Chinese New Year celebrations (held for *Chun Jie,* the Spring Festival) in many Australian cities are well attended by the population as a whole, often in the city's 'Chinatown' area. Public activities might include fireworks, dragon dances, special costumes, music and dance and demonstrations of noodle-making. These popular public events also accompany many private activities, such as family reunions, religious observances and gifts of money to children. Another popular Chinese celebration is the Lantern Festival (*Yuan Xiao Jie*), which may include children of many ethnic origins making and parading lanterns in their schools, in their communities, or in Chinatown.

FESTIVAL OF LEADLIGHTS
Held in late October since 1988 in the Perth suburb of Subiaco, Western Australia, this fundraising festival is organised by the Save the Children

Fund, but involves substantial local cooperation. On a selected Saturday night, all residents of Subiaco are asked to turn on their interior lights to allow the glow to shine through the numerous leadlight windows that are a feature of the suburb. Before the illuminations begin there is a party at the local community centre, where maps are sold detailing various street routes along which one may walk or slowly drive. The festival, growing each year, in 1993 featured exhibitions of stained glass arts, entertainment and related events. The event is currently held every second year. *See also Customs*

FETES *See Bazaars; Community Fairs*

FIELD DAYS
Usually organised in the country by, or in the interests of, suppliers of commercial agricultural goods, such as tractors and related implements, and also by pastoral concerns to show off their breeding stock. Despite their commercial purpose, field days are usually occasions for serious socialising, eating, drinking and gossip, as well as opportunities to look over new equipment, products and animals. *See also Agricultural Shows;Customs*

FIESTA
A general term, of Spanish-language origin, for any period of feasting and celebration. The exact date and occasion on which a particular fiesta occurs may vary from country to country and even from village to village. In the Philippines, for example, some villages have their fiesta on the day of the Immaculate Conception (8 December). Generally the fiesta is attached to a formal observance of the Catholic Church, though some also involve local saints and events. Regardless of their cause, fiestas may be characterised by any or all of the following: excessive eating and drinking, processions, carnivals, sporting and artistic competitions and displays, games, theatre, the wearing of special festive clothing or decoration, and all-round enjoyment. In Fitzroy, Melbourne, the Johnston Street Fiesta has become popular in recent years in that suburb's 'Spanish precinct'. *See also Customs; Feste; Festivals; Religious Lore*

FIRST DAY OF THE MONTH
Children in some parts of Australia may greet the first day of the month with this rhyme and the accompanying actions: 'A pinch and punch for

the first of the month', to which the usual reply is 'A hit and a kick for being so quick'. It is a British belief that it is lucky to be born on this day, and that being born on New Year's Day is especially propitious, as is being born on the 'Horses' Birthday', 1 August. *See also Customs; Folk Belief; Horses' Birthday, The*

FISHER'S GHOST

Famous ghost of ticket-of-leave convict Frederick Fisher, murdered and secretly buried at Fisher's Creek (NSW) by his business partner, George Worrell, in 1826. The authorities were unable to locate the body until a local man claimed to have seen Fisher's bloodied ghost, which directed him to the grave. A local festival of growing size and reputation has been a regular event in nearby Campbelltown for many years. *See also Folklorism; Ghosts*

FITZPATRICK, CONSTABLE

The policeman who allegedly attempted to molest Ned Kelly's sisters in the family home. Ned Kelly (probably) shot Fitzpatrick in the wrist, an act that precipitated the gaoling of Kelly's mother Ellen, and thus the bushranging outbreak that made Ned Kelly a folk, and later national, hero. *See also Bushrangers; Kelly, Ned*

'FLASH JACK FROM GUNDAGAI'

Hero of a late nineteenth-century shearing song, who has shorn all round the country and claims to be able to 'do a respectable tally myself whenever I like to try'. The 'One-Tree Plain' referred to in the song was part of Tom Patterson's Ulong station on the Riverina. *See also Bush Ballads, Pastoral Industry Lore, Shearers*

'FLASH STOCKMAN, THE'

Popular bush recitation and song in which the stockman boasts of his prowess as horseman, fencer and shearer and ends with versions of the lines:

> *In everything I do you can cut me fair in two,*
> *'Cause I'm far too bloody good to be in one.*

See also Bush, The; Bush Ballads, Folk Poetry, Pastoral Industry Folklore

FLIES

Long a notorious menace throughout the country, flies have in recent years become less of a problem due to biological controls. Flies nevertheless feature in a good deal of bush folklore, especially relating to weather forecasting, and still retain something of the status of a perverse national icon. 'The Australian salute' is a continuous wave to keep flies off the face, and it has been said that the Australian accent, often produced with little opening of the mouth, derives from the need to keep out the flies. *See also Bush, Eco-Lore; The; National Icons*

FLOWERS

There is considerable folklore in Australia surrounding flowers. Much of this is derived from British custom. It includes the giving of flowers on occasions such as weddings, birthdays, anniversaries, Valentine's Day and Mother's Day. Flowers are also closely associated with many Christian activities, such as church decoration and some harvest customs, and are the usual accompaniment of mourning. In the Greek Orthodox Church, the Epitaph (representing Christ's grave) is decorated with flowers and carried in procession on the eve of Good Friday.

May Day customs such as maypole dancing also involved flowers, as do some children's games (making daisy chains) and adolescent divinations relating to the faithfulness of real or imagined sweethearts in which petals are plucked to decide if 'he loves me' or 'he loves me not'. The 'language of flowers', a system by which particular flowers are associated with wedding anniversaries, and different flowers are said to have different meanings when given as gifts, is largely a commercialisation of fragments of folk tradition involving flowers. Some flowers may be associated with ill luck, including wattle, when in the house. It is often considered unlucky to combine red and white flowers in an arrangement, especially if the flowers are for a sick person. Arum lilies are also widely considered to be unlucky in the house, also an English folk belief. *See also Eco-Lore, Folk Belief, Jack-in-the-Green, May Day*

FO DAN (Chinese), PHAT DAN (Vietnamese), WESAK (Laotian, Thai, Sinhalese)

On this day in May or June, Chinese and Vietnamese Buddhists celebrate the birth of Buddha, and Sri Lankan, Cambodian, Laotian, Thai and Sinhalese Buddhists celebrate the birth, enlightenment and death of the Buddha. In all cases, this is the most important Buddhist religious celebration and involves popular celebratory activities such as hanging flower garlands and streamers, cleaning the home and statues of Buddha. In many parts of South-East Asia it is customary for songbirds to be released from cages, a reflection of the Buddha's traditional love of animals and concern for their freedom. *See also Chinese Folklore in Australia; Customs; Religious Lore*

FOLK ALLIANCE AUSTRALIA

Established in 1996, the FAA fosters and promotes the folk community and the folk arts through 'education, advocacy, professionalism and field development'. It has organised National Conventions and National Folk Weeks; publishes a regular newsletter and other titles, including the *Folk Directory*; and generally raises awareness of folk arts in Australia and internationally. *See also Folk Arts; Folk Festivals; Folk Revival*

FOLK ART

It is regrettable that in Australia the term 'folk art' is often used in a very narrow sense to mean painting of stylised designs on wooden household objects such as bread boards or larger blanket boxes. Certainly these practices have a base in some European traditions (usually unspecified), but folk art, in Australia and elsewhere, is much more varied than this.

The Australian National Gallery in Canberra has a significant collection of Australian folk art which includes items such as the Convict Quilt, Aboriginal woven baskets, Harold Aisen's tin sculptures of Jewish life, home-made soft toys, pottery, weather vanes and nineteenth-century decorative objects made from shells, hair and ferns. What characteristics do these objects have which caused our leading *art* gallery to collect and display them? Why are they designated as art, and not simply as handcraft?

The leading American folklorist Henry Glassie wrote that art of any kind must have an aesthetic quality which stimulates the senses, aesthetic as opposed to *anaesthetic*, a concept which we readily understand as deadening the senses (or putting us to sleep!). Any object which we call 'art' must engage us; perhaps stimulate us to wonder, to admire, to catch our breath, to move us to tears, or sometimes to anger or rejection. It must embody more than simple clever workmanship.

Folk art is normally produced by people who have had no formal art training, although they may have learned the skills and concepts of their work from another person, perhaps a family member. It is often produced for a practical reason, but there is always more to it than this. The catalogue to an exhibition of folk art held in 1983 by the Canadian Museum of Civilisation (*From the Heart: Folk Art in Canada*, 1983, pp. 11–12) noted that elements present in the production of folk art might include *reflection, commitment and fantasy*. A wooden fire engine or jumper made for a child's birthday involves commitment; a religious sculpture or icon may involve both reflection and commitment; and many whimsical toys and embroideries (such as the Westbury Quilt [1900–1903] held in the Australian National Gallery) embody a strong sense of fun and fantasy, as well as a commitment to religious, patriotic and domestic ideals.

Art is often distinguished from craft in that craft is held to have an essentially utilitarian purpose (such as the many interesting home-made letter-boxes which are an amusing feature of Australian, particularly rural, life). By contrast, art is sometimes held to be 'purely aesthetic'. This distinction is hard to maintain, as art and craft often overlap. A pottery jug fashioned to resemble a cockatoo may have been made for pouring milk, but if its aesthetic quality stimulates the senses, as Henry Glassie would say, it is art. *See also Crafts; Quilts*

FOLK ARTS

A term that has grown up since the 1960s to describe the usually revivalist performance of folk song, music, dance, tale, verse and related expressions. A number of community organisations are involved in folk arts, including various state and territory Folk Federations, the Victorian Folklife Association, the Folk Alliance Australia and the Storytellers' Guild, to name only several among a large number of groups. *See also Folk Alliance Australia, Folk Festivals, Folklorism, Folk Revival*

FOLK BELIEF

Frequently referred to as 'superstition', folk belief is a large field that includes beliefs about luck, predicting the future, what allegedly happened in the past or, as in urban legends, somewhere else in the present. Belief is often accompanied by practices that reflect the underlying tenet, such as not walking under ladders, or throwing spilled salt over the left shoulder, for fear of incurring bad luck. More elaborately, belief may also underlie customary behaviour, such as pilgrimage, the construction of shrines and grottoes, and the processioning and associated celebrations of village saints. Surveys of folk beliefs, or 'superstitions', such as those carried out through the Western Australian Folklore Archive and elsewhere in the country, confirm the remarkable range and variety of folk beliefs within the Australian community. The most commonly encountered Anglo-Celtic folk beliefs relate to bad luck, such as those mentioned above, and that the breaking of a mirror will bring seven years' bad luck and that a black cat crossing one's path is an ill omen, especially if it occurs on a 'Black Friday'. Less often encountered but by no means rare are beliefs that it is unlucky to open an umbrella inside the house, to place shoes on a table or to put a new calendar up before the old year is out. Opals are widely considered unlucky in Australia. In Greek tradition it is unlucky to sweep at night and in Italian belief oil spilled on a floor brings bad luck. Other beliefs concern good luck, as in the Vietnamese Chinese belief that money will come to the household if a dog or bird should enter and the Italian belief that carrying a silver coin ensures good luck. The full range of folk beliefs common to the English-speaking world are alive and well in Australia, as are the considerable repertoires of such beliefs held by other language groups, as well as a range of indigenous beliefs. Belief is also a factor in some forms of folk medicine in weatherlore. *See also Customs; First Day of the Month; Folk Medicine; Ghost Lore; Opals; Urban Legends; Weatherlore*

FOLK COSTUME

Distinctive styles of dress worn by folk groups either as an expression of their sense of national, ethnic, regional, occupational or other identity; or to mark special occasions including life cycle events such as birthdays, weddings and funerals. Some examples include the characteristic bush dress of the farmer or grazier, the stockman, the swagman; the many national and ethnic costumes worn in Australia; the garb worn by members of youthful groups such as 'Westies', 'Goths' and 'Bogans', and occupational garbs. Often the wearing of special, new, distinctive, colourful, whimsical or otherwise out-of-the-ordinary dress is associated with customary observances such as festivals, celebrations, commemorations and the like. *See also Customs; Fancy Dress; Jack-in-the-Green; Mufti Day*

FOLK DIRECTORY

An annual guide to folk arts performers, events, services, organisations, publications and radio programs, the *Folk Directory* was originally published by the Australian Folk Trust. Since 1999 it has been published by Folk Alliance Australia. Elements of the directory are available on the latter organisation's website. *See also Folk Alliance Australia; Folk Festivals; Folk Revival*

FOLK FEDERATIONS

Encouraged by the folk revival of the 1950s and 60s, folk federations were established in most states and territories to coordinate and further the activities of folk clubs, organise concerts, festivals and social events and publish newsletters. In Victoria the Victorian Folk Music Society and in the Australian Capital Territory the Monaro Folk Music Society respectively took on this role. These organisations were at the base of the Australian Folk Trust, a national peak body from 1966 to the 1990s. The role of the Trust has, to a great extent, been assumed by Folk Alliance Australia. *See also Folk Alliance Australia; Folk Festivals; Folk Revival*

FOLK FESTIVALS

In Australia, what are called folk festivals are usually those organised by folk revival organisations. These include the Queensland Folk Federation, which runs the annual Woodford (formerly Maleny) Folk Festival, probably Australia's largest. There is also the independent National Folk Festival, held each Easter in Canberra. Smaller folk festivals are held in each state. The Port Fairy Folk Festival, held each year at Port Fairy in Victoria, is a popular and successful example of regional folk festivals. Much of the content of folk festivals features revival performers, including some from overseas, as well as Aboriginal and other substantial culturally diverse participation. Festivals feature not only concerts, but skills training in music and dance, and 'workshops' which are often well-researched and sometimes multimedia presentations, possibly on historical topics such as Federation.

Folk festivals in Australia are growing in numbers and strength from year to year, possibly because of the sense of community as well as the artistic performance which they offer. This growth has led to increasing consideration by festivals of their role in Australian society, and increased interest in continuous musical and craft traditions as well as in revived activities. A major influence has been the Smithsonian Folklife Festival, held every July in Washington DC by the Smithsonian Institution. This festival features only continuous traditions, not revived ones, and focuses each year on a different region in the United States. Each year it also presents the folk traditions of a different foreign country, and Australia has twice been invited to participate: in 1990 and 1991. The Australian government distinguished itself by making Australia the only foreign country to ever have refused the Smithsonian's invitations. The Woodford Folk Festival now has an agreement with the Smithsonian Institution to send interns to Washington for study and training purposes, and continues its connection with the Australian Studies Centre at the University of Queensland, which has organised discussion forums at the Festival. Many who are not members of folk clubs attend folk festivals in Australia, and they are becoming an increasingly significant part of Australian cultural and intellectual life. See also Folklorism; Folk Revival

FOLK HEROES

Heroes and heroines are celebrated in the folk traditions of all cultures, past and present. Australian folklore has its share of such real and legendary characters, and these include humorous heroes (the Drongo, Jacky Bindieye and Tom Doyle), bushranger heroes (Ned Kelly, the Wild Colonial Boy) as well as indigenous heroes of struggle (Yagan and Jandamurra), occupational heroes (Crooked Mick and Jackie Howe of shearers' tradition)' some political figures (Pig-Iron Bob), sporting heroes (The Don, Cazaly, Les Darcy) and animals (Phar Lap, Red Dog). Interestingly, explorers rarely appear in Australian folklore, at least as far as present field collection reveals. The closest approximation is, perhaps, the ill-fated gold-seeker, Lasseter.

Australia, like most other cultures, has comparatively few folk heroines. The list includes Kate Kelly and Black Mary, whose fame, such as it is, depends mainly on their relationship to a hero. Other possible inclusions might be recently-beatified Mary McKillop, Grace Bussell of Western Australian fame, and contemporary sporting celebrities such as Dawn Fraser. A feature common to many folk heroes is their unacceptability to some groups. Thus Ned Kelly, although now a national as well as a folk hero, is considered a villain by many. The same is true, unsurprisingly, of political heroes.

Heroic types (as opposed to individuals) are also a feature of Australian folklore, including the bushman in various guises, such as the overlander, the bullocky, the shearer and the swagman; as well as the urban larrikin, the digger, and the battler. *See also Bushrangers, Crooked Mick, Doyle, Tom; Drongo, The; Folk Tales; Jacky Bindieye, Lasseter's Reef, Political Lore, Sports Lore,*

FOLK HUMOUR

Like folk humour around the world, Australian tradition has an extensive repertoire of humorous stories, songs, verse, jokes, e-lore and other forms. Much of this involves the kind of ethnic and gender slurring and stereotyping found in the jokes of all cultures, with the obviously unique content of slurs against indigenous Australians. Australian folk humour is also characterised by an emphasis on anti-authoritarianism, with humour about bosses and authority figures being common. Satirising and otherwise undercutting authority and accepted norms is also a feature of other folk traditions, though in its Australian expressions it tends to be of the dry, laconic and often sardonic kind. Bush yarns are perhaps the best example of this type, and these are often equated with popular notions of national identity. Australian folklore, especially that of the bush, is full of characters noted for their wit and other humorous attributes, including Cornelius Kenna, Jacky Bindieye and Snuffler Oldfield, among many others. Folk humour may also be a vehicle for expressing popular scepticism about, or lack of respect for, the decisions and actions of institutions, as in the case of 'dingo jokes' and other folklore related to the Azaria Chamberlain affair. *See also Azaria Chamberlain; Dad and Dave; Dingo Jokes; Tom, Doyle; Drongo, The; Galloping Jones; Jackie Bindieye; Jokes; Cornelius Kenna; National Icons; Racist Folklore; Snuffler Oldfield; Tom'n'opless; Yarns*

FOLKLORE

What is folklore? Folk culture is sometimes described as 'the culture of everyday life', as distinct from high or elite culture (as encompassed by universities, opera, art galleries, for example) or commercial popular culture (television, pop music, comics and magazines). The term 'folklife' is also commonly used (often interchangeably with 'folklore'), to indicate that it is *living culture* which is being considered, and not only the 'customs...of the olden time' as the antiquary William Thoms, who introduced the term into English research studies in 1846, indicated.

This Guide has attempted to represent, for Australia, all these features, and to include at least representative samples of all the types (genres) of folklore as well as of the many groups of people possessing that lore. Many attempts have been made to summarise the vast field of 'unofficial culture' called folklore. Graham Seal's *The Hidden Culture: Folklore in Australian Society* (1989, second edition 1998), was the first published textbook of Australian folklore. Folklore is omnipresent in everyday life. Every time you tell a joke or a yarn, every time you knit a jumper or build a chook-house, every time children play skippy or hopscotch, every time you celebrate Christmas or a birthday...this is folklore. *See also* INTRODUCTION

FOLKLORE OF STRUGGLE

A substantial body of Australian song, verse, legend and related lore involves political, industrial and economic conflict and hardship. Much convict lore casts the transported convict as the victim of a harsh legal and penal system. A good deal of this lore involves the Irish antagonism towards the English, a theme that is also found in bushranging traditions, especially those associated with Ned Kelly. There is also a good deal of legendry surrounding the industrial conflicts and economic recession of the 1890s and of the Great Depression of the 1930s. The song 'Waltzing Matilda' was inspired by events, real or alleged, related to the shearers' strikes of the early 1890s. Strikes, lockouts and political conflicts, including those of indigenous peoples demanding acceptable wages and conditions, have produced their own bodies of lore. Unions, especially those of rural workers and the building, metal and stevedoring industries, have strong traditions of struggle that include song, story, and material culture objects including union banners and icons such as 'The Southern Cross' flag of the Eureka Stockade. The anti-Vietnam War movement of the 1960s and 1970s produced some folk protest material, especially in the form of songs, while picket lines, street protests and demonstrations draw heavily on a range of traditional chants, costumes and tactics. The 'Internationale' and 'The Red Flag' are still sung and venerated in Australian Labor Party circles.

Then raise the scarlet standard high,
Beneath its shade we'll live and die;

Though cowards flinch and traitors sneer,
We'll keep the Red Flag flying here.

See also Bushrangers; Convict Lore; Labor Lore; Political Lore

FOLKLORISM

Folklorism refers to the processes through which folklore moves beyond its original context and is used for other purposes. Typical examples of this include the adaptation of customs as tourism spectacles; the commercialisation of customs and other forms of folklore, including foods, medicines, designs and songs; and the revival of obsolete or moribund traditions, as in the case of Morris dancing, bush dancing, song, costume. *See also INTRODUCTION; Folklore; Folk Revival; Waltzing Matilda*

FOLK MEDICINE

Folk medicine includes healing practices, medicines and a wide variety of beliefs. Australia has quite a rich body of folk medicine derived from European, Asian and indigenous sources. Increasingly, this body of knowledge is receiving notice from the mainstream medical community as 'alternative medicine' grows in popularity. It is also receiving considerable attention from Aboriginal legal bodies because it represents part of the intellectual property of indigenous Australia, for which royalties and other payments are being requested. These matters are of considerable importance considering the possible worldwide potential of some traditional plants such as smoke bush in the treatment of HIV and AIDS. An important report on Australian indigenous cultural and intellectual property rights entitled *Our Culture: Our Future* (Janke 1998) recommends the establishment of an indigenous Australian centre for traditional medicines.

Currently, many Australians identify the therapeutic value of eucalyptus and tea tree oil. Lemon juice and honey (with some whisky, if you're lucky) is a well-loved treatment for colds and flu, and old-fashioned washing 'blue' or vinegar are used for insects and jellyfish stings. Many popular Queensland beaches have bottles of vinegar placed in racks for immediate treatment during the 'stinger' season.

Chinese herbal medicine has been used in Australia by people of all ethnic backgrounds since the first Chinese immigrants arrived in the early nineteenth century, and today many conventionally trained doctors are also using Chinese acupuncture techniques. Other non-mainstream forms of medicine include naturopathic and homeopathic medicine, although, as 'folk medicine' is usually practised in the home rather than by professionals, it is doubtful whether these should be included in the category. Many Australians of Celtic and Mediterranean (and other) origins wear St Christopher and other religious medals to protect them against car accidents and other misfortunes. The scope of belief in folk medicine ranges from amused acknowledgement (to notions such as the 'giving away' of warts to another person, or paying someone a small coin to take them away) to more serious belief in forces such as the 'Evil Eye'. *See also Eco-Lore; Evil Eye, The; Folk Belief; Folklore; Goanna Oil; Indigenous Folklore*

FOLK POETRY

A large and significant form of folkloric expression especially prominent in, though not unique to, the bush tradition. There is a close connection between folk poetry and folksong. Lyrics of songs may be recited as verse, while verse may be sung. As well as the ballad form, folk poetry may include toasts, stump speeches in which political speechmaking is whimsically but pointedly parodied, tank messages and some speech forms related to rhyming slang, such as 'Things are crook in Tallarook; no work in Bourke'. Humour, frequently sardonic, is the dominant mode of Australian folk poetry, though the commemorative, elegiac and sentimental modes are also heard. Some of 'Banjo' Paterson's poems, or at least fragments of them, have passed into folk tradition. The first words of 'The Man from Snowy River' ('There was movement at the station'), and the line from 'Clancy of the Overflow' ('Clancy's gone to Queensland drovin', and we don't know where he are'), have clearly passed into folk idiom and are often quoted in many different contexts. Poems by many other poets have also become part of folk tradition. *See also Bush Ballads, Folk Songs; Lawson, Henry; Paterson, A.B. ('Banjo'); Recitation, Spider from the Gwydir, The; Tank Messages, Toasts*

FOLK REVIVAL

In the 1950s there was an upsurge of popular interest in folk traditions arose in several countries, including the United States and Australia. Common explanations for this upsurge link its appearance with the end of World War II, a growing appreciation of the culture of 'the common man' and, in Australia at least, a concern for national identity in the face of international (particularly American) mass culture influences. The 'revival' encompassed several types of action which represented new developments in Australian cultural life, namely field recording of folksongs, instrumental music and stories; publication of 'bush ballads' derived mostly from printed sources, and the establishment of folk clubs and folklore societies.

The first field collector to make sound recordings of Australian folklore, mostly in south-eastern Australia from the 1950s, was the late John Meredith AM, and his collection is housed in the National Library of Australia. Somewhat earlier, in the 1940s, Dr Percy Jones had collected by hand notation a small number of bush songs which were popularised by the American folk singer Burl Ives during his Australian tour in the early 1950s. Percy Jones' collection, sadly destroyed by fire in the Ash Wednesday bushfires of 1983, included 'Click Go the Shears', 'Botany Bay' and 'The Wild Colonial Boy'. The first publication in the Australian folk revival was Vance Palmer's *Old Australian Bush Ballads* (1950), a number of which were taken from 'Banjo' Paterson's *Old Bush Songs* (1905), with 'music restored by Margaret Sutherland'. The folklorist Ron Edwards (1966) acknowledged the importance of the Palmer/Sutherland book, noting 'that the revival did not start until both words and music were available'.

The folk clubs and societies founded in the 1950s popularised these 'Australian folk songs' through 'singabouts', concerts and eventually through festivals. Bush bands such as The Bushwackers gave popular performances and played for equally popular bush dances. The folk clubs and societies formed state folk federations which are mostly still vigorous organisations today. It is worthy of note that in the United States, folk music entered the mainstream of popular culture through performing groups such as Peter, Paul and Mary. Some folk songs such as 'Hang Down Your Head Tom Dooley' became commercial 'hits' during the 1950s and 1960s. *See also Dance; Folk Festivals; Folklorism*

FOLKSONGS

A large and important genre of folklore, including lullabies, dandling songs, nursery songs, children's play songs, work songs, drinking songs, bawdy songs, ritual songs, ballads, lyrical songs and others. Many folk songs derive from popular and, occasionally, art song repertoires, while others appear to be the creations of local singers and poets, usually anonymous, that have caught the popular interest and so passed into folk tradition. Most fieldwork and research into Australian folk song has been directed at the rich traditions of the bush, including indigenous material. Awaiting collection , however, are considerable song traditions among migrant groups of all ethnicities and among occupational, religious and other groups. *See also Bawdry; Bush Ballads; Bush Band; Bush Music; Folk Revival; Migration Lore; Transportation Ballads*

FOLK SPEECH

Australia is widely recognised as a country rich in folk speech, which includes slang, idiomatic and colourful sayings, phrases and insults, as well as the jargons and argots of occupational and lifestyle group of all kinds. Folk speech also includes rhyming slang and naming practices related to places, people and events. General Australian folk speech, or slang, has long been felt to be a powerful signifier of Australian identity and was famously used in a poem of that name by W. T. Goodge, celebrating the delights of the Australian vernacular. It begins:

> 'Tis the everyday Australian
> Has a language of his own,
> Has a language, or a slanguage,
> Which can simply stand alone.

The poem goes on to mention a great number of now mostly obsolete folk speech terms, such as 'dickin pitch to kid us' (a lie), 'tin-back' (a party) and 'clinah' (woman) and ends:

> And our undiluted English
> is a fad to which we cling,
> But the great Australian slanguage
> Is a truly awful thing!

In more recent years the entertainer Barry Humphries has drawn extensively on aspects of folk speech in the creation of such figures as Barry ('Bazza') MacKenzie and Edna (now Dame Edna) Everage. Some of Humphries' more elaborately colourful idioms appear to be his own invention, though a few of these seem to have entered the vernacular, 'drier than a dead dingo's donger' being one such example. Australian folk speech has been documented and discussed in Graham Seal's *The Lingo: Listening to Australian English* (1998). There is no question that

Australians enjoy using and hearing the many aspects of their folk speech, such as the colourful metaphors 'lower than a snake's belly', 'flat out like a lizard drinking' and 'better than a poke in the eye with a burnt stick'. *See also Affectionate Diminutive; Bastard; Bawdry; Bloody; National Icons; Rhyming Slang*

FOLK SPORTS

Most major sports played in Australia, and elsewhere, have their origins in folk games of one kind or another, including football (the origins of soccer go back to at least the twelfth century in England), cricket, golf, basketball, bowls, baseball, equestrian sports, track and field and other such activities. It has been suggested that Australian Rules Football may have been influenced by Aboriginal practices. Some sports also continue to be played in folkloric situations, especially cricket, tennis and football, which are often played casually in car parks, streets, parks and beaches across the country. Folk sports often arise in occupational situations, such as the Stawell Gift (Vic.) and the Nullarbor Muster and the Jarrah Jerker's Jog (both WA). Some of these may involve displays of occupational expertise, as with camp-drafting and woodchopping. The Tolmie Sports in north-eastern Victoria have been held each February since 1887. *See also Highland Games; Jarrah Jerker's Jog; Picnic Races; Sports Lore; Sports Weekend; Stawell Gift; The; Turf Lore*

FOLK TALES

A large and varied form of folk expression heard in many forms throughout Australian tradition. Includes legends of heroes, events, yarns of colourful characters, tricksters and animals, 'fairy' tales, 'urban' or contemporary legends, stories of the supernatural and of lost treasures, how places came by their names, personal experience stories, occupational tales, tall tales and 'bulldust' of all kinds. *See also Ah Foo, Jimmy; Bindieye, Jacky; Crooked Mick; Dad and Dave; Doyle, Tom; Drop Bears, Fairy Tales; Folk Heroes; Folk Humour; German Charlie; Galloping Jones; Ghost Lore; 'Hungry' Tyson; Kenna, Cornelius; Lasseter's Reef; Legendary Animals; Lone Pine Seedlings, The; Min Min Lights; Palmerston, Christy; Ragged Thirteen, The; Red Dog; Slouch Hat, The; Sunffler Oldfield; Speewah; Storytelling; Tom'nOpless; Urban Legends; White Woman of Gippsland, The; World's Greatest Whinger; The; Yarama; Yarns; Yowie*

FOODWAYS

'Foodways' is the term used by folklorists to describe not only what people eat, but also the customs and practices surrounding its preparation and consumption. Despite the number of colleges and institutions in Australia (mostly TAFE) concerned with the training of chefs, caterers and the like, plus the many adult education courses featuring ethnic cuisine and *cordon bleu* cooking, most people's basic cooking and food management skills are learned at home, in a true folkloric process of direct transmission. People who have not learned these skills in their families – and their children – can be doubly disadvantaged.

It is hard to identify a specifically Australian cuisine. In recent years some traditionally indigenous foods such as kangaroo and crocodile meat have begun to be consumed in the wider community, but widespread consumption of native produce is still in its infancy (*see Bush Tucker*). Australian cooking has a strong base in British foods such as roast lamb (mutton in previous generations) but is now strongly influenced by non-British immigrant traditions. This writer has on numerous occasions stated her belief that Australians couldn't live without Chinese food, provided by the Chinese restaurants which may exist in even the smallest and remotest country towns. Today, these local establishments are also likely to be Thai or Vietnamese, and some of their techniques (such as the stir-fry) are now part of everyday Australian cooking. From at least the middle of the nineteenth century, Australians obtained most of their fresh vegetables from Chinese market gardens, and they are a tradition that continues.

Post-World War II immigration has enormously enriched Australian foodways. Pasta is now a staple in home cooking, and pizza has joined fish and chips as a favourite fast food or take away. Previously little-known vegetables such as broccoli, zucchini, snow peas and capsicums are popular, as well as olives, sun-dried tomatoes and a huge variety of cheeses. A somewhat comical development in recent consumption habits is the fad for bottled water; more comical in some places (such as Melbourne, renowned for its pure water) than others. At the height of this fashion one Monash University lecturer spoke of lecturing to a class of jack-in-the-boxes, constantly drinking bottled water, and constantly leaving the room to visit the toilets. (Of course his lecturing style may also have been a factor.)

Food is surrounded by cultural practices and rituals, and the linking of special foods to special occasions (*see Christmas; Easter*). Customs will involve both eating and non-eating. Jewish families may lay the table with special foods on Friday evenings, at the beginning of the Sabbath, and also on special occasions such as Passover. Muslim families will fast from sun-rise to sun-down during the month of Ramadan. For many Christian churches, Lent, the month leading up to Easter, is a period for self-restraint in eating and in other ways. Other occasions featuring special foods might include the elaborate, multi-tiered wedding cake (usually white), and the 'fairy bread' associated with children's birthday parties, i.e. thin bread and butter with 'hundreds and thousands' (multi-coloured sprinkles). Guests at a wedding reception will expect to take home a piece of wedding cake, perhaps to put under their pillows so as to dream of a future spouse, and children at a birthday party will expect to take home (at least) a bag of sweets (lollies) and a piece of birthday cake.

Australians asked to identify a national dish might mention pavlova, the meat pie, or Vegemite. Pavlova is a large meringue topped with cream and fruit (particularly passionfruit), and there are many theories about the origin of this dish, allegedly created by 'a leading chef' in honour of the Russian ballerina Anna Pavlova during an Australian tour. Vegemite is a commercially produced by-product of the beer industry, but it has entered both folk and popular culture as an Australian icon. Meat pies are a strong contender for a national dish, and there are some regional variations, such as the 'floater', common to Adelaide and Sydney, which combines the pie with mashed peas, a uniquely British foodstuff. Regional influences in Australian food show themselves mostly in names for foods, such as 'rockmelon' in some States and 'canteloupe' in others. A type of luncheon sausage is variably known as Devon, Strasbourg, Polony or German sausage in different parts of Australia, although the term 'German sausage' went out of favour during the World Wars fought against Germany.

Backyard barbecues and picnics are popular food-related pastimes: Michael Symons' definitive book on the history of eating in Australia is titled *One Continuous Picnic*. Today's picnics are likely to include wine as well as beer or soft drinks, all kept cool in an insulated box usually called an 'Esky', after a particular early brand of cooler. The inclusion of wine reflects a change in Australians' drinking habits in recent generations, and the proliferation of vineyards throughout the countryside. *See also Barbecues; Bush Tucker; Vegemite*

FOREIGN ORDERS

Also 'foreigners', 'foreignies'. These are all terms used in Australia for the practice of using an employer's time, goods or equipment to produce something for an employee's private benefit. Using the office photocopier to run off a hundred copies of a handbill advertising a weekend garage sale is one example of this practice. The foreign order is not unique to this country – the French call it 'la perruque', the wig – but it is a custom much in keeping with the traditional relationships of workers and bosses. *See also Customs; Folk Speech; Work Lore*

FORTY DAYS

At Royal Military College Duntroon, an observance to celebrate the fact that there were only forty more days to go before graduation, and hence the end of the academic year. The day was characterised by a relaxation of the usual military discipline and formality and the newest cadets were allowed to address senior 4th Class cadets by their forenames. Members of 4th Class would read out the 'Marriage Stakes' a 'book' giving odds on which members of the graduating class would be married within one year of graduation. It is reported that a version of the pop song 'Forty Days and Forty Nights' was usually sung on this occasion by members of 4th Class. If so, this would be a 1950s addition to the custom, which is said to have been current from the 1930s until the end of the 1960s. An example of a social levelling custom, sometimes found in hierarchical organisations. *See also Customs; Free Dress Day; Mufti Day, Work Lore*

FRANK THE POET

Francis MacNamara (1811–?), a convict transported from Ireland in 1832, was the composer of a number of poems and ballads, including 'The Convict's Tour to Hell' and probably the song 'Moreton Bay', paraphrased in Ned Kelly's 'Jerilderie Letter'. John Meredith and Rex Whalan published an in-depth study of MacNamara's life and work in 1979. *See also Convict Lore, Irish Influences on Australian Folklore; Kelly, Ned; Logan, Captain; 'Moreton Bay'; Transportation Ballads; Treason Ballads*

'FREEDOM ON THE WALLABY'

A famous poem written by Henry Lawson in sympathy with the shearers' strike of 1891, this presented a radical expression of the life and viewpoint of the itinerant bush worker. Some considered it to be seditious, especially the lines:

> *We'll make the tyrants feel the sting o' those that they would throttle;*
> *They needn't say the fault is ours if blood should stain the wattle.*

Often appearing in various versions and to a number of tunes, it has been suggested that it was derived from a traditional song known as 'Australia's on the Wallaby', to the tune of which it is frequently sung. *See also Bush Ballad, Folk Songs, Folklore of Struggle, Labor Lore, Lawson, Henry, Pastoral Industry Folklore, Shearers*

FREE DRESS DAY

Occupational custom that developed in Australia during the 1990s (though it is also observed elsewhere) in which workers come to work – often on a Friday – dressed in casual clothes. Sometimes a modest penalty or fine is collected for a good cause. It is apparently in decline in recent years. *See also Customs; Folk Costume; Forty Days; Mufti Day*

'FREEHOLD ON THE PLAIN, THE'

Bush song lamenting the loss of a squatter's selection through the combined depredations of bad seasons and the banks. Typical of a class of such songs that includes 'The Broken-Down Squatter', the chorus of which runs:

> *For the banks are all broken, they say,*
> *And the merchants are all up a tree.*
> *When the big-wigs are brought to the bankruptcy Court,*
> *What chance for a squatter like me?*

Both songs were included in Paterson's *Old Bush Songs* (1905). *See also Bush Ballad; Free Selector; Old Bush Songs; Paterson, A.B. ('Banjo')*

FREE SELECTOR

One who, in New South Wales and Victoria, was from the 1860s able to 'select' (i.e. occupy) what was then considered government land. The selector and family could live and work on the land and ultimately 'alienate' (buy) it from the government after sufficient improvements had been made. Conflict between selectors and the earlier group of landholders, usually known as 'squatters' in folklore, was the cause of much tension during the late nineteenth century and was a major factor in a number of bushranging outbreaks, especially that of Ned Kelly. Selectors generally had access only to the poorer land, away from water and transport and, in folklore at least, were notoriously poor and disadvantaged, as described in ballads such as 'Oh, Give Me a Hut', or 'The Free Selector', whose opening verse enjoins the listener:

> To rejoice at the victory John Robertson's won,
> Now the Land Bill is passed and the good times have come.

A later verse describes the utopian hopes raised by free selection:

> No more with our swags through the bush need we roam
> Imploring of charity to give us a home,
> For the land is unfettered and we may reside
> In a home of our own by some clear waterside.

See also Bush; The; Bushrangers; Cocky; Folk Speech; 'Freehold on the Plain, The'

FREMANTLE DOCTOR
Cool afternoon sea breeze experienced in the Fremantle and Perth areas in Western Australia. There are many other 'doctors' along the Australian coast. See also Brickfielder; Cockeye Bob; Eco-lore; Folk Speech; Southerly Buster

FUNERALS
Many customs surrounding funerals have remained constant over generations, if not centuries, but there are some newer aspects of funerals in the twenty-first century. The decline in religious observance has made way for persons other than clergy to officiate at funerals, and sometimes a family friend or leading member of a community will conduct the proceedings. The actual burial or cremation will still be arranged by an accredited funeral director or crematorium, but the tradition may end there. Today, some individuals and their loved ones opt to combine the funeral itself with the wake, and to regard the occasion as a cheerful celebration of the deceased's life rather than as a mourning ceremony or a simple marker of their passing. A number of speeches may be given,

some humorous, and the eating and drinking at the gathering may include toasts to the departed. Floral tributes, usually in the shape of wreaths or sheaths, are important elements of funeral services, usually accompanied by a card identifying the sender, expressing sympathy, condolence and perhaps other sentiments; although these are sometimes replaced, by request, with a donation to a favoured charity. A custom which is probably not more than one generation old involves the placing of flowers and wreaths at the location of fatal road accidents. Usually these roadside markers are of limited duration, but they may sometimes be kept up for a considerable time.

The best-known form of folk funeral custom in Australia is probably the 'wake', a simultaneous sending-off of the departed and a celebration of continuing life, assisted by liberal amounts of food and alcohol. The funeral customs of the broad Anglo-Celtic community may relate to this concept, to a greater or lesser degree. Depending upon the circumstances wakes, especially within the Irish-Australian community, can be more like a celebration than a mourning.

In other cultures, the notion of sending the soul of the departed to the afterlife is also strong. In Greek tradition men and women wear black and the women are expected to indicate their grief through loud weeping, while the men drink coffee and brandy outside the house of the deceased or of the family. Widows were traditionally expected to wear black after the death of the husband, though this custom seems to have declined markedly in Australia in recent years. *See also Customs, Family Folklore, Religious Lore, Roadside Shrines and Memorials*

FURPHY

One of the rare words in Australian folk speech with a dated origin. A 'furphy', as used in Australian folk speech, is a rumour or unsubstantiated or discredited report or idea. The term is usually held to have originated among Australian troops in Egypt during 1915 where the water carts in use were manufactured by J. Furphy and Sons of Shepparton (Vic.), the maker's name being prominently displayed on the vehicle. As gossip and rumour were exchanged by men gathering at the carts, the term 'furphy' evolved as a general descriptor for a falsehood. Like a number of other items of digger folk speech, the word survived the war and passed into the general Australian vernacular, where it is still heard today. *See also Digger, Folk Speech*

G

GALLIPOLI

Anglicisation of the Turkish name *Cannakale*, a peninsula in the Dardanelles where, during World War I, Australian and New Zealand troops landed on the morning of 25 April 1915. This marked the first time this country's troops had fought a military action as Australians rather than as colonials, and the event is popularly considered to have represented the birth of Australia as a nation. The event is closely related to the extensive folk traditions of the digger and Anzac. *See also* ANZAC, *Anzac Day, Dawn Service, Digger, Lone Pine Seeds, The; National Icons*

GALLOPING JONES

A historical figure of northern Queensland folklore, said to have died in 1960, Jones was a bush fighter, a trickster, a drinker, a stock-stealer and a bank robber. His antics included stealing stock, selling the animals and stealing them back again the very same night. Once he was arrested by a policeman and an Aboriginal tracker for illegally slaughtering a cow. The evidence was the cow's hide, prominently marked with someone else's brand. On the way back to town, Jones and his captors camped. Jones managed to get the policeman and his assistant drunk and, when they fell asleep, rode off into the night. However, instead of escaping, he returned a few hours later with a fresh cow hide which he substituted for the one carried by the policeman. Next day the party arrived in town where Jones was tried for his crime. When the evidence was pulled from the bag it was found to bear Jones' own brand, and the case was dismissed.

In another story, Jones is again captured by a young policemen whom he fools into letting him go behind a bush to relieve himself. Of course, Jones escapes and the policeman has to return to town without his captive. When he reports his failure to the sergeant, who is in his usual 'office', the pub, there is Jones, washed and shaved and having a beer. The embarrassed policeman threatens to shoot Jones, but the trickster just says that he had felt the need for a clean-up and a drink, and that now he will be happy to stroll down to the lockup.

Many stories concerning Galloping Jones are also told of a similar Queensland folk character called Snuffler Oldfield. Galloping Jones traditions are very much in the mould of the larger-than-life pioneer heroes of the American west, with more than a touch of the trickster who usually outsmarts everyone else. *See also Folk Humour, Oldfield, Snuffler; Yarns*

GARAGE SALE

An economical custom by which householders sell off their unwanted furniture and other goods to anyone who happens to be passing. Garage sales are often held when a family moves house. Usually advertised by handwritten signs, garage sales these days are also often widely advertised in the columns of local newspapers, which sometimes provide advertisers with pre-printed placards to be placed at corners to indicate the direction of the sale.

One of a number of forms of folk commerce in Australia, the garage sale is, like the car boot sale and the trash-and-treasure market, an import from the United States in the years since World War II. All these activities mark a shift in public attitudes towards raising money for one's own use through the sale of unwanted goods. Personal fundraising was once a source of shame and a badge of poverty, perhaps requiring a furtive visit to the pawnshop, but nowadays garage sales are often convivial occasions which may be organised by people at all levels of society. Trash-and-treasure markets and car boot sales are usually more elaborate affairs, and they may be organised at weekends by groups such as Rotary in order to raise funds for charity. In this case the individual seller will usually pay a fixed fee to the organisers in return for a space in a public place such as a week-day car park and the right to pocket their own profits. Other aspects of folk commerce worth noting include barter, which may operate as a simple *quid pro quo* such as sharing surplus lemons and vegetables among neighbours, or as an elaborate system of credits which may be paid off in labour as well as goods. *The Trading Post* newspapers are undoubtedly commercial operations, but they incorporate some folkloric elements through the honesty system which, for some categories of sales at least, leaves it to the seller to advise the paper and pay a commission if a sale is made. *See also Customs; Markets*

GARDINER, FRANK

Francis Christie was the real name of the bushranger known to history and folklore as 'Darkie' Gardiner. Born near Goulburn in New South Wales in 1830, Gardiner's father was a Scottish migrant and his mother an Irish-Aboriginal named Clarke. Sentenced to three years' hard labour for cattle-stealing in 1850, Gardiner escaped and left the colony. By 1852 he had returned to New South Wales, being arrested again in February 1854. Thereafter he was in and out of gaol on a succession of stock-stealing charges until 1862, when at Eugowra Rocks he masterminded Australia's most spectacular robbery of the nineteenth century. With eleven others (one of whom was probably Ben Hall), Gardiner robbed the Forbes Gold Escort of £4000 in cash, over 200 ounces of gold and the Royal Mail. Most of the loot was recovered fairly soon after the robbery and in 1864 Gardiner was captured in Queensland, where he was living under an assumed identity. Gardiner was sentenced to thirty-two years' hard labour. After ten years of constant lobbying by his family, Gardiner was released and exiled, eventually going to America, where he is said to have opened a saloon on the San Francisco waterfront and to have been killed there in a gunfight during the 1890s. His traditions include a ballad and legends relating to the proceeds of the Eugowra Rocks robbery. See also Bushrangers; Dunn, John; Folk Heroes; Gardiner's Gold; Gilbert, John; Hall, Ben; Vane, John

GARDINER'S GOLD

Also sometimes known as Ben Hall's gold, this is a portion of the booty from the Eugowra Rocks robbery of 1862 allegedly buried by the members of the Gardiner–Hall gang and never recovered. The gold has been the subject of considerable legendry, including the return of Gardiner's adult sons from America in an attempt – perhaps successful – to locate and regain the booty. See also Gardiner, Frank; Hall, Ben; Lost Treasures

GAY AND LESBIAN MARDI GRAS

This event is usually said to have begun as the 'Gay Mardi Gras' in Sydney in 1978 as a local response to the American Stonewall riot of 1969. There is, however, a tradition that the event had its origins in smaller public displays by gays in the Paddington area in previous years. Whatever its exact origins, the 'Gay and Lesbian Mardi Gras', as it is now known, has become one of the largest and most spectacular public festivals in Australia. Its centrepiece is a vast parade of street theatre, floats, dancers, singers and almost anything else in various forms of spectacular dress and undress. Originally established as an event to express the activities of the gay community, the Gay and Lesbian Mardi Gras is now well on the way to becoming an institutionalised event, with participation by tens of thousands of 'straight' Australians and tourists.

The title 'mardi gras' (usually translated as meaning 'fat Tuesday') indicates the event's inspiration in the street festivals of France and Europe generally. In France the event is held on the first day of Lent and is characterised by excessive eating and drinking, followed by the beginning of the Lenten period of fasting the next day. Other well-known 'mardi gras' events are those of New Orleans and Rio de Janeiro. *See also Coming Out (1); Customs*

'GENTLE ANNIE'

Parody of the well-known song of the same name written by Stephen Foster in 1856. A light-hearted and slightly tongue-in-cheek love song, it is one of relatively few such songs collected in the bush tradition. The second verse gives the flavour:

> *Oh, your mutton's very sweet, Gentle Annie,*
> *And I'm sure it can't be packed in New South Wales.*
> *But you'd better put a fence 'round those cabbages*
> *Or they'll all be eat up by the snails.*

See also Bush Ballad; Folk Songs; Old Bush Songs

GERMAN CHARLIE

A shanty-keeper of German origin to whom a number of humorous statements in mock German are traditionally attributed, such as 'Der man dat shall take two drinks of my rum, and then vill not vight his own fader, he is plutty gowardt'. Folklorist and writer Bill Scott collected a number of these tales, which often deal with the problems encountered by migrants. *See also Folk Humour; German Influences on Australian Folklore; Migration Lore; Yarns*

GERMAN INFLUENCES ON AUSTRALIAN FOLKLORE

German communities, notably in and around the Barossa Valley in South Australia, have developed a distinctive tradition of foodways, speech, custom and belief. Noris Ioannou's *Barossa Journeys: Into a Valley of Tradition* (1997) investigates many aspects of the German traditions of this well-defined geographical area. These include:

- handcrafts/arts (including quilts, furniture, pottery, tin art, needlework, musical instruments, stained glass)
- architecture (distinctive, often near-medieval in style, with a strong English rural gentry influence and, more recently, the odd touch of provincial France)
- customs: occasional (*federschleissen* or featherstripping, singing, music); periodic (festivals, agricultural calendar customs, harvest thanksgiving, rites of passage, courting/marriage, tin kettling or *Polter Abend*, christening and funerals)
- foodways (recipes, cooking techniques, foods, associated prayers)
- folk medicine (herbalism, homeopathy)
- beliefs (these include orthodox religious beliefs as well as folk beliefs and the unofficial side of Christian dogma in relation to the devil and magic, such as hexes, witchcraft, the meaning of certain visual motifs used on gravestones and churches, weatherlore and predictions, among others)
- folk tales (stories, legends of lost villages, German traditions)
- songs, rhymes, childlore
- folk speech, especially 'Barossa Deutsch'.

The author shows how all these elements are connected, and how that interconnectedness is, as for all folk groups, the essence of the sense of identity and of place for the Barossa German community.

Ian Harmstorf also surveys the extent and variety of German folklore in South Australia in *The Oxford Companion to Australian Folklore* and, more broadly, in his *The Germans in Australia* (1985). The development from the 1960s of the Oktoberfest, mostly as a commercial and entertainment event, has nevertheless introduced many aspects of German folklore to the broader Australian community, especially in relation to food and drink. Other German influences on Australian folklore include the possible German derivation of the term 'matilda' and elements of the wedding anniversary custom. The game of two-up is also called 'swy', an echo of its origins in the similar German game, 'zwei' being German for 'two'. *See also Essenfest; Festabend and Schutzenfest; Oktoberfest; Tin Kettling, Two-Up; 'Waltzing Matilda'*

GESTURES

Signs made with various parts of the body, especially the hands, are found in folk tradition around the world. In Australia we have adopted and adapted a number of (usually insulting) gestures from the common pool of English-language gestures, as well as gaining a range of others from more recent migrant traditions. Some examples of the insulting are the inverse 'v-sign', consisting of a raised and often crooked index and middle fingers of the right hand; the raised single index, or sometimes middle finger of either hand (adapted from American usage); and the now almost obsolete raised thumb, a crude version of the thumbs-up sign, which is much more commonly used to mean everything is all right. An inverse v-sign behind another's head indicates that person is a cuckold. 'Cocking a snook' (also called the 'Shanghai gesture'), an old gesture involving the thumb being placed on the nose and the fingers of the hand, sometimes two, being waggled in mocking derision is widely known in Europe and was common in British – and probably Australian – tradition in the nineteenth century, though rarely seen today.

The single or double-handed raised v-for-victory sign among sportsmen has now been almost entirely replaced by punching the air with the fist. Still common, especially among children, is the crossing of the middle and index fingers to avert bad luck or ensure good (or, with both hands held behind the back, as tacit permission to tell a lie). Various gestures exist among southern European groups for warding off the influence of the evil eye, and Vietnamese people have certain taboos related to the pointing of body joints, including the elbow. *See also Evil Eye, The; Satanism*

GHOST CATTLE OF YALLOURN

In the Gippsland Hills of Victoria during the middle of the nineteenth century a cattle stampede almost destroyed the town of Moe. Since then, many have heard the sounds of cattle moving around when none can be seen. Some local explanations for these sounds include earth movements associated with the open cut coal mines at Yallourn, adjacent to Moe. *See also Ghost Lore*

GHOST LORE

Australian folklore contains many ghost traditions. As in most other cultures, these stories tend to derive from violent or unusual deaths, either of individuals or groups of people; a considerable number involve animals. Ghost and other supernatural traditions are invariably associated with particular locations, including geographical sites, ships, hotels, theatres, houses, almost any old public buildings, and even beneath Sydney Harbour. A significant number of haunting traditions are associated with workplace accidents. New ghost traditions are also continually being created, as a look at Richard Davis' *The Ghost Guide to Australia* (1998) will confirm. Likewise, older traditions, such as the Black Horse of Sutton (NSW), which was a harbinger of death to a Monaro family, the eerie rumbling wagon sounds once heard in the Murdering Sandhills near Narrandera (NSW) but now not reported for over a century, and the weeping woman ghost of old Pinjarra Bridge (WA), fade with the generations. A representative selection of old and new traditions are contained in this book, but there are many others, including ghosts of famous individuals such as the explorer Robert O'Hara Burke, the bushranger Johnny Gilbert and the navigator William Dampier. Among Australia's numerous haunted houses are Bungaribee House (NSW), a house at Drysdale on the Bellarine Peninsula (Vic.) and even Yarralumla, the official residence of the Governor-General in Canberra (ACT) since 1927. Many geographical locations are also associated with supernatural traditions, such as Devlin's Pound in Western Australia; the New South Wales town of Berrima, which has a headless ghost; and the area between Hughenden and Winton in Queensland that is the home of the well-known Min Min Light(s). *See also Alkimos Ghosts, The; Black Lady of Mount Victoria, The; Blue Lady of New Norcia, The; Fisher's Ghost, Ghost Cattle of Yallourn; Ghosts of Garth, The; Hardhat Haunting, Min-Min Lights*

GHOSTS OF 'GARTH', THE

A ghost tradition. On the banks of the River Esk, near Fingal in Tasmania, stands a mid nineteenth-century residence named 'Garth'. The two-storey stone house was originally built by a young settler for his intended bride back in England. But when he returned to England to marry his fiancée he found she had jilted him for another. Desolate, the young man returned to the unfinished house and hanged himself in the courtyard. With the upper storey left just as the builders abandoned it over a century past, the house is haunted by the disappointed suitor's ghost. It is said that some years after the young Englishman hanged himself, a child, running in fear of being punished for some mischief by her convict nurse, fell into a well near the abandoned house. Attempting to save the little girl, the convict woman was drowned in the well along with the child. Both lie buried at 'Garth', and the ghosts of the child and her would-be saviour, as well as that of the young Englishman, still haunt the house. *See also Ghost Lore*

GILBERT, JOHN

Bushranger and member of the Frank Gardiner-Ben Hall confederacy, and also the subject of considerable celebration in his own right. Gilbert appears in a number of ballads about Ben Hall and figures in considerable legendry in and around his home (in the Forbes district of New South Wales), including a ghost tradition. He was also commemorated in the poem 'How Gilbert Died' (1894) by A.B. Paterson, who was brought up in the area: '...the smallest child on the Watershed can tell you how Gilbert died'. *See also Bushrangers, Folk Heroes, Gardiner, Frank; Hall, Ben*

GIPPSLAND WHITE GIRL, THE *See White Woman of Gippsland, The*

'GIRL WITH THE BLACK VELVET BAND, THE'

Nineteenth century transportation ballad of Irish derivation in which a young man, beguiled by a 'a pretty little young maiden' whose 'eyes ... shone like diamonds', is led into being her accomplice in picking a watch from a gentleman's pocket. He is arrested and transported for the crime 'far away to van Diemen's land/Away from my friends and relations/And the girl with the black velvet band'. Said to have been widely sung in the outback during the 1880s. *See also Convict Lore; Transportation Ballads*

GIRLS' NIGHT OUT

All-female night out of eating, drinking and perhaps a visit to a venue featuring male strippers. Not earlier than the 1960s. *See also Customs; Hens' Night*

GLENROWAN STATION

Scene of the Kelly gang's last stand against the authorities in late June 1880, and focus of a number of Kelly songs and traditions. As the ballad 'Kelly Was Their Captain' claims:

> *It was at the Glenrowan Station where the conflict raged severe,*
> *When more than forty policemen at the scene then did appear.*

No credit to their bravery, no credit to their name,
Ned Kelly terrified them all and put their blood to shame.

See also Kelly, Ned

GOANNA OIL

The *Report of the Committee of Inquiry into Folklife in Australia* (1987, p.
55) described Goanna Oil and Salve as 'sufficiently legendary, old-
established and the subject of folk beliefs to be accorded folk status'.
'Goanna Oil' does not contain oil derived from goannas any more than
Singapore's famed Tiger Balm contains tigers, but it has a whiff of the
bush and of Aboriginal medicine sufficient to make numbers of
Australians swear by its magical properties. Goanna Oil is one of a
number of commercial products which Australians have taken to their
hearts, including Vegemite, Aeroplane Jelly, Mortein Fly Spray and Flick
Pest Control Products, often as the result of hugely successful radio or
television advertisements. A sure sign of folkloric status is when the
jingle in question is the subject of parody, as in the 1950s Cold War era
parody of 'the Flick man':

> *How can you be sure*
> *There are no Russians in the floor*
> *Soviets in the door*
> *Communists galore?*
>
> *Get an A-Bomb, that's your answer*
> *Remember one flash*
> *And they're ash.*

See also Aeroplane Jelly; Folk Medicine; National Icons

GOING AWAY

After the formalities of the wedding and reception, it is permissible for
the bride and groom to slip away to their honeymoon. For this purpose,
the bride will change from her wedding dress into new clothes, these
being thereafter known as her 'going away dress' or 'going away outfit'.
Traditionally, the 'going away' vehicle is decorated with 'just married'
messages, bunting, streamers and tin cans or other noise-making objects.
(*see also Tin Kettling*). The couple escape to their supposedly secret

honeymoon location, leaving their friends and relatives to party on into the small hours at the expense, usually, of the parents-in-law.

It is often Greek practice for the newlyweds to go straight from the marriage ceremony to their honeymoon. When they return, they have an open house for the wedding guests, who come to congratulate them on their marriage. *See also Customs; Tin Kettling; Weddings*

GOING 'O.S.'

Since the beginning of free settlement in Australia, making a return visit 'home' to Britain was an important event in the lives of those who could afford it. In the years following World War II, the 'trip to England' or to 'England and the Continent' became a rite of passage for young middle-class people, often for six months or a year, before 'settling down' to serious career or family activities. Initially the trips were made by boat, but with the growth of international air travel, and the lowering of air fares, more and more young Australians of all social classes made the trip 'o.s.' (overseas). Destinations for overseas travel became more varied, and visits to Asia became more frequent, with Thailand and Bali (in Indonesia) some of the most favoured and cheapest holiday locations. It is not clear as at the end of 2002 whether the growth of international terrorism, and in particular, the tragic bombing in Bali on 12 October 2002, will curb young Australians' desire to 'go o.s.'. *See also Customs*

GOLDRUSH LORE

The various goldrushes in Australia since European settlement have brought large numbers of people into the country, especially after the strikes in New South Wales and Victoria in the 1850s, and in Western Australia during the 1890s. The goldfields generated a great deal of lore and legend, especially in the form of song, verse and tall story. Well-known gold ballads include 'The Miner', 'Look Out Below', 'Tambaroora Gold', 'The Old Palmer Song', 'With My Swag All On My Shoulder' ('Denis O'Reilly') and 'Pint Pot and Billy', among others. Chinese miners featured in a number of gold ballads, usually in a derogatory manner. A number of goldfields songs of the eastern Australian rushes are derived from the compositions of Charles Thatcher, 'The Minstrel of the Goldfields'. Gold was also a major motivation for the bushranging of the 1860s that also generated a great deal of folklore, especially in relation to figures like Ben Hall, Frank Gardiner, 'Thunderbolt' and Daniel 'Mad Dog' Morgan.

Gold itself is the object of considerable folkloric belief, including the efficacy of gold wedding rings for eradicating sties in the eye, and gold earrings were worn by seafarers both to strengthen the eyes and to prevent drowning. It is also often said that European sailors wore a gold earring so that wherever they died or drowned, the payment would be there on hand for a Christian burial and prayers, either at sea or on land. The use of gold coins at sea, such as placing one beneath the mast to avoid bad luck, is also an old tradition. *See also Bushrangers, Digger, Lost Treasures, Racist Folklore, Ragged Thirteen, The; Thatcher, Charles*

GOORIANAWA
Nineteenth century shearing song in which a shearer recalls the tough stations he has shorn during his life, none being as hard as Goorianawa (NSW): 'Spare me flamin' days, I never saw before/The way we had to knuckle down at Goorianawa.' *See also Pastoral Industry Folklore, Shearers, Work Lore*

GOVERNORS, THE
In 1900 Jimmy Governor, his brother Joe and accomplice Jacky Underwood between them murdered nine white people and seriously wounded three others. The first five deaths occurred at Breelong, near Gilgandra in central western New South Wales, when Jimmy Governor, the ringleader, is thought to have taken offence at slurs cast on his wife. On 20 July 1900 he and Underwood murdered his employer's wife, three children and a local schoolmistress. The three Aborigines then escaped into the bush and began a bushranging spree that lasted several months. Underwood was subsequently arrested, and the Governor brothers murdered a woman and child and two more men. Joe Governor was eventually shot by pursuers, and Jimmy Governor and Jacky Underwood were hanged in January 1901.

There are a considerable number of folk traditions relating to Jimmy Governor and his accomplices – usually referred to as 'the Breelong Blacks' – in the central west region of New South Wales. The late John Meredith collected a number of ballads on the subject in this region, though these seem to have circulated in written rather than oral form. The Governor story was the basis of Thomas Keneally's celebrated novel *The Chant of Jimmie Blacksmith* (1972), subsequently made into a well-known, if controversial, film. *See also Indigenous Folklore; Racist Folklore*

GRAFFITI

One of the world's oldest forms of protest or self-expression, graffiti has traditionally consisted of anonymous writings, usually brief, on public spaces such as walls or, more privately, inside lavatory cubicles. Graffiti written by ancient Romans in occupied Britain in the first century AD has been found, and they are still written in Australia today. Some classic slogans on Australian walls have included 'Pig Iron Bob', a reference to Prime Minister Robert Menzies' battles with waterside workers who (prophetically) refused to load pig-iron for Japan shortly before the beginning of World War II. In a lighter vein is the question and response publicised by the historian and football enthusiast Ian Turner in the 1970s:

> *What would you do if Jesus came to Hawthorn?*
> *Get him to move Peter Hudson to full forward.*

Every year's new graffiti reflects its era: 'End the Vietnam War', 'No war for oil', 'Dead men don't rape' and 'If he beats you, leave' all say something about the preoccupations of the time. Whereas graffiti in public places is usually concerned with political or social issues, writings in lavatories (what folklorists call *latrinalia*) are usually more individual. A study done by Gwenda Beed Davey in the 1990s showed that women writing in lavatories are more preoccupied with personal issues. Davey's study documented cries from the heart, dialogue and debate about religion, politics and sexual preference, philosophical pronouncements and advice to the lovelorn. The biggest single group of graffiti included 'pronouncements' about the writer's favourite topic, and the opinions given (more or less forcefully) – as well as on religion, politics and sexual preference – concerned ecological issues, incest, bodily functions, school and tourism. Some examples included

> *We're here, we're queer*
> *And we're proud*

and

> *Grass is green and other shades*
> *I'll stick to that*
> *And not get AIDS.*

Considerable controversy has raged (and still rages) about the status of spray-can painting on walls, such as railway cuttings, and in and on railway carriages. Is it art? Is it vandalism? Is it original – or is it mindless copying from mostly American books of spray-can designs? Like more conventional graffiti, does it have anything to say? *See also Folk Humour; Folk Art; Folklore of Struggle*

GRAFTON JACARANDA FESTIVAL

Held annually since 1934 over several weeks in October–November, this event is usually reckoned to be the oldest festival in Australia celebrating a harvest or flowering of a plant, in this case the spectacular blue-flowering Jacaranda tree. The festival involves floral displays, garden competitions, processions, fairs, the selection and processioning of a 'festival queen', sporting events and entertainments. *See also Customs; Festivals*

GRANVILLE TRAIN DISASTER, THE

On 19 January 1977, eighty passengers were killed and over eighty injured when a Blue Mountains commuter train ploughed into the Bold Street Bridge at Granville station in New South Wales. Each year since the tragedy a memorial service has been held near the site of the crash. *See also Disasters; Roadside Shrines and Memorials; 'Sunshine Rail Disaster, The'*

GREAT AUSTRALIAN ADJECTIVE, THE *See Bloody*

GREAT DEPRESSION, THE

The severe economic depression of the 1930s is always 'the Great Depression' in Australian folklore. The effects on workers and families were so drastic that the era remains potent in folk memory several generations later. There is a solid body of depression lore, including songs and ditties like 'On the Steps of the Dole-Office Door', which includes a reference to New South Wales Premier Jack Lang, who 'closed up the banks, it was one of his pranks/And sent us to the dole-office door'. Other songs and poems of the era deal with forced evictions, strikes, lock-outs, the need to 'hop a rattler' (or train) in order to find employment, relief work, dole rations and 'happy valleys', the shanty towns in which many formerly comfortable Australians were forced to live. A number of depression songs, such as 'Hallelujah, I'm a Bum' show the influence of American folk and popular culture on Australian tradition, an influence boosted by the development of radio during the 1930s and the rise of recording artists in the Australian country and western style, a genre that also influenced Aboriginal traditional singers such as Dougie Young, composer of 'The Land Where the Crow Flies Backwards'. *See also Disasters; Folklore of Struggle; Labor Lore*

GREEK FOLKLORE IN AUSTRALIA

The Greek-speaking community in Australia is one of the largest groups of non-English-speaking background, and one with a high degree of language maintenance. According to the 1996 Census, 259,019 persons over five years of age speak Greek at home. The Greek language is maintained in the family, by the Greek Orthodox Church, by newspapers and a variety of organisations, and by the large number of 'ethnic schools' for children operating outside regular school hours. Language maintenance is also assisted by the many dance groups for both children and young adults in most Australian cities.

The best-known manifestations of Greek folklore in Australia are probably to do with food, music and dance. All three are often combined in popular restaurants and tavernas in cities and towns, and the clientele is likely to include Anglo and other ethnic Australians as well as those of Greek parentage. Food specialties are likely to be grilled lamb and fish, *taramasalata* and *tsatsiki* (fish roe and garlic/yoghurt/cucumber dips), pastries such as baklava and the traditional sweet, thick Greek coffee. The music may be *rebetika*, sometimes called the 'Greek blues', as well as other Greek folk or popular music, and the dancing will often be provided by the diners. Many Australians of all ethnic backgrounds can manage the simpler steps in Greek dancing, or are at least willing to 'have a go'. Musical instruments will almost certainly include the popular bouzouki as well as perhaps *baglama*, *lyra*, *outi* and *sandouri*.

Popular Greek *Glendi* festivals featuring music, dance and food are regularly held in a number of locations, such as Melbourne's Lonsdale Greek precinct. There is also much Greek folklore in Australia which is not on public display. Stathis Gauntlett and Anna Chatzinikolaou, from La Trobe University in Melbourne, in the *Oxford Companion to Australian Folklore* (1993), write that private observances brought to Australia by early Greek settlers have included:

Veneration of small private icons (to this day unobtrusively kept in wallets or stuck to the sun-visors of cars, trucks and taxis), traditional naming practices and celebration of (saints') name-days, evil-eye superstitions (matiasma), right-foot-first superstitions (podariko), and hospitality rituals at inaugurations, ceremonies and other special occasions (kerasma, kilyva, vasilopita, etc).

They also referred in the same publication to 'traditional proverbs, cliché dialogues, tales, jokes, anecdotes…and…Greek folk songs'.

The Greek Orthodox Church in Australia has maintained many folk traditions such as wedding customs, Easter customs (including dyeing and cracking Easter eggs), and various 'blessing of the waters' rituals carried out at seaside locations. Some folk customs have adapted to the southern hemisphere and to Australian life: for example, a number of Australian 'bush bands' now include bouzouki among their instruments. Perhaps the most striking change in Greek folk traditions in Australia is in the language. Australian-Greek is now considered by many linguists to be a distinct 'ethnolect' including hybrid words such as *milkbaraki* (a little milk bar/shop) as well as other linguistic changes. *See also Rebetika; Weddings*

GRIFFITHS, SAM

Properly Samuel Griffiths (1845–1920), Queensland Premier from 1883 to 1888 and 1890 to 1893. He appears in a song named after him in which the subject of 'coloured' – or 'kanaka' – labour from the South Pacific islands is treated from the perspective of the bush worker. *See also Political Lore*

GROG

Folk speech for alcohol since at least the early nineteenth century, and a common accompaniment of much folkloric activity. Also features frequently in folklore, especially that of male occupational groups such as shearers, drovers and diggers, and of youth groups such as larrikins, surfies and student revellers, including those taking part in 'Schoolies Week' on the east coast or its west coast equivalent, 'Leavers'. In these contexts grog is often associated with violence and the consequences of over-indulgence. There is a large body of folklore surrounding the intake of alcohol, including drinking games, folk speech, customs such as 'the shout', and folk medicine involving (alleged) remedies for hangovers. *See also* 'Across the Western Plains'; Chook Raffles; Kirup Syrup; National Icons, Pub, The; Student Revels

GROTTOES

These are often Catholic shrines to the Virgin Mary, but may be graced with statues of other saints and may be built in back yards. Many of these statues were discarded by Catholic clergy in the reforming zeal of the 1960s and after, only to be rescued by laity and re-erected in the garden grotto, or sometimes within the house itself. *See also Customs, Pilgrimage, Religious Lore*

GUMLEAF PLAYING

Leaf playing might be considered by many older Australians as a traditional Aboriginal activity, although there is little evidence of this practice among traditional Aboriginal societies. Certainly some Aboriginal people did play leaves in the inter-war years, and some missions organised 'leaf orchestras' to play for church services. Like the musical saw, leaf playing was sometimes included in vaudeville performances in the same era. Kevin Bradley (of the National Library of Australia) described in the *Oxford Companion to Australian Folklore* (1993) four of the most common styles of playing leaves. He also notes that the leaves played were not necessarily gum leaves, and that the practice was not exclusively Australian. *See also Bush, The; Folk Music, Making Do*

'GUMTREE CANOE, THE'

One among relatively few romantic bush songs, probably derived from a popular song. The singer pictures himself afloat with his Julia in a gum-tree canoe 'With my thumb on the banjo, my toe on the oar/I'll sing to my Julia, I'll sing as I row...'. *See also Bush Ballads; Folk Songs; 'Gentle Annie'*

GUY FAWKES' NIGHT

Traditionally celebrated in Australia since at least 1805, Guy Fawkes' Night takes place on 5 November, and continues the British tradition of celebrating the Gunpowder Plot of 1605, when Catholic activists including Guy Fawkes attempted to blow up the British Houses of Parliament. A bonfire is built on which effigies or 'guys' are thrown, together with the exploding of fireworks such as bungers, rockets, Roman candles and Catherine wheels. Some crackers are hand held, such as sparklers, while others are attached to nearby fences or set in bottles or on poles. A few generations ago almost every suburb or country town would hold its own cracker night, but fear of accidents, fires and injuries and the lack of open spaces in suburbia, along with restrictions on the sale of fireworks to the public, have all contributed to the decline of cracker night. Bonfires are still lit, however, and Guy Fawkes still appears on 5 November in places such as the town of Moe in Victoria. Many adults can still recite at least part of the old rhyme:

> Please to remember the fifth of November
> Gunpowder, treason and plot.
> I see no reason why gunpowder treason
> Should ever be forgot.

See also Cracker Night; Customs; Empire Day

H

HAJJ

One of the five pillars of Islam, the *Hajj* or pilgrimage to Mecca in Saudi Arabia takes place from the eighth to the thirteenth of *Zul-Hijja* on the Muslim calendar (around July). Adult Muslims make great efforts to perform this pilgrimage at least once in their lives, often travelling to Mecca in family and friendship groups. *See also Customs; Family Folklore; Pilgrimage; Religious Lore; Reunions*

HALL, BEN

A bushranger hero of the Forbes (NSW) region (1837–1865). In his extensive tradition Ben Hall is a victim of injustice on the part of 'the Crown', is courteous to women, even-handed and kind. Hall features in a number of celebratory and often elegiac ballads, including 'The Streets of Forbes', 'The Death of Ben Hall', 'Bold Ben Hall' and 'Dunn, Gilbert and Ben Hall'. In the song usually titled 'My Name is Ben Hall' the bushranger robs a squatter (wealthy landowner), but in proper outlaw hero style returns him five pounds to see him to the end of his journey. In another version of this ballad there is a suggestion that the bushranger is betrayed by his 'false wife', and also that he shares the results of his robberies in Robin Hood style – 'With my friends in the bush I'll distribute this wealth.' It is said that Ben Hall's share of the gold from the Eugowra Rocks robbery is buried somewhere in the Weddin Mountains (NSW). Other lore about Hall involves his shooting by police, allegedly twenty or more times, and the belief that a woman subsequently gave birth to a son fathered by Ben Hall and that the child had birth marks exactly matching the number and location of Hall's wounds. Ben Hall's grave in Forbes is still tended and decorated by local people. *See also Bushrangers, Folk Heroes and Heroines, Gardiner, Frank; Gardiner's Gold; Gilbert, Johnny*

HALLOWEEN

Celebrated on 31 October, the last night of the year according to the Celtic calendar, Halloween (also Hallowe'en) is a popular festival in the Celtic countries, in parts of Britain and in the United States. It is also gaining in popularity in Australia, where it has attracted criticism from the Christian church in recent years, partly due to its importance on the witches' calendar, where it is called *Samhain*, the name by which it is still known in Ireland. Although widely held to have origins in pre-Christian beliefs, there is no historical evidence to connect it with the dead or with any pagan rituals. It is only since the nineteenth century in Britain and America that Halloween has developed its now familiar spooky dimension, acknowledged by children dressing as ghosts or monsters and 'trick or treating' – visiting houses and demanding sweets, money or drinks on pain of harmless mischief to the household. Halloween has been observed in Australia only since c. 1980, mainly in the form of children's 'trick or treat' activities, adopted directly from the American tradition. A possible explanation for the recent growth of Halloween in Australia is that currently popular horror novels and movies about aliens and the supernatural may have contributed to the craze. It also seems that primary school teachers, searching for October–November seasonal activities, have been instrumental in promoting the custom amongst their pupils. As well, retailers have been enthusiastic suppliers of Halloween paraphernalia as a handy stop-gap in the period between Father's Day and Christmas.

Halloween is closely connected with the Christian feasts of All Saints Day (1 November) and All Souls' Day (2 November). These two days were once known as 'Hallow Tide' and commemorate respectively the lives of past, present and future saints and the souls of deceased family and friends. Graves may be visited and tended on All Souls Day. Halloween is also traditionally believed to be a favourable time for divining the future of one's love life. The methods used involved, amongst other things, candles, mirrors, 'bobbing for apples', eating salted fish, hempseed, and even mashed potato. *See also Children's Folklore, Customs, Religious Lore, Trick or Treat*

HANDCLAPPING GAMES

Handclapping games are one of the most popular of children's traditional games, usually played by primary school girls. They can mostly be observed in the playground, but will often be played to pass the time out of school hours. As well as rhythmical hand movements including clapping, they almost always involve a verbal chant such as the very old rhyme:

Mary Mack, dressed in black
Silver buttons down her back.
She likes coffee,
She likes tea,
She likes sitting
On a black man's knee.

Some of these chants are very long, such as the life-cycle chant 'When Suzy was a baby', which ranges from Suzy's babyhood to death and status as a ghost/angel. The games are usually played by two, though sometimes larger numbers may be involved, perhaps in a circle of up to ten players. Lindsay and Palmer (1981) gave detailed descriptions of twenty-five different clapping games observed in Brisbane primary schools during the 1970s, and the Australian Children's Folklore Collection at the Museum of Victoria includes many dozens more. One of the most well known is 'A Sailor Went to Sea':

A sailor went to sea, sea, sea,
To see what he could see, see, see;
But all that he could see, see, see
Was the bottom of the deep blue sea, sea, sea.

The text of the rhymes may vary, although they are surprisingly stable over time and place. Many handclapping games popular in Australia are also found in other English-speaking countries, and in foreign-language versions elsewhere. *See also Australian Children's Folklore Collection; Children's Folklore; Games*

HARDHAT HAUNTING
There is said to be a ghostly hardhat diver in Sydney Harbour, NSW, just beneath the Harbour Bridge. Tradition has it that the diver, who is never named, was killed during the construction of the Bridge (c. 1929–32). The ghost was reported by two divers in the 1960s and has been seen on several occasions since. *See also Ghost Lore; Work Lore*

HARVEST CUSTOMS
These vary greatly from place to place. In some rural areas it is still customary for the local church to hold a special thanksgiving service for the successful completion of the harvest. Such 'harvest festivals' generally

derive from the invention of a Victorian minister of religion in Cornwall, who instituted the first in 1843. Contrary to popular belief, harvest customs, like most other 'old' folk customs, are not survivals of 'pagan' sacrificial or seasonal rituals. It was common until well into the twentieth century for churches in cities and suburbs to also hold thanksgiving services, often involving offerings of fruit and vegetables. In some churches the observance may still be kept. Sometimes in conjunction with these, or independently, special meals and accompanying celebrations were organised, such as the 'shearing supper', and some of these continue.

Shearing suppers and carnivals were the Australian equivalent of the British 'harvest home' and other European harvest customs. At the end of the shearing season a celebration might be held on the station, often elaborate, and involving horse races, sports and a dance, as well as liberal amounts of food and alcohol. These have a more convincing folkloric pedigree. Often accompanied by excessive indulgence, at least in the eyes of the Victorian church, such customs were a major reason for the invention of the harvest festival or harvest thanksgiving. *See also Blessing of the Fleece; Blessing of the Fleet; Customs; Picnic Races*

HENLEY-ON-TODD REGATTA

A 'yacht' race of wildly improvised craft along the dry bed of the Todd River, Alice Springs (NT) on the first Monday in August. Established in 1961, this festive event derives more than a little of its continuing popularity through its implied satirisation of the famous Henley Regatta in England. *See also Customs; Folk Humour; Folk Sports*

HENS' NIGHT

A women's social custom, often taking place on the same night as the groom's 'Bucks' Night', this may involve the bride-to-be, her bridesmaids, female friends and possibly their mothers dressing in their sexiest clothes for a party. This may take place at a private house or a restaurant, and be continued at a night club. Like the male event, there is an emphasis on alcohol, usually the 'cocktail' or some other exotic and expensive drink. Small presents are also given, sometimes with a sexual connection. A male stripper may complete the evening, which usually ends before midnight. Whatever form these nights take, they provide an opportunity for a good time:'Hens' Nights are not restricted to wedding preliminaries and are now a common occasional custom. *See also Customs; Girls' Night Out; Weddings; Women's Folklore*

HEXHAM GREYS, THE

The Hexham (NSW) Greys are large mosquitoes, usually said to be enormous enough to wear hobnail boots and to drill their way into the bodies of their victims. Similar legends and tall tales are told about these and other insects in many parts of the country. *See also Flies; Folk Humour; Legendary Animals; Yarns*

HODJA, THE

Nasreddin Hodja is a character much-loved in Turkish folklore, and well known to adults and children of Turkish background living in Australia. The honorary title of 'hodja' indicates that Nasreddin is a scholar, immediately recognisable by his scholar's headdress or *kavuk*, and by his faithful donkey. Turkish-Australian schoolchildren in Richmond, Victoria, told a story about Nasreddin's *kavuk*. On one occasion Nasreddin is upbraided for his inability to read a poorly written letter. 'How can you wear the kavuk, when you can't read this letter?' demands the letter-owner. 'You wear the kavuk, and see if you can read the letter!' replies Nasreddin. Nasreddin's scholarship and wisdom are sometimes faulty, though he can talk himself out of most difficult situations. Nasreddin Hodja is both a wise man and a fool, an upholder of authority and a challenger of the powerful. His character is also well known in Greece, the Balkans and the Middle East, and in other areas formerly occupied by the Ottoman Empire. Stories told about Nasreddin Hodja can be lengthy, or simply clever retorts, as in the example above. *See also Folk Heroes; Folk Humour; Migration Lore*

HOGMANAY *See New Year's Day*

HOLIDAYS

Holidays come in an almost infinite variety of forms and can be taken at any number of locations, including at home. Common holiday customs in Australia may involve a camping trip by car, often interstate or at least covering a great distance, a holiday at a 'beach shack' (in Western Australia and elsewhere) or 'weekender', or in a caravan or a trip overseas to Bali, Hong Kong, Singapore or further afield. Cities often have favoured and habitual holiday locations, such as Bateman's Bay for

Canberra and Rottnest Island ('Rotto') for Perth. Other traditional locations include the Gold Coast and the islands of the Great Barrier Reef in Queensland, though in recent years many Australians have become more adventurous in their holiday destinations. *See also Customs; Family Folklore; Work Lore*

HOLY DAN

Pure-spoken bullock-driver in a well-known bush recitation in which the God-fearing Dan steadfastly refuses to blaspheme as his animals progressively die during a Queensland drought. Finally, all but one of his twenty bullocks die:

> *Then Dan broke down – good, Holy Dan*
> *The man who never swore.*
> *He knelt beside the latest corpse*
> *And here's the prayer he prore.*

> *'That's nineteen thou hast taken, lord*
> *And now you'll plainly see,*
> *You'd better take the bloody lot,*
> *One's no damn good to me…'*

Immediately Dan uttered these words the sky opened and rain lashed down, causing a flood in which Holy Dan was drowned. *See also Bullockies; Folk Humour; Recitation*

HOOP SNAKES

Mythic creatures of tall-tale tradition. These snakes are said to form into hoops and bowl themselves at intruders in the bush. *See also Drop Bears; Folk Humour, Legendary Animals*

HOPE CHEST *See Trousseau*

HOPPY (HOPSCOTCH)

Hopscotch, commonly called 'hoppy' in Australia, is a popular children's game played by both boys and girls, but more commonly by girls usually of primary school age. A pattern of numbered squares is drawn or scratched on the ground with chalk or a stone, and frequently a special stone or 'taw' is thrown or kicked inside them, and children hop on one leg from one square to another. Players are usually 'out' if the taw lands on a line, or if they hop on a line or lose their balance, or if they hop into a square containing a taw. Common pattern variations include the 'aeroplane' and 'snail' (a spiral of squares). Children will often vary the size and proportions of the hopscotch grid according to the age of the players, so that pre-painted hopscotch grids in the playground may not be ideal; teachers would be better advised to provide the children with chalk. *See also Australian Children's Folklore Collection; Children's Folklore; Games*

HORSES

The horse appears frequently in Australian rural tradition, as beast of burden and as the bearer of the bushman hero of myth, as well as of the closely related figure of the bushranger. A legendary horse is 'the small and weedy beast, with a touch of Timor pony, three parts thoroughbred at least' that carried the Man from Snowy River, and the Light Horse Brigades of World War I that were immortalised in Charles Chauvel's 1941 film *Forty Thousand Horsemen*. Horses are also central to the lore of the turf, or horse racing: one racehorse, Phar Lap, has become a national icon. In more modern times, some horseracing scandals such as the Fine Cotton horse substitution or 'ring in' have passed into folklore. *See also Bush, The; Bushrangers; Horses' Birthday, The; 'Man from Snowy River', The; Phar Lap; Turf Lore*

HORSES' BIRTHDAY

From the mid nineteenth century, when horseracing (popular in Australia from around 1900) became organised and regulated, 1 August became the day marked in the Australia calendar as the official 'horses' birthday'. This was in order to regulate the age of horses entered in age-related races (for two-year-olds, for example). This date is not internationally recognised, but varies according to the breeding seasons in different parts of the world. According to Australian folk belief, anyone born on 1 August is lucky. *See also Folk Belief; Horses; Turf Lore*

HOUSEWARMING

A party held in a newly occupied house. The new occupants invite friends and family to celebrate their taking possession of the new home, so that the conviviality of the occasion 'warms' the new living quarters. A custom common throughout the world, its continuation in Australia is an indication of the perpetual human urge to mark significant new stages of life with social activity, the location of much folklore. *See also Customs, Family Folklore*

HUGHIE

Familiar form for God, or the rain gods, as in the farmer's plea, 'Send 'er down, Hughie.' Also used by surfers in the form 'Send 'em in, Hughie', asking for rideable waves. Of obscure origin, thought to be probably late nineteenth century. *See also Beach Lore; Bush, The; Folk Belief; Folk Speech*

I

INDIGENOUS FOLKLORE

Just as the tenets of other religious belief systems are not folklore, the central beliefs, customs and expressions of Aboriginal and Torres Strait Islander spirituality are not folklore. Early anthropologists and collectors of Aboriginal culture frequently referred to these materials and activities as 'folklore'. Modern folklorists do not. However, as with all cultures and creeds, indigenous peoples have extensive folk traditions outside their spiritual and mythic beliefs and practices. These include foodways, medicines, art, craft, stories, songs, games, children's lore – in which area a considerable amount of fieldwork and research has been carried out – and a variety of other forms.

There is a two-way traffic between indigenous and non-indigenous traditions. Aboriginal and Torres Strait Islander peoples have adapted many introduced traditions, especially those associated with music, folk speech and some heroic figures like the navigator Captain Cook and bushranger Ned Kelly. Non-indigenous Australians have likewise adapted elements of indigenous tradition, including tales and beliefs about fabled creatures like the bunyip and the yarama; names for places, plants and animals; traditional art and craft designs and other elements of Aboriginal culture, such as the didgeridoo. *See also Bunyip; Bush Music; Children's Folklore; Coo-ee; Cook, Captain; Corroboree; Folk Speech; Games; Kelly, Ned; Jacky Bindieye; Jacky-Jacky; Jandamurra; Racist Folklore; Yagan; Yarama; Yowie*

INITIATION CUSTOMS

Many trades and groups have initiation rituals, ranging from innocuous pranks like asking a new starter to 'fetch a left-handed spanner' to brutal forms of ceremonial mistreatment practised in some sectors of the armed forces and other male-dominated groups, such as male-only boarding schools and university colleges. These ceremonies are often longstanding or, if not, are often claimed to be by those who carry them out. Some notorious cases of initiations have been revealed in recent years both in the armed forces and in some universities. *See also Bastardisation, Customs, Work Lore*

INSULT AND INVECTIVE

All folk traditions have extensive repertoires of insulting terms, sayings, jokes and other forms of derogation, usually humorous in nature, though usually wounding for their targets. These include insulting terms and jokes about those of 'other' race, nation, ethnicity, colour, religion or other form of perceived difference. Australian tradition is also rich in insults related to appearance ('he has a head like a bagful of busted boils'), stupidity (nong, drongo).

Children's folk speech is especially fertile, as revealed in June Factor's *Kidspeak* (2001), which lists terms and variations including dumbo, dummy, spastic, spazzo, spaz, fuckface, fuckhead, etc. *See also Folk Humour, Folk Speech, Jokes*

IRISH INFLUENCES ON AUSTRALIAN FOLKLORE

The traditions of the large numbers of Irish who were transported or migrated to Australia in the nineteenth century had a powerful influence on colonial folklore. The Irish influence is especially strong in the lore of convicts, migrants and bushrangers. St Patrick's Day was one of the earliest calendar customs observed in Australia after settlement. As in Britain and the USA, the folk stereotype of the Irish as stupid is prevalent in much of the lore of this period, and continues in the form of the 'Irish joke' and other types of modern folklore, such as e-lore and humorous tales that feature 'an Englishmen, an Irishman and an Australian'. Building on its nineteenth-century foundations, the continuing migration of Irish people has ensured that the influence of Irish tradition on Australian folklore is broad and profound. It is found in most forms of folklore, including folk song and music, dance, folk tale, humour, custom and national mythologies like that of Ned Kelly and the Eureka Stockade. Many aspects of the Irish influence on Australian folk tradition are revealed in Bill Wannan's *The Folklore of the Irish in Australia* (1980) and in his earlier compilation *The Wearing of the Green* (1965). *See also Convict Lore; Doyle, Tom; Frank the Poet; Kelly, Ned; Migration Lore; St Patrick's Day; Transportation Ballads*

IRISH JOKES

Many different countries have designated a particular nationality or ethnic group or minority as the butt of derogatory humour, and generate jokes that feature their alleged stupidity. Canadians mock Newfoundlanders ('Newfies'), Americans mock Poles ('Polacks'),

Germans mock East Friesians, Indians mock Bengalis and Australians frequently pick on the Irish: 'What's at the top of an Irish ladder? A Stop sign.' Often an apparent result of injustice, poverty or lack of education suffered by, or inflicted on, that group at some time, it is notable that jokes about their alleged inferiority in fact 'blame the victim'.

So-called 'Irish jokes' have to be considered in the wider context of the racist joke, although most Irish jokes are likely to be less unpleasant than some circulating in Australia about Aboriginal people and Jews. Humour is a very potent way of circulating racism, in that it is often hard for a listener to object to a racist joke, for fear of being thought humourless or offending the teller (who may be a friend). And so the cycle of racism continues. *See also Folk Humour; Jokes; Racist Folklore*

ISLAMIC NEW YEAR
A religious custom observed on the first day of the month of *Muharrum* (mid to late September) which celebrates the flight of the Prophet Mohammed from Mecca to Medina in 622 AD. Generally, the story of this flight is told and, in some Islamic countries such as Egypt, there may also be fairs, and gifts such as sweets and new clothes given to children. *See also Customs; Folk Costume; Foodways; Religious Lore*

'ISLE DE FRANCE, THE'
Transportation ballad c. mid-nineteenth century in which an Irish convict being transported to Australia for seven years is wrecked upon the Isle de France (Mauritius). In a most unlikely resolution, he is pardoned by the Queen. *See also Convict Lore, Irish Influences on Australian Folklore, Transportation Ballads*

ITALIAN FOLKLORE IN AUSTRALIA
Italian is the second most commonly spoken language in Australia, after English. Early Italian immigrants came from a wide variety of regions in Italy, and as well as standard Italian, many different dialects are spoken. There is a proliferation of Italian clubs and associations in Australia including the Veneto Club in Melbourne, the APIA Club in Sydney, the Marco Polo Club in Queanbeyan (NSW) and the Verdi Club in Alice Springs (NT). The family, these clubs and the Catholic Church are the main institutions in Australia helping to maintain rich and complex Italian folk traditions. In some cases, individual musicians and folk clubs or festivals have helped to revive partly forgotten traditions. The

musician Kavisha Mazella played a leading role in the formation of the Fremantle Women's Choir and the Melbourne equivalent, La Voce della Luna. Both choirs have retrieved fragments of Italian folk songs, including some songs about migration, and these songs have been performed publicly at folk festivals, in concert and in theatrical performances.

Religious processions are of great importance in Italo-Australian folk culture. Fremantle's Blessing of the Fleet is held annually in this popular fishing and tourist town near Perth (WA). Other festivals may be secular, such as the Lygon Street Festa in Melbourne's University suburb of Carlton, which celebrates the food and restaurant culture of the area. Australia as a whole has taken to its heart the Italian food traditions of espresso, latte and cappuccino coffee, pasta and pizza, and this last may have nudged the Australian meat pie from its place as the favourite national 'fast food'.

When considering 'Italian folklore', it is important to remember that most of Italy was united as a single country only in the mid-nineteenth century, and that its regional, social and economic diversity is enormous. Many Italian folk traditions are not as well known to the wider Australian public as are food and festivals, and these private traditions remain within families or communities and as the subject of anthropological studies. Private customs range from traditional cooking and preserving practices (such as home-made tomato paste, sausage and wine) to family relationships and private devotions to the Virgin Mary, the *Madonna*. Some items of folk speech have become Italianised, such as 'billicano' for billycan. The Italian version of bowls, bocce, has also become popular in recent years. *See also Blessing of the Fleet; Bocce; Customs; Easter; Festivals; Tooth Fairy, The; Village Saints' Processions*

J

JACK-IN-THE-GREEN

Male figure appearing in some forms of English traditional drama, usually said to date from the medieval period. The 'Jack' was enclosed in a light wooden frame around and through which was wound greenery and ribbons. This figure led a procession through villages, usually collecting money or soliciting drinks. Jack-in-the-Green also appeared in the occupational traditions of British chimney sweeps, whose May Day processions were similar in some aspects to much traditional drama, or 'mumming'. As revealed in K. Leech's *Jack-in-the-Green in Tasmania 1844–1873* (1989), Australian sweeps in Tasmania and New South Wales were still keeping up this tradition until well into the nineteenth century. Similar customs are known throughout Western and Eastern Europe and Russia, including the Slavic figure of 'Green George'. *See also Customs, May Day, Work Lore*

JACKS

Jacks or 'knucklebones' is a children's game traditionally played with boiled-down sheep's knuckles, but often played today with commercially produced plastic knuckles or other tokens. The basic movement involves holding five knuckles in one hand, tossing them in the air, and trying to catch as many as possible on the back of the same hand. The player then generally tries to pick up the fallen jacks while tossing others in the air, in a sequence which increases in complexity, and sometimes involves extra jacks and specific extra movements while the jacks are aloft. Lindsay and Palmer identified more than twenty different games played in Brisbane (Qld) in the 1970s. These included Scatters, Cut the Cabbage, Thread the Needle, Jingles, Jumps, Eggs in the Basket and Horse in the Stable. Many of these games are still played today. Like many other examples of children's lore, Jacks or Knucklebones were not exclusively played by children in older times, and are known to have been played by Roman soldiers in Britain in the first century AD. *See also Australian Children's Folklore Collection; Children's Folklore*

JACKY-JACKY

Hero of an unusual song in which Jacky-Jacky represents all Aboriginal people robbed of their traditions by European settlement. One verse goes:

> White fella come and take Jackie's country,
> Spread their fences across his land;
> Now poor Jacky has to pay his taxes
> And his hunting days are gone.

This song, well known in Aboriginal communities, ends:

> Now the country short of money,
> Jackie Jackie sits and laughs all day;
> White fella want to give it back to Jackie,
> No bloody fear, he won't have it that way.

See also Folk Humour, Folklore of Struggle, Indigenous Folklore

JANDAMURRA

Tribal name (variously spelt) of the Bunaba outlaw also known in Anglo-Australian tradition as 'Pigeon'. Jandamurra is a hero of the indigenous resistance to European incursion in north-west Australia, his activities spanning the period 1888–1890. Jandamurra is also representative of the international tradition of the outlaw hero, well represented in Australia through the folklore of bushranging. *See also Bushrangers; Folk Heroes; Folklore of Struggle; Indigenous Folklore*

JARRAH JERKER'S JOG

Run in November each year from the south-west Western Australian town of Nannup, this race is a marathon in which men and women carry railway sleepers made of Jarrah, an extremely dense and heavy West Australian hardwood. *See also Customs, Folk Sports, Work Lore*

JEWISH NEW YEAR *See Rosh Hashanah*

'JIM JONES'

Powerful convict ballad, thought to be from c. 1830s, though not collected until 1907, in which a defiant Jim Jones vows to escape from his chains and join Jack Donohoe and other bushrangers. He swears then to 'give the law a little shock', to 'kill the tyrants one and all' and 'shoot the floggers down'. Usually sung to the tune most commonly known as 'Irish Molly-O'. *See also Convict Lore; Transportation Ballads*

JIMMY SAGO

Fictional character in a song titled 'Jimmy Sago, Jackeroo' (c. 1880) in which Jimmy, a 'new chum', is given ironic and sarcastic advice about how to behave in Australia by a bushman. As a jackeroo, or trainee overseer, Jimmy Sago is seen as a member of the upper classes and so automatically on the side of the boss and unlikely to survive the rigours of bush life and labour. *See also Bush, The; Migration Lore; New Chum*

JIMMY WOODSER

A term for one who drinks alone, probably from the late nineteenth century. *See also Folk Speech; Grog; Pub, The*

JOHNNY CAKES

Small dampers, or unleavened bread, that appear in bush lore as basic survival food, or 'tucker'. Johnny cakes are the subject of at least one well-known ballad with the chorus:

> *With my four little johnny cakes all nicely cooked,*
> *A nice little codfish just off the hook;*
> *My little round flourbag sitting on a stump,*
> *And my little tea-and-sugar bag looking nice and plump.*

See also Damper, Folk Speech, Foodways

JOHNNY TROY

Known in Australia only through a song and a brief reference in Francis MacNamara's poem 'The Convict's Tour to Hell', Johnny Troy is especially interesting as an example of a folk hero who has a busy life in American tradition, while having apparently dropped from Australian folklore entirely. In his ballad, Troy is brave, defiant and altogether a fine specimen of the noble convict and outlaw hero. Troy is also mentioned in company with other convict and bushranger heroes in Francis (Frank the Poet) MacNamara's 'The Convict's Tour to Hell', composed 1839, and in the best-known of the ballads about convict bushranger Jack

Donohoe. *See also Convict Lore; Frank the Poet; Irish Influences on Australian Folklore; Transportation Ballads*

JOKES

'Banjo' Paterson's barber in his poem 'The Man from Ironbark' was a 'humorist of note', although his practical joke (pretending to cut the bushie's throat) was, alas, high on stupidity and low on real humour. Practical jokes are not a large part of Australian folk culture, except in certain limited contexts such as initiation rituals (see *Bastardisation*) and usually drunken events such as 'bucks' nights' for young men who are about to be married. In keeping with the important place which folk speech plays in Australian life and culture, most jokes in Australia are verbal, and most of the forms are international, although the content may be very local. Children begin telling jokes at a very young age, with riddles and 'knock-knocks' as some of the earliest favourites:

> *Why did the orange stop in the middle of the road?*
> *Because it ran out of juice.*

> *Knock knock.*
> *Who's there?*
> *Peter.*
> *Peter who?*
> *Pee tonight before you go to bed.*

These types of children's jokes are largely international, as also are highly topical jokes about disasters, such as the ones about the NASA space shuttle tragedy or the aeroplane crash which killed John F Kennedy Jnr:

> *Where do the Kennedys go for their vacation?*
> *All over Martha's Vineyard.*

Today, these jokes are circulated by email, but in pre-Internet times, they appeared seemingly with the speed of light even in distant countries. So what might constitute a specifically Australian joke? Some writers, such as Bill Wannan, Ron Edwards, Bill Scott and Graham Seal, have emphasised qualities such as irony, exaggeration and anti-authoritarianism, exemplified in the joke about the old swaggie who is offered a lift by the local squatter. The swaggie refuses, saying 'You can open your own bloody gates.' Phillip Adams and Patrice Newell, writing in *The Penguin Book of Australian Jokes* (1994, p. 26), state that most Australian jokes are 'the world's jokes, dressed up in Akubras and Drizabones', and note the difficulty in finding a 'differentiation of Australian humour'. Nevertheless they do include a version of one classic – 'politically incorrect and distinctly chauvinist' – which in its austerity, brevity and basic decency speaks of an ethos that links us to the time of Lawson. This goes roughly as follows:

> *A couple of farmers on neighbouring properties are working together to repair a broken-down fence. One says to the other: 'I reckon I might have a bit of a break now that the shearin's done. Head on down to the Big Smoke.'*

> *'Yeah? I hear Sydney's pretty good. What route will you take?'*

> *'Oh, I reckon I'll take the missus. After all, she stuck by me through the drought.'*

See also *Dingo Jokes; Folk Humour; Irish Jokes; Racist Folklore*

JOLLY SWAGMAN, THE
Legendary figure in the famous Australian song, 'Waltzing Matilda', the words of which were written by A. B. ('Banjo') Paterson in 1895. The song, in various versions, recounts how the jolly swagman (rural tramp) steals a sheep. Upon being caught by the squatter, or local landowner, and the mounted police, the swagman prefers to drown himself in the waterhole rather than be taken alive. 'Waltzing Matilda' has become the unofficial national anthem of Australia and the swagman represents the anti-authoritarian hero common to much Australian folklore. *See also National Icons, Paterson, A.B. (Banjo); Swagman, Waltzing Matilda*

JUDGE MACEVOY
A probably mythical figure who 'trembled and gave up his gold' when robbed by the Wild Colonial Boy in his ballad.

K

KANGAROO

This native marsupial appears in Aboriginal myth and European folklore in various roles. In many indigenous belief systems the kangaroo is the great spirit ancestor. In European lore the kangaroo appears as an outwitter of humans, as in the long-lived yarn and contemporary legend usually known as 'The Well-dressed Roo', where an animal thought to be dead ends up hopping into the bush supposedly wearing the jacket – and bearing the wallet – of a naïve and astounded tourist or city-slicker who has dressed it up for a photograph. The kangaroo is also admired for strength and toughness, as in phrases like 'tough as an old man kangaroo'. As well, the colloquial phrase 'to have kangaroos loose in the top paddock', indicates mental incompetence or instability.

The popular 1970s children's television series 'Skippy' featured a kangaroo, and the term 'Skippy, the bush kangaroo' is still often heard, as is the theme tune of the series. So widely watched was this series, in Australia and overseas, that among children 'a Skippy' or 'a Skip' has become a playground term for a native-born Anglo Celtic Australian. *See also Folk Speech; National Icons, Skippy, the Bush Kangaroo*

'KANGAROO VALLEY PANTHER, THE' *See Legendary Animals*

KARAGIOZIS

Comic hero of the Greek shadow puppet theatre, from whom it takes its name. Karagiozis, meaning 'black-eye', is a hunchback, bald and very ugly but with a sense of humour and trickster's cunning. He heads a cast of colourful characters drawn from legend and history and is continually getting himself into awkward situations in his attempts to feed himself, usually pretending to have skills which he does not possess, such as those of a doctor or dictator. He is assisted by his colleagues, who usually end up bearing the brunt of Karagiozis's antics. Typically the Karagiozis plays have a sharp element of social and political satire, with Karagiozis himself identified with the poor and oppressed.

Karagiozis, which has oriental origins, is documented in the Ottoman Empire during the seventeenth century and appears to have arrived in

Greece via Turkey in the early nineteenth century. Greatly popular in Greece, since the 1920s the hunchback hero, aided by his commercial appropriation into children's literature and later television, has been exported throughout the world in the wake of the Greek diaspora. Similarly, Karagiozis has a usually affectionate, though sometimes controversial, place in Greek communities in Australia. *See also Children's Folklore; Folk Humour; Greek Folklore in Australia; Punch and Judy*

KELLY

An axe, after a proprietary brand of the early twentieth century. *See also Folk Speech, Work Lore*

KELLY, DAN

Daniel Kelly (1861–1880), the younger brother of Ned, was a member of the Kelly gang of bushrangers. He is featured in a number of Kelly ballads and traditions, which include the belief that he was not killed at Glenrowan but secretly escaped to South Africa or the USA. *See also Bushrangers; Kelly, Ned*

KELLY, DAVIS AND FITZROY

Names of the three policemen said to have killed Jack Donohoe, the 'Wild Colonial Boy' in the ballad of the same name:

> *Three mounted troopers rode in sight, Kelly, Davis and Fitzroy*
> *And swore that they would capture him, the Wild Colonial Boy.*

KELLY, KATE

Ned Kelly's younger sister (Catherine Ada 1863–1898), who features in Kelly tradition as his helper – 'the girl who helped Ned Kelly'. According to folklore, she dressed as a man in order to fool the police into chasing her, thus allowing the bushranger and his accomplices to escape. She is also said to have brought food, clothes and ammunition to the outlaws' bush hideout. In fact, it was Ned Kelly's elder, married sister, Maggie Skillion, who carried out these acts. *See also Black Mary; Folk Heroes; Kelly, Ned*

KELLY, NED

Edward 'Ned' Kelly (1854/5–1880). Bushranger and folk hero who has become an Australian national icon, venerated by some, despised by others, taken for granted by most. Kelly's real and alleged activities between 1878 and 1880, when he and his accomplices Joe Byrne, Steve Hart and Ned's younger brother, Dan, defied the forces of law and authority in north-eastern Victoria, are the subject of a considerable body of folk song, verse, story and belief. After a long period of conflict with the authorities and some local landholders, Ned Kelly and his companions took to the bush in October 1878. They were pursued by four policemen, Sergeant Kennedy and Constables McIntyre, Scanlon and Lonigan. At Stringybark Creek the bushrangers ambushed the police. Ned Kelly shot three of them dead and MacIntyre escaped. Ned Kelly was outlawed and an extremely large reward was placed on his head. Over the following eighteen months the Kellys robbed banks and homesteads in north-eastern Victoria and across the border in New South Wales. In February 1879, after robbing a bank at Jerilderie, Ned Kelly wrote the lengthy and autobiographical 'Jerilderie Letter', as it came to be known, as a justification of his actions.

Despite massive efforts the police were unable to catch them, a situation exacerbated by the considerable sympathy and support the Kellys had aroused among small selectors and some sectors of the urban population. In late June 1880 the Kelly gang took over the inn at Glenrowan Railway Station, filled it with hostages and planned to derail a train carrying police sent to capture them. The plot was foiled by a local schoolteacher Kelly allowed to leave the inn, who warned the police. Wearing their famous armour, three of the bushrangers were killed by police gunfire, along with some of the hostages. Ned Kelly was badly wounded, captured, nursed back to health, tried, found guilty of murder and hanged in old Melbourne Gaol on 11 November 1880.

In common with certain other bushrangers who became folk heroes, Kelly lore paints the outlaw as a man wronged by the police and the government – 'Now the Governor of Victoria was an enemy of this man', claims the song 'Kelly Was Their Captain'. Kelly is also portrayed as brave, clever, an outstanding bushman who outsmarts the police at almost every turn, who offers no violence to the poor and weak and eventually 'dies game' at the end of a rope, traditionally (though almost certainly not) uttering the final resonant words 'Such is life' or, in some versions, 'Tell 'em I died game.' Ned Kelly is the Australian culmination of a long tradition of outlaw heroes reaching back to the mythical Robin Hood and embracing selected other celebrated criminals, such as the English Dick Turpin, the Irish William Brennan and the American Jesse James, among others. In many ways Kelly is the most perfect representative of this powerful tradition and is the only such figure to have moved beyond the realms of folk and media heroism to take his place as a national hero, if a controversial one. Ned Kelly's ambivalent status is reflected in Australian folk speech in phrases such as the complimentary 'Game as Ned Kelly', as against the complaint that someone may 'charge like Ned Kelly' (that is, overcharge). Ned Kelly has also become a folk hero to some Aboriginal groups, who see him as representing something of their own struggle against oppression. The origins and development of the Kelly legend have been traced in Graham Seal's *Ned Kelly in Popular Tradition* (1980), published in an updated edition as *Tell 'em I Died Game: The Legend of Ned Kelly* (2002). *See also Bushrangers; Folklore of Struggle; Kelly, Kate; National Icons; Sherritt, Aaron*

KENNA, CORNELIUS

Legendary acid-tongued wit of Victoria's western district, who always has a ready retort in the numerous yarns about him. In one of these, 'Corny', as he is generally called, is served an under-measure whisky. As he looks disapprovingly at the glass, the barmaid indignantly points out that the whisky is thirty years old. Kenna replies that the whisky is very small for its age. *See also Folk Heroes; Folk Humour, Yarns*

KENNEDY, SERGEANT

Policeman murdered by Ned Kelly at Stringybark Creek on 26 October 1878. Continues to be a hero to the Victoria Police while featuring in Kelly folklore as a villain. *See also Folk Heroes; Kelly, Ned; Work Lore*

KERNEWEK LOWENDER

A biennial festive custom held in South Australia in mid-May. Over the Adelaide Cup long weekend, in the strongly Cornish-influenced towns of Kadina, Moonta and Wallaroo, the *Kernewek Lowender* is held on odd-numbered years only. This 'Cornish Festival' involves all things Cornish, including food, music and games, as well as some recent additions such as fireworks and a display of vintage cars. The British tradition of maypole dancing is continued, as is the 'Furry Dance', or flower dance, a traditional Cornish custom still extant in Britain, where it is performed in the village of Helston on each 8 May (The Feast of the Apparition of St Michael) or the nearest Saturday to that date. Although the South Australian *Kernewek Lowender* was initiated only in 1973, the original Furry Dance is thought to be of considerable antiquity, being well established by the sixteenth century. *See also Cousin Jacks; Cousin Jennies; Curling; Customs*

KIRUP SYRUP

Legendary, and allegedly deadly, homemade wine from the West Australian town of Kirup. *See also Grog; Foodways; Pub, The*

KITCHEN TEA *See Shower Tea*

KNITTING

Knitting is among the most folkloric of handcrafts as it is almost always learned, initially at least, in a face-to-face situation within the family (or by direct transmission, as folklorists would say). This writer remembers her grandmother painstakingly teaching her the basic techniques with a patter of instructions which included 'put the collar on the dog' (loop the wool around the knitting needle). Knitting is usually done by women, but sometimes by men in isolated situations, such as at sea. The knitted object may be extremely simple, such as a long scarf in a favoured football team's colours, usually involving a plain stitch; or extremely complex, such as a cable knit or Aran sweater, which may involve special needles such as a circular steel loop.

Hand-knitting is often done as a gesture of affection: knitting a jumper for a boyfriend (for example) may cost more in buying the wool than a ready-made jumper from a store. Folk culture and commerce have a close relationship in relation to knitting, as wool, knitting needles and patterns are produced by commercial firms such as Paton's. It is sometimes said that knitting did not become a common pastime until World War I, when women were encouraged to knit socks and other items for the troops. *See also Crafts; Making Do; Women's Folklore*

KNOCKING

The practice of disparaging the ideas, suggestions, actions and achievements of others. Related to the widely lamented but persistent

Australian custom of 'cutting down tall poppies'. *See also Customs;
Cutting Down Tall Poppies; Folk Speech; National Icons*

KREVATTI *See Shower Tea*

KRISHNA JANMASHTAMI
An Indian Hindu celebration of the birthday of the Lord Krishna, falling
on the eighth day of the Hindu month of *Shravan* (August/September).
Janmashtami involves fairs, arts and crafts, processions, some fasting and
much feasting. *See also Customs; Religious Lore*

KULIN BUSH RACES, THE *See Picnic Races*

KYNETON CAT, THE *See Legendary Animals*

L

LABOR LORE

The folklore of the Australian Labor movement – the Australian Labor Party and the trade unions – is rich, extensive and usually passionately held, as suggested by the folk phrase 'true believers' to denote those who believe fervently in the aims and objectives of these organisations. Labor lore includes the large body of occupational folklore as well as the mythology and iconography of Labor and the trade unions, complete with its pantheon of heroic figures such as Prime Ministers Curtin and Chifley, and villains such as William 'Billy' Hughes. The traditions are usually held to begin at the Eureka Stockade of 1854, though in recent years they have been extended to the convict era with the celebration of the Vinegar Hill uprising of 1804. The Southern Cross constellation of stars used on the flag of the rebellious diggers at Eureka is a powerful symbol of the union left, and replicas of the Eureka flag are still flown on large building sites across the country. Labor tradition also includes the events in the life of Ned Kelly; the 1890s maritime strikes and shearers' strikes, especially the incidents among shearers at Barcaldine (Qld); and the political, industrial and social events of 'the Great Depression' of the 1930s. There is also a vast body of lore – legends, verse and song – associated with individual strikes, lockouts, sit-ins and other confrontations between Labor and capital and between Labor and the state. These actions and events are often celebrated in visual form in the trade union banners displayed proudly at public rallies and parades, an extensive and persistent tradition manifested especially on significant dates such as May Day. The phrase 'maintain the rage', referring to the dismissal by the Governor-General of the Whitlam Labor Government in 1975 has passed into Australian folk speech, and is used in many different contexts. *See also Folklore of Struggle; Irish Influences on Australian Folklore; May Day; Political Lore; Tree of Knowledge; The; Work Lore*

LACE-MAKING

Lace-making in Australia is often associated with immigrant women from countries such as Malta and Italy, but it has been practised in

Australia by women of many ethnic origins for many years. The Moe lace-makers in Victoria's La Trobe Valley represent a multicultural interest in the handcraft which was documented in 1994–6 by Gwenda Davey during the Moe Folklife Project. *See also Craft; Migration Lore*

'LACHLAN TIGERS, THE'

Title of a shearing song with a rousing chorus beginning 'A lot of Lachlan Tigers, it's plain to see we are...' Like most shearing songs, this one celebrates the shearers' lifestyle and work ethic. The 'Lachlan Tigers' are a contract shearing gang proud of their ability at their demanding occupation. *See also Folk Songs; Pastoral Industry Folklore; Shearers; Work Lore*

LAGERPHONE

As the name implies, this musical or percussion instrument is made of beer bottle tops loosely nailed along a piece of wood like a broomstick which is stomped and rattled to produce a considerable sound, and sometimes played with a stick like a bow. Although it is usually found in a 'bush band', the lagerphone, like the 'bush bass' (tea chest) does not appear to have been a widespread traditional Australian bush instrument, but was adopted during the folk revival of the 1950s and 1960s, possibly under the influence of the British skiffle bands popular at the time. More common bush instruments played in colonial times would have been the fiddle and concertina – and often the piano, even in remote locations. According to Peter Ellis, writing in the *Oxford Companion to Australian Folklore* (1993), the lagerphone may have derived from the 'Jingling Johnny', a stick covered with bells or shells and used by shepherds in Napoleonic times. Such devices were also used in European military bands from the seventeenth century. *See also Bush Band; Bush Music; Folk Revival; Musical Instruments*

LAMINGTON DRIVE

A traditional fundraising method in Australia. Made from sponge cakes cut into squares or oblongs and dipped in chocolate icing and then shredded coconut, lamingtons are said to have been named after Baron Lamington, Governor of Queensland 1895–1901, and have been associated closely with Australian cuisine since at least 1910. Their sale – often now commercialised – was and is a favourite method of raising money for community groups, schools and charities. *See also Chook Raffle; Customs; Foodways*

LAMMAS DAY

Celebrated on 1 August. A festival marking the start of the harvest season in the early English church, but suppressed during the Reformation. It was revived in 1843, from which time it has been moved to later in the season and now marks the end of the harvest rather than its beginning. This time is also an important evening on the occult calendar, especially for followers of Wicca, or witchcraft, for whom it is a time for the celebration of male–female union, usually involving a ritual marriage and magic for the health of the coven and a good harvest. This observance harks back to the earlier Celtic feast of Lughnasa(d). *See also Folk Belief; Religious Lore*

LARRIKIN

The term 'larrikin' was not used to describe a member of a gang of hooligans until the 1860s, though the gambling, swearing, womanising, drinking and petty crime undertaken by the bearers of the name had been a problem in the colony of New South Wales from at least the early 19th century. Larrikins so-named, however, appear only in late nineteenth-century folk expressions such as the poems 'The Woolloomooloo Lair' ('My Name it is McCarty') and 'The Bastard from the Bush'. Larrikinism has contributed a great deal to general Australian folk speech (including terms such as 'stoush', 'blue' and 'bludge'), and the much-romanticised and exaggerated qualities of the larrikin are much vaunted in notions of national identity, mainly due to the literary efforts of late nineteenth-century and early twentieth-century writers such as Henry Lawson, Will Dyson and, especially, C.J. Dennis. For such an influential social phenomenon, it is surprising that there has been only one substantial study, James Murray's *Larrikins: 19th century Outrage* (1973). *See also Bloke, Folk Speech; National Icons*

LASSETER'S REEF

Legendary 'lost' reef of gold allegedly discovered by Lewis Harold Bell Lasseter somewhere in the Peterman Ranges (SA) in 1897. The fabulous richness of the lode and the many unsuccessful attempts to find it – one of which resulted in Lasseter's death in 1931 – have made the term a by-word for hopeless causes. The considerable legendry of Lasseter and his claimed find resonates strongly with other Australian lost treasure traditions, as well as with others around the world. *See also Folk Heroes; Lost Treasures; National Icons*

LAWSON, HENRY

Henry Archibald Lawson (1867–1922) was a writer whose verse often derived from traditional materials, and which verse in turn also passed into folk tradition. His short stories were conscious literary craftings of the oral yarn genre and sometimes used traditional plots and themes, as in 'The Loaded Dog'. *See also 'Bastard from the Bush, The'; Bush Ballad; Folklore of Struggle; 'Freedom on the Wallaby'; Labor Lore; 'Loaded Dog, The'*

LAZY HARRY

Proprietor of the shanty, or shack, named after him and celebrated in the song 'On the Road to Gundagai' (not to be confused with the song in which 'the dog sat on the tucker-box nine miles from Gundagai'). Shanties, combination public houses (often illegal), brothels and hostelries were notorious among itinerant bush workers as places where one could be 'lambed down', or seduced into drinking away, losing, spending, gambling or otherwise being parted from all one's hard-earned pay. This theme appears in a number of bush folk songs, including 'Across the Western Plains' ('The Jolly Grog and Tobacco') and some versions of 'The Wild Rover'. *See also Bush, The; Pastoral Industry Folklore*

LEATHER PLAITING

A well-documented handcraft, usually undertaken by men, but also by some country women. The Australian folklorist Ron Edwards, a practitioner of this craft, has produced a number of booklets on leather-craft and a major book, *Bush Leatherwork* (1984). The titles of Edwards' booklets indicate the range of uses of leather plaiting: *Bridles Plaited and Plain, Braided Belts, Whipmaking and Stockmen's Plaited Belts*, and all are illustrated with Edwards' fine and detailed drawings. *See also Crafts*

LEAVERS

West Australian end of secondary school custom. A rite of passage in which students travel to various holiday locations, such as Rottnest Island and elsewhere, for some days of celebration and excess to mark their release from secondary education. School leavers are known as 'schoolies' in New South Wales and Queensland. *See also Customs, Schoolies' Week*

LEGENDARY ANIMALS

Cryptozoology is the study and pursuit of mythical animals, including yaramas, yowies and bunyips. Australian folklore is rich in such creatures, and especially in 'Alien Big Cats' (or 'ABCs'). There are many traditions about these elusive beasts, usually said to have escaped from a circus or travelling show of some kind and to live in the bush, appearing occasionally to kill off local livestock. Another popular explanation is that they are the escaped mascots (e.g. cougars) of American forces stationed in Australia during World War II. Australia's legendary animals include 'The Charters Tower Cougar' (Qld), 'The Dromana Mountain Lion' (Vic.), 'The Emmaville Panther' (NSW), 'The Kangaroo Valley Panther' (NSW), 'The Kyneton Cat' (Vic.), 'The Marulan Tiger' (NSW), 'The Mount Spec Cougar' (Qld), 'The Nannup Tiger' (WA), 'The Tantanoola Tiger' (SA), 'The Townsville Cougar' (Qld) and 'The Waterford Panther' (Qld). There are also both real and imaginary insects (legendary usually for their size), including flies and mosquitoes. The imported species, cane toads, also have an extensive folklore of their own. A useful and balanced overview is provided by Malcolm Smith in *Bunyips and Bigfoots* (1996), and Bill Scott includes much of his fieldwork and research in this area in *The Long and the Short and the Tall* (1985) and *Pelicans and Chihuahuas and Other Urban Legends* (1996). *See also Ants; Bunyip; Drop Bears; Folk Tales; Hexham Greys; The; Hoop Snakes; Tasmanian Tiger; Yarama; Yowie*

LENT

Lent is an occasion in the Christian calendar which, like Christmas and Easter, is observed to some degree by Australians who are not churchgoers or otherwise religious. A period of fasting and penitence in preparation for Easter, it begins on Ash Wednesday, the fortieth weekday before Easter, and ends on Easter Saturday. It is common in a workplace for a person, usually a woman, to announce that he or she is 'giving up chocolate for Lent'. These seemingly trivial observances appear to acknowledge, as in many religions, the virtue of self-restraint or sacrifice. These virtues are also acknowledged in events such as the sponsored 'forty-hour fasts' undertaken by some community organisations, including schools, to raise compassion and money for aid organisations or groups such as refugees. *See also Customs, Easter, Religious Lore*

'LIMEJUICE TUB, THE'

A nineteenth-century shearers' and swagman's song bemoaning the rigours of shearing: 'shearing's hell in New South Wales'. Popular due to its fine tune and rousing chorus:

> *Here we are in New South Wales,*
> *Shearing sheep as big as whales*
> *With leather necks and daggy tails*
> *And hides as tough as rusty nails.*

and ending with the lines:

> *At home, at home I'd rather be,*
> *Not humping my drum [carrying a*
> *swag] in the back countree.*

See also Folk Songs, Pastoral Industry Folklore, Shearers, Work Lore

LITTLE DIGGER, THE

Folk name for World War I Prime Minister William 'Billy' Hughes, who also appears in a number of anti-conscription ditties of the era, notably a parody of the popular song 'Mr Booze' ('Mr Hughes, Mr Hughes, you're a mischief-maker, Billy Hughes...') and 'Billy Hughes' Army':

> *Why don't you join, why don't you join,*
> *Why don't you join Billy Hughes' army?*
> *Six bob [shillings] a week and nothing to eat*
> *Great big boots and blisters on your feet*
> *Why don't you join?, etc.*

See also Folk Speech; Labor Lore; Political Lore; War Lore

'LOADED DOG, THE'

Title of a famous short story by Henry Lawson (also treated by Jack London), based on an internationally distributed folk tale about hunters who tie a lighted stick of gelignite or other explosive to a dog's tail, hoping to blow up their prey. But instead of disappearing into the prey's burrow or lair, the animal lopes faithfully back to the hunters, usually blowing up their means of transport, belongings and sometimes themselves. (The dog in Lawson's story retrieves the explosive, rather than having it cruelly tied to its tail). Versions of this old story are still told as contemporary or urban legends throughout Australia, and elsewhere. *See also Dogs; Folk Tales; Lawson, Henry; Urban Legends*

LOCAL LORE

The folklore peculiar to a locality or region or known, to a greater or lesser degree, by most inhabitants of reasonably lengthy standing. Local lore is synonymous with a sense of place, of belonging and of local community identity, and reflects the structures of meaning that have developed over time. Its most typical forms are local legends, songs and poems about people, events and places; stories about placenames and local natural features; and beliefs – usually inaccurate and prejudiced – about places and people that are not local. If the locality is rural or semi-rural, it may also include vast repositories of knowledge and belief about local flora and fauna. In these areas, local traditions may be amalgams of settler and indigenous lore. Noris Ioannou's *Barossa Journeys: Into a Valley of Tradition* (1997) is one of the few published Australian studies of local lore. *See also Doyle, Tom; Eco-Lore, Flowers, Folk Medicine, Indigenous Folklore; Palmerston, Christy; Place Names*

LOGAN, CAPTAIN PATRICK

Captain Patrick Logan, Commandant of Moreton Bay (Qld) penal station from its establishment in 1826. Noted as a strict disciplinarian, his death at the hands of Aborigines in the Mt Irwin (now Mt Beppo) area in October 1830 was the cause of considerable celebration among the convicts at Moreton Bay. Logan features in the song known as 'Moreton Bay' which records the harshness of the penal station and the convicts' joy at the news of Logan's death. Also titled 'The Convict's Lament' and 'The Convict's Arrival', the lyrics of 'Moreton Bay' may have been the work of Francis MacNamara, 'Frank the Poet'. *See also Convict Lore; Frank the Poet; Irish Influences on Australian Folklore; 'Moreton Bay'; Transportation Ballads*

LOLLYBAGGING

Reported as a Christmas custom in the strongly British area of Kwinana-Rockingham (WA), and similar to the Halloween 'Trick or Treat'. *See also Children's Folklore; Customs*

LONE PINE SEEDLINGS, THE

Seedlings allegedly gathered from the remaining pine tree at Lone Pine on the Gallipoli peninsula. There are numerous such seedlings held by individuals, families and organisations throughout Australia and New Zealand, where they are the object of considerable veneration, especially by those with military backgrounds and/or connections. *See also ANZAC, Digger; Folk Belief; Gallipoli*

LONIGAN, CONSTABLE *See Kelly, Ned*

LOST TREASURES

What may seem to be uniquely Australian legends of lost treasures, such as Lasseter's Reef and the Silver Reef, display many of the traditional elements of 'lost treasure' folklore from around the world. Firstly, there is a fabulously rich treasure of some kind. It is lost and in a remote and/or mysterious location. It is often guarded by fierce native peoples, who sometimes put a curse on the treasure and/or those who search for it. If there is no curse, then some form of ill-luck will attend the discoverer(s) of and/or searchers for the trove. An intrepid male explorer stumbles on the trove but, barely surviving, loses the location in the course of struggling back to civilisation with a sample of the find. But there is a map. If there isn't a map, there will be a diary, journal or other document which is either too cryptic to be useful or has conveniently and usually mysteriously also disappeared. The map/document and tales and legends of the trove entice future hopefuls to search in vain, and often terminally, for the wealth. The treasure remains 'lost'.

There are 'lost reef' and related traditions in the Monaro district ('Lindo's Reef') in New South Wales; and on the Cape York Peninsula ('Dead Man's Secret') in north-west Queensland between Cloncurry and Georgetown; and there is the cache of sovereigns supposedly hidden on Lord Howe Island when a whaling brig, *George*, was wrecked there in 1830. Other 'lost treasures' in Australian folklore include the plunder of bushrangers: Frank Gardiner's alleged stash of gold is still missing, and Ben Hall and 'Thunderbolt' also have well-developed hidden/lost treasure tales attached to them. In addition, there is said to be an idol or god in the form of a giant dog made of tortoiseshell on Moa Island in the Torres Strait, and there are legends of buried or sunken treasure troves throughout the country and around the coastline. Some, though by no means all, of these are documented in Kenneth Byron's *Lost Treasures in Australia and New Zealand* (1964). *See also Dead Horse Treasure, The; Folk Tales; Gardiner's Gold; Lasseter's Reef; Silver Reef, The*

LOWRY, FRED

Fred Lowry (1836–1863), a bushranger of the Bathurst (NSW) region, is the subject of numerous extant local traditions and at least one ballad, a version of which was collected by John Meredith and Chris Sullivan in 1983. In common with most bushranger lore, Lowry is presented as a brave, defiant hero who goes down gamely in a shoot-out with the cowardly police. He also seems to have had a reputation as a smart dresser and ladies' man. Legend has it that Lowry was the bushranger whose last words were 'Tell 'em I died game'. The 'last words' of folk heroes are a small but significant aspect of folklore. *See also Bush Ballad; Bushrangers; Folk Heroes; 'Such is Life'*

M

MACLEAN HIGHLAND GATHERING
Held on Good Friday and Easter Saturday since 1893, this is a celebration of Scots traditions – sports, competitions, song, music, dance, food, Scotch whisky – in and around the town of Maclean (NSW). *See also Customs, Folk Sports, Highland Games*

MACNAMARA, FRANCIS *See Frank the Poet*

MCLAREN VALE WINE BUSHING FESTIVAL
Held in the McLaren Vale area of South Australia over Friday, Saturday and Sunday of the last weekend in October, this is said to be an adaptation of the supposedly centuries-old British tradition of 'bushing', which involves the hanging of ivy bushes on tavern doors to announce the arrival of the latest European vintages. This event, established in 1973, involves wine tasting, eating, dancing, processions and exhibitions of arts and crafts, and may even telescope into the following month, incorporating Melbourne Cup Luncheons. The event also spans Halloween and includes a formal 'Halloween Ball'. *See also Customs, Folklorism*

'MAGGIE MAY'
A song about a Liverpool prostitute named Maggie May who is transported to Van Diemen's Land for robbing her clients. Probably of early music hall origins and widely sung by sailors. *See also Convict Lore; Maritime Lore; Transportation Ballads*

MAHOGANY SHIP, THE
Legendary wreckage of what is usually said to have been a Portuguese sailing ship buried under the sands of Warrnambool (Vic.). *See also Folk Belief; Folk Tales; Lost Treasures*

MAKING DO
The phrase 'making do' refers to the resourcefulness and improvisation skills of Australians in the two centuries since 1788, particularly among

people living in poverty or hardship in both city and bush, or in isolated areas where distance made it difficult and expensive to obtain both basic necessities and luxuries. The Wagga Rug, made from leftover clothing and fabric scraps sewn onto chaff bags, is a representation of the art of 'making do'; as was the traditional bush ability to replace a fan belt or repair a motor part with almost any material that came to hand. The tradition of 'having a go' still exists in the DIY (Do It Yourself) practices of Australian families. Unlike in some other countries, many Australian householders will still paint their own houses, repair their own fences, and sometimes (unfortunately, and illegally) attend to their own electrical wiring. Commerce readily supports the DIY tradition in Australia, and suburban and country hardware stores are available to supply the necessary materials. This may be thought to suggest that commerce is taking over the folk traditions of 'making do', but DIY is far from dead. A female acquaintance of this writer recently tired of waiting for her husband to build an extension to the house, and took to the offending wall with a chain saw. Initiative lives. *See also Backyard, Crafts; Customs*

PADDY MALONE

An Irish emigrant who appears as the stereotypical new chum in a number of folk songs, including 'Paddy Malone in Australia' and 'Paddy's Letter'. *See also Irish Influences on Australian Folklore; Migration Lore; New Chum*

MALTESE FOLKLORE IN AUSTRALIA

Much Maltese folklore is based on religious observances. The popular festivals are usually celebrations of saints' days such as Our Lady of Victories (*il Vitorja*) and other saints important to the Maltese village of origin. Processions at festas will often be led by a parish band, and folk dancing groups are a prominent part of the festivities. The most significant Maltese custom is the Feast of our Lady, on 8 September, commemorating the repelling of Turkish invaders of the island in 1565. Other days of significance include 21 September, the National Day, commemorating independence from Britain, Republic Day, on 13 December, and Freedom Day, commemorating the day on which the last British soldier left the island, on 31 March 1979. In recent years 7 June, or *Sette Guigno*, has been observed in remembrance of a workers' uprising in 1919. The Maltese harvest festival custom *Mnarja*, takes place in June.

One interesting aspect of Maltese folk culture in Australia concerns the *ghanejja*, in which singers and guitar players perform partly fixed and partly improvised songs (*ghana*) that may include satirical comment on community identities and their activities. In the last few years, the National Library of Australia has been recording these musicians as part of its Oral History and Folklore program. After some years of neglect, *ghana* music is receiving increasing attention both in Australia and in Malta, and from musicologists internationally. Like Greek *rebetika* music, *ghana* music, formerly rejected as 'lower class', is undergoing a revival.

Despite Maltese communities' rich community and folk life, expressed through religion, family gatherings, clubs, picnics and sport such as football and *bocce*, the Maltese language has not been maintained in Australia in second and third generations to the same extent as languages in some other immigrant groups, such as the larger Greek communities. The reasons for this are speculative, but are likely to include the widespread use of English in Malta itself, and its history, before independence, as a British possession. There is also a high degree of marriage outside the Maltese community in Australia.

As with all immigrant communities in Australia, the Maltese have been affected by the Australian experience, much of which persists in folk memory. Present-day Maltese still talk about 'the children of Billy Hughes', the 214 Maltese men who travelled to Australia in 1916 on the ship *Gange*, and who were initially refused entry on racist grounds, being instead rerouted to New Caledonia. There are at least two folk songs about this sorry episode still sung in Australia.

Other Australians are becoming increasingly familiar with a traditional Maltese culinary treat, the little *pastizzi* (cheese pastries) now readily available frozen in supermarkets. Maltese foodways are just one example of the rich folk traditions of Malta maintained in Australia by the large Maltese communities in Melbourne and Sydney, and smaller communities in Adelaide, Perth, Wollongong (NSW) and Mackay (Qld). *See also Customs; Folklore of Struggle; Migration Lore*

'MAN FROM SNOWY RIVER, THE'
Poem composed by A. B. ('Banjo') Paterson and published in 1890. The rhythm of the verse, together with its heroic bush theme has made the poem part of Australian tradition. It is not only recited widely but has also generated many parodies, such as 'The Man from Kao-Magma', Kao-

Magma being a once well-known proprietary brand of antacid liquid. *See also Bush Ballad; Horses; Paterson, A.B. ('Banjo')*

'MARANOA DROVERS, THE'
Bush ballad, also known as 'The Sandy Maranoa' and usually sung to 'Little Old Log Cabin in the Lane'. 'The Maranoa Drovers' is a spirited, if romantic, evocation of the rough and tumble life of the drover in Queensland and New South Wales during the late nineteenth century. Attributed to a Queensland drover named A.W. Davis. *See also Bush Ballads; Pastoral Industry Folklore, Work Lore*

MARBLES
This popular children's game is played by both girls and boys, usually in the school playground, provided it has not been banned in case it causes fights. There are many different games and many different types of marbles, each with their own distinctive name, such as a glassie, cat's eye, steely, bird cage and Tom Bowler. Some games mentioned by Lindsay and Palmer (1981) are 'Holesies', 'Poison', 'Rings', 'Cat and Mouse' and 'Five Times Keepers'. As in many children's games, a great deal of skill is required, both in the physical movements and in negotiating the process of the game. In some Australian schools children have adopted the 'Chinese flick', a highly effective two-handed flick introduced by Chinese and Vietnamese children, and first documented by Heather Russell (1986). Marbles has an ancient history, and children can be seen playing marbles in Flemish artist Pieter Brueghel's famous painting 'Children's Games' (1560). *See also Australian Children's Folklore Collection; Children's Folklore; INTRODUCTION*

MARITIME LORE
There are considerable bodies of such tradition associated with the pearling industries of Broome (WA) and the Torres Strait, involving Indigenous Australian elements combined with Malay, Filipino, Japanese, Chinese, 'Kanaka' and Anglo-Celtic influences. Various sectors of the fishing industry – coastal, deep sea and inland – are known to have rich repertoires of song, story, custom, belief and material culture, as with the traditions of cray-pot making in Fremantle (Portuguese, Italian, Anglo-Celtic) and elsewhere in Western Australia. Traditions of deep-water mariners, including whalers, tend to be international rather than specific to Australia, as in the case of

worksongs (shanties) and other sailor lore, including arts and crafts (such as scrimshaw, ropework, ships and other objects in bottles), folk beliefs and occupational customs such as the Dead Horse Shanty (a folk play and accompanying song) and Crossing the Line. 'Bound for South Australia' and a variant known as 'The Codfish Shanty' are among the few sea-songs with specifically Australian references.

Like many aspects of Australian folk tradition, the lore of the maritime industries and activities remains largely undocumented; these observations are liable to perhaps considerable future amendment. In recent years some institutions, including the National Maritime Museum in Sydney, have begun to use oral history interviews to enhance their material collections. *See also Crossing the Line; Indigenous Folklore; Pearler's Light, The; Pearler's Ghost, The; Work Lore*

MARKETS

An ancient tradition of buying and selling which is still hugely popular in Australia. Markets are traditionally held outdoors, perhaps sheltered by awnings, and are temporary establishments which at the end of market day will be dismantled until the next week, or month. There are exceptions to this in the big city markets, such as Melbourne's much-loved Queen Victoria Market, which has permanent buildings, although most of the stalls for food, clothing and household wares are temporary. All manner of goods are sold at markets, and smaller community markets usually feature crafts made by local residents. Some of markets' ancient customs survive, such as the cries of butchers at Melbourne's 'Vicky Market'. This writer has heard one butcher there peddling his 'laaaaamb chops', in the best tradition of mediaeval street cries. Recent years have seen a revival of 'farmers' markets', where farmers bring fresh produce into the suburbs to sell directly to householders. *See also Bazaars, Community Fairs; Garage Sales*

'MARULAN TIGER', THE' *See Animals, Legendary*

'MARYBOROUGH MINER, THE'

Song about the travels, trials and crimes of a gold digger whose career seems to span an amazingly long period, from the convict era until the 1890s, at which time he claims to have 'chanced my arm at Cue' (WA). Adapted c. 1960s by English folklorist A.L. Lloyd (1908–1982) from an earlier song, 'The Murrumbidgee Shearer' and widely, if controversially, sung during the Australian and British folk revivals. *See also Folk Festivals, Folk Revival, Goldrush Lore*

MATE

Widespread form of male address characteristically, though not uniquely, Australian. Derived from British usage and probably in use from the earliest years of settlement, the term has in recent years been extended to females. Like the term 'bastard', able to convey a multitude of meanings, from the affectionate to the aggressive. *See also Bush, The; Folk Speech; Mateship*

MATESHIP

The code of male bonding and camaraderie often said to lie at the core of Australian national identity. Endemic in the folklore of the strongly male-oriented bush tradition and also implicit in the traditions of the digger, though rarely explicit in the folk expressions of that group. *See also Bush, The; Digger; Lawson, Henry; Mate*

MATILDA

Another name for a swag, possibly derived from German usage for a camp follower, and the basis of A.B. ('Banjo') Paterson's poem 'Waltzing Matilda'. *See also German Influences on Australian Folklore; Swag, Waltzing Matilda*

MAY DAY

The first day of May traditionally marks the start of summer in the northern hemisphere; it has been, and still is, the time for much customary activity, including the crowning of May Queens, dancing around the maypole and related practices. Maypole dancing has often been carried out, especially by schoolchildren, in Australia, notably on the Moonta Peninsula of South Australia, where there has been a strong Cornish presence since the nineteenth century (*see Kernewek Lowender*). Maypole dancing in Australia, however, is often more an institutionalised exhibition than a folk custom. Another nineteenth century British custom to persist for some time in Australia was 'Jack-in-the-Green'.

May day and the month of May in general have extensive folk belief associations. These include the ancient (Roman) belief that it is unlucky to marry in May; that it is a month dangerous because of the prevalence of fairies and other occult visitants; that May flowers are unlucky; and that May dew and rain is good for one's complexion, for medical cures and for divining the identity of a future husband. The evening of 30 April, or 'May Eve', is an important time in the witchcraft (Wicca) calendar, marking the beginning of the northern hemisphere Summer.

May 1, or May Day, is also important in the calendar of the international socialist and labour movements, having been established as a day of significance through the struggle for an eight-hour working day, especially in the United States during the 1880s. Since 1890, internationally, it has been a day for parading the red flag and for picnics. In the Australian states, May Day is usually marked by a parade and various festive activities on the Sunday nearest to 1 May, except for the Northern Territory, where it is celebrated on 6 May; and in Queensland. Labour Day in Queensland (1 May) marks the gaining of the eight-hour working day by stonemasons in 1858. Originally known as 'Eight Hours Celebration Day', the event was celebrated first on 1 March 1865. In 1893 the day was moved to coincide with May Day. Today, the actual celebrations of May Day in Queensland may be on varying dates. *See also Customs; Folk Belief; Jack-in-the-Green; Labor Lore*

MEAT PIES

An Australian icon, the meat pie is sometimes nominated as Australia's 'national food'. Usually eaten with tomato sauce (or 'dead horse', in rhyming slang). Interestingly, a major brand of Aussie meat pie has a folkloric name: 'Four'N Twenty' pies are named from the ancient nursery rhyme:

> *Sing a song of sixpence,*
> *A pocket full of rye;*
> *Four and twenty blackbirds*
> *Baked in a pie.*
> *When the pie was opened*
> *The birds began to sing;*
> *Wasn't that a dainty dish*
> *To set before the King?*

For many years 'Four N'Twenty's' advertising included pictures of the 'four and twenty blackbirds'. In recent years the blackbirds have, sadly, been dropped from the ads. A variation on the plain meat pie is the 'floater', a pie served with mashed peas. This is a very British dish, as is the meat pie itself. Gourmet pies include the British pork pie and other more exotic variations on the basic product such as curry or chilli pie. *See also Foodways; National Icons*

MELBOURNE CUP, THE

Since 1861 the Melbourne Cup, a handicap horse race, has been run over two miles (now 3200 metres) at Melbourne's Flemington racecourse on the first Tuesday in November. Since that date, 'The Cup' has become one of the few folk customs observed nationally. In workplaces across the country the tradition is to 'down tools' while the race is being run in order to see who will win the 'sweep' (in which horses are assigned by lottery, with the owners of the placegetters' tickets taking the pot) customarily organised on the day of the event. The custom of getting dressed up to attend the Cup has developed into one of its most spectacular and extravagant features. Women may attend the Cup in large, and often bizarre, hats, which range from the expensive to the home trimmed; while male attire varies from morning suits to fancy costume. This good-humoured ostentation has inspired a characteristically parodic folk reaction: in pubs and restaurants across the country on Cup Day the bemused visitor will see groups of women lunching in outlandish hats. In the hamlet of Kulin, far south of Perth, the Kulin Bobtail Cup is held on the same day, but the contestants are lizards. In Victoria this day is a public holiday. *See also Customs; Folk Sports; Horses; National Icons; Phar Lap; Sports Lore; Sweeps; Turf Lore*

MID-AUTUMN MOON FESTIVAL

Held on the day of the full moon in the eighth month of the Chinese calendar (late September–early October), this festival is celebrated by peoples of Chinese derivation throughout the world. Essentially an autumn harvest thanksgiving festival, in parts of Vietnam it is known as the children's *Tet* or New Year. 'Mooncakes' made with sweets and nuts are prepared in the family home, and gifts are exchanged, usually foodstuffs and usually tagged with red to indicate luck and prosperity.

As the traditional date for this festival occurs in the Australian spring, it is sometimes celebrated at this time in defiance of the seasons, and sometimes in the Australian autumn. For instance, since 1984 the Autumn Moon Lantern Festival has been held for one day each year in Melbourne's Chinatown. This commercially oriented version of the

Mid-Autumn Moon Festival involves the making of lanterns, singing, dancing, games and riddling. *See also Chinese Folklore in Australia Folklore; Customs; Family Folklore; Foodways*

MIDSUMMER EVE

St John's Eve and St John's Day are celebrated on 23 and 24 June respectively. The fact that the Christian feast of St John (marking his nativity) falls on the day following the pagan Midsummer Eve meant that earlier fire festivals were incorporated into this observance throughout Europe, Ireland and Britain. It is therefore difficult to distinguish the official and the folkloric aspects of this observance. St John's Day is particularly celebrated amongst people of Cornish extraction and is also central to Scandinavian folk belief and custom.

In Australia, areas with a strong Cornish presence, especially in South Australia, celebrate Midsummer Eve with bonfires and with explosive charges, as befitted a community with strong mining links. *See also Customs; Folklorism; Religious Folklore*

MIGRATION LORE

As a country with a population substantially based on immigration, Australia has many related traditions. The 'new chum' was an early figure of folk fun during the colonial era. From the early arrival of Irish convicts to the influx of Chinese diggers on the goldfields in the 1850s, to the post-World War II mass migration programs, until today, folk prejudices about newcomers and/or people of non-Anglo-Celtic origins were given full rein in folk speech ('bog Irish', 'chinks', 'wogs', 'pommies', 'reffos', 'towel-heads') and in jokes ('What's that whining sound you hear in a jumbo jet full of migrants after they turn off the engines? The British.') In addition, a wide array of reprographic and electronic lore (faxes and emails) may be circulated, trading on folk stereotypes such as alleged government 'gifts' to migrants of cars, colour television sets, etc.

Migrants also have their own lore, consisting typically of stories about the hardships and trials of travel to Australia; of settling in, or not; of learning the language (both formal English and Australian folk speech). A good example of this is the wealth of stories attached to the arrival of the 'Dunera Boys' at the Bonegilla migrant camp, and to the Snowy Mountain Scheme in the post-World War II period. An important aspect of migration lore is the bringing of new traditions to the community. This is a double-edged process; it has a positive potential for intercultural understanding and the maintenance of traditions within a migrant group but it may also have negative aspects, in that tension may be caused over such matters as conflicting social mores or religious beliefs (the wearing of traditional clothing with occupational uniforms, for example, or the practice of Christmas customs in schools with non-Christian pupils).

Migrant groups also bring extensive bodies of folk expression and practice into the country, especially in relation to folk customs, many of which are of great age, but some (such as 'Christmas in July'), are newly developed. Migration has also brought many new folk musical influences to Australia, including the traditions of Greek *rebetika* and South America. Some languages widely spoken in Australia such as Greek, Italian, German and Dutch have developed local variations in grammar and vocabulary which, in some cases, represent unique dialects (Australian Greek, for example). *See also Chinese Folklore in Australia; Customs; German Influences on Australian Folklore; Greek Folklore in Australia; Irish Influences on Australian Folklore; Italian Folklore in Australia; Maltese Folklore in Australia; New Chum*

MIN-MIN LIGHTS
Variously located in south-west Queensland, though best known around Hughenden, the Min-Min lights are an Australian version of the British will-o-the-wisp and similar apparently supernatural dancing lights caused by the spontaneous combustion of marshy gases. It is said that 'min-min' derives from an Aboriginal language and that the lights are regarded by Aboriginal people as evil spirits. *See also Folk Belief, Ghost Lore, Indigenous Folklore*

MOONDYNE JOE
Joseph Bolitho Johns (1831–1920), or Moondyne Joe, was transported as a convict from England to Western Australia in 1853. He absconded, was captured and escaped repeatedly throughout the late 1880s. Johns' skill at escaping made him a Western Australian bushranger hero. While the only song extant about Joe is a parody of the nursery rhyme 'Pop Goes the Weasel', in its brevity can be detected that set of tensions and conflicts between unpopular authority and those suffering beneath it that typically underlie outlaw heroes. Joe's ability to survive well in the bush was due to a network of sympathisers, always a prerequisite for an outlaw to be 'heroised'. Folk traditions about Moondyne Joe include

numerous stories about his escapes, his cleverness and his buried gold. *See also Bushrangers; Folk Heroes; Lost Treasures*

MOPPS, CHARLIE
The man who invented beer, according to this widespread drinking song, also a favourite of sailors, with the refrain 'God bless Charlie Mopps, the man who invented beer'. *See also Folk Songs; Grog; Pub, The*

MORANT, HARRY 'THE BREAKER'
Henry Harbord Morant (1865–1902), aka Murant, was noted in the bush in the late 1880s and the 1890s as a fine horsebreaker and minor bush balladist. Executed by the British army during the Boer War on a charge of murdering prisoners, Morant has in recent years become an alleged 'folk hero', mainly due to a number of books about him and a successful feature film about his life and death. Folklorists have found little to suggest that Morant was an especially notable figure in his day; in fact he seems to have been widely disliked, even feared by his peers. It was suggested by the late John Meredith in his *Breaker's Mate: Will Ogilvie in Australia* (1996) that the apparently depressive Morant may have committed the Gatton (Qld) murders, a brutal and still unsolved sex crime of December 1898. *See also Bush, The; Bush Ballad; Folk Heroes; Folklorism*

'MORETON BAY'
Nineteenth-century convict ballad (probably written by Francis MacNamara, 'Frank the Poet') also known as 'The Convict's Lament' and 'The Death of Captain Logan', in which a convict laments his harsh treatment in various penal stations and especially at the hands of Captain Logan of Moreton Bay. Logan is killed by Aborigines, an event that causes great rejoicing among the convicts. This song is also notable in relation to Ned Kelly, who paraphrased one of its verses in 'The Jerilderie Letter'. The song verse goes:

> He said, 'I've been a prisoner at Port Macquarie,
> at Norfolk Island and Emu Plains,
> At Castle Hill and cursed Toongabbie –
> at all those places I've worked in chains;
> But of all the places of condemnation
> and penal stations of New South Wales,

To Moreton Bay I found no equal,
for excessive tyranny each day prevails.'

The relevant lines of 'The Jerilderie Letter' (with original spelling, punctuation and grammar) are:

... [they] were doomed to Port McQuarie Toweringabbie Norfolk island
and Emu plains and in those places of tyranny and condemnation many
a blooming Irishman rather than subdue to the Saxon yoke were flogged
to death and bravely died in servile chains...

See also Logan, Captain; Convict Lore; Folklore; Frank the Poet, Irish Influences on Australian Folklore; Transportation Ballads; Kelly, Ned

MORGAN, DANIEL 'MAD DOG'

Bushranger hero Daniel Morgan operated along the Victoria and New South Wales border between 1863 and 1865, stealing horses, robbing travellers and occasionally occupying farms and stations. Evidence suggests that he may have been emotionally unbalanced, but he was not the pathological killer painted by the police and the press. In fact, Morgan had considerable support and sympathy, particularly in Victoria, where he was known as 'the traveller's friend'. The circumstances of Morgan's bushranging were brutal, ending in his death and disfigurement by police at Peechelba station (Vic.) in April 1865, as commemorated in the ballad 'The Death of Morgan':

Oh, Morgan was the traveller's friend, the squatters all rejoice
That the outlaw's life is at an end, no more they'll hear his voice.
Success attend all highwaymen that do the poor some good;
But my curse attend a treacherous man who'd shed another's blood...

See also Bushrangers, Folk Heroes

MORRIS, MORRIS DANCING

Although Morris dancing is usually thought of as British, the word 'Morris' comes from Morisca, and is an English version of a Moorish dance, described by Funk and Wagnalls' *Standard Dictionary of Folklore, Mythology and Legend* as 'a ritualistic form of battle mime'. The battles may not only be between armies but also between the seasons, and the dance is often a celebration of fertility. A group of Morris dancers is usually six or ten men wearing white trousers, shirts and hats, with bells on their legs and ankles, and equipped with sticks and handkerchiefs. Australia has a number of Morris groups, often including Australians of British birth. Women also participate in Australian Morris, and there are a number of all-women's groups, such as 'The Fair Maids of Perth' in Western Australia. The dances include vigorous leaping, and thumping or striking with sticks. Stick dances include 'Shepherd's Hey' and handkerchief dances include 'Country Gardens'. Australian-born pianist, composer and folk collector, Percy Grainger (1882–1961) arranged the music for both of these dances for piano.

The dancers in the Morris are often accompanied by traditional characters such as the hobby horse and the jester or fool, derived from English tradition. However, one group from the Northern Territory includes a realistic-looking crocodile as one of its 'associates'. *See also Dance; Folklorism; Folk Revival*

MOSQUITOES
These insects, known throughout the country as 'mozzies', appear in folklore as outsize creatures that perform outlandish feats, including carrying cows away (Giru, Qld) and eating bullocks, then picking their teeth with the horns (Hexham, NSW). Similar tales are told around the country. The hated biters also find their way into sayings such as that addressed by a parent to a troublesome child: 'If you don't be good I'll whack ya – like a mozzie on Mount Kozzie' (Australia's highest mountain, Mount Kosciuszko in New South Wales). *See also Flies; Folk Speech; Hexham Greys, The; Legendary Animals*

MOTHER'S DAY
Mother's Day (held on the second Sunday in May) has its roots in post-Civil War America. After a number of localised observances of a day dedicated to mothers, dating back to 1868, Mother's Day was instigated by Anna Jarvis on the second Sunday in the month, 9 May 1907 in Philadelphia. In England it has been combined with the older tradition of Mothering Sunday, which was in decline by World War II when American troops introduced the American Mother's Day. Traditionally the fourth Sunday in Lent (the forty-day period before Easter, beginning on Ash Wednesday) was 'Mothering Sunday', so-called because servant girls were allowed to visit their mothers on this day, taking a 'simnel

cake', a fruit cake whose twelve decorative balls were believed to represent the Twelve Apostles. Mothering Sunday is still observed among Anglicans around the world. Simnel cakes are still cooked in Australia.

Mother's Day is a bonanza for the commerce and retail worlds, but it is also the occasion for the expression of affection and appreciation within the family, with the giving of cards and presents to 'mum' and the customary preparation of breakfast in bed by other family members – a symbolic act that acknowledges the traditional role of mother in the home. Mother's Day is also notable for the visiting of elderly parents and grandparents by sons, daughters, in-laws and grandchildren. The flower traditionally given in Australia on this day is the white chrysanthemum, (though in America and in some fifty other countries where the day is observed, the custom is often to give carnations) usually in a bunch or potted. Whether this is a whimsical relationship to the last syllable of the flower's name – a favoured folk interpretation – or to the traditional language of flowers (the chrysanthemum, depending on its colour, is generally held to represent love and truth) is unclear. *See also Customs; Family Folklore; Father's Day; Folk Belief*

MOUNT KEMBLA MINE EXPLOSION COMMEMORATION

On 31 July 1902 ninety-six miners were killed in an explosion at the Mt Kembla Coal Mine in New South Wales. On each anniversary since then a memorial service has been held at the Mt Kembla Anglican Church. *See also Customs; Disasters*

MOUNT SPEC COUGAR, THE *See Legendary Animals*

MUCK-UP DAY

Known by this name in many places, this is the traditional day of mischief that marks the end of secondary school for graduating/exiting students. The mischief may be relatively harmless, as in hanging smelly fishheads around the school and throwing flour and/or water bombs. However, overenthusiasm can often lead to acts of vandalism to school property and damage to private property, such as teachers' cars. Many schools now encourage students to funnel this energy into some entertaining way of raising money for charity. *See also Customs; Student Revels*

MUFTI DAY

Increasingly common in business during the 1990s, a day on which employees are allowed, even encouraged, to wear 'mufti', or casual clothes in the workplace; but said to be on the decline as business reverts to more traditional approaches and dress. Also called 'Casual Friday' or 'Free Dress Day' in schools and workplaces. At many secondary schools Mufti Day is often associated with raising money for charity, with students bringing a small donation to school to pay for the privilege of dispensing with uniforms and dress code. The term 'mufti' became widely used in World War II, when it denoted the wearing of plain clothes by anyone entitled to wear a uniform. *See also Customs; Work Lore*

'MURRUMBIDGEE SHEARER, THE'

Lively and colourful nineteenth-century shearing song appearing in Paterson's *Old Bush Songs* and forming the basis of A.L. Lloyd's later, controversial adaptation 'The Maryborough Miner'. In the original song, the shearer has had a chequered career of prospecting for gold, burning the sheds of uncooperative squatters and robbing gold escorts. He finishes up by spending 'ten years on Cockatoo', Sydney's colonial island prison. *See also Bush, The; 'Maryborough Miner, The; Old Bush Songs, Pastoral Industry Folklore*

MUSEUM OF CHILDHOOD (WA)

Located at Perth's Edith Cowan University, the Museum of Childhood holds large collections of children's play materials and related items and is a repository of the social history of childhood. *See also Australian Children's Folklore Collection, Children's Folklore*

MUSICAL INSTRUMENTS

Many of the instruments used in contemporary bush bands are not traditional Australian folk instruments, and certainly were not used for social dancing in colonial days. The guitar, lagerphone, bush bass and washboard were incorporated into bush bands during the folk revival of the 1950s and 1960s, probably influenced by the popular skiffle bands of the time. More authentic 'folk instruments' are the fiddle, concertina, tin whistle and the piano. The epic struggle to bring a piano into a nineteenth-century settler community in New Zealand, described in Jane Campion's film *The Piano*, was by no means unusual in Australia. There is a lengthy and scholarly entry on musical instruments written by Peter Ellis in the *Oxford Companion to Australian Folklore* (1993). *See also Bush Bands; Bush Music; Dance*

N

NANNUP TIGER, THE

The Nannup Tiger (WA) is often said to be the survivor of an almost extinct species of carnivorous marsupial known as *Thylacinus cynocephalus* (a striped wolf-like creature). It has been reported as far north as Geraldton and as far south as Esperance.

Reports of the Nannup Tiger seem to date back almost to the earliest European settlement of the southern corner of Western Australia, being especially frequent in the late 1960s and early 1970s. It is thought that this increase in sightings was due to climatic conditions which forced the 'tiger' into the wooded areas around Nannup. Various attempts have been made to capture the Nannup Tiger, though so far with no success. Similar traditions of legendary animals abound throughout the country. *See also Legendary Animals; Tasmanian Tiger*

NATIONAL ICONS

Many of our most cherished icons of national identity are derived from and/or closely related to folklore, including Ned Kelly, Les Darcy, the swagman, the digger in the form of the volunteer private soldier, two-up, the Melbourne Cup, Phar Lap, Australian Rules Football, cricket, beer, the beach, the backyard shed, the utility ('ute', usually with a cattle dog in the tray), the bush, gum trees, the dingo, the kookaburra ('laughing jackass'), flies, and the song 'Waltzing Matilda', among others. Many folk notions also related to the Australian sense of national identity are expressed in folk speech forms such as 'a fair go', 'she'll be right', 'knocking' and 'cutting down tall poppies'. While national identity is related to folklore in most countries, in Australia there is an especially close connection, first explicated in Russel Ward's *The Australian Legend* (1958). *See also Bush, The; Folk Humour; Folk Speech*

NATIONAL LIBRARY OF AUSTRALIA

The National Library of Australia in Canberra is this country's main repository of documented folklore in Australia, especially sound recordings. The NLA was established in 1960, and from its inception has had a commitment to folklore. One of its first purchases for its new Oral

History Section was the John Meredith collection of sound recordings from the 1950s, which included traditional songs, instrumental music, stories and children's games. Meredith's collections (resumed in the 1980s) were accompanied by a number of outstanding photographs, published by the National Library as *Real Folk* in 1995. Since the 1960s the Library has assisted numerous collectors to carry out recording projects of folklore in Australia, including in Aboriginal communities and in immigrant communities whose family language is not English. *See* CHRONICLE

NEW CHUM
A person new to Australia, especially from Britain. From convict slang for a fellow prisoner c. late eighteenth-early nineteenth century, though still widely used throughout the nineteenth century in goldfields ballads ('The New Chum Chinaman') and bush songs. *See also Folk Speech; Malone, Paddy; Migration Lore*

NEW YEAR'S DAY
A calendar celebration and a secular holiday, 1 January marks the start of a new year according to the Christian calendar. New Year's Eve, 31 December, is traditionally a time of eating, drinking, dancing and generally behaving in an uninhibited manner. At the stroke of midnight the New Year is welcomed in with joined hands and the singing of 'Auld Lang Syne', sometimes in a circle; and cheers, kisses, embraces and wishes of 'Happy New Year'. As well as the folk custom of well-wishing, New Year is traditionally associated with new beginnings, with hopes for happiness and prosperity in the coming twelve months, and with 'New Year's resolutions', such as to give up smoking, drinking, procrastination, or otherwise to adopt behaviour or attitudes perceived to be positive.

The still-observed Scots and northern English tradition of 'first footing' takes place on New Year's Eve, or 'Hogmanay' as it is called in those regions. The traditional belief that the first foot to cross the threshold would determine the luck of the household for the rest of the year made it desirable that this 'first footer' should be a person of good omen. In Scots tradition, this was a dark-haired male carrying a lump of coal. Originally, the first footer also bore money and bread or other food, symbols of wealth and plenty, but now coal, ensuring adequate winter fuel, is generally felt to be sufficient. It is also traditional that the first footer be given a good helping of Scotch whisky. Persons considered unlucky are those with squints, flat feet, red hair, and women. With variations, this custom is also known in many other parts of England and on the Isle of Man.

In the Greek Orthodox religion 1 January is not only New Year's Day but also traditionally marks the death of St Basil, a revered founder of the Greek church. Special foods are prepared in Greek Orthodox homes, particularly the St Basil's Cake (*vassilopitta*) in which a coin is usually placed. The cake is cut and distributed to all members of the family in order of age, beginning with elders.

In the Orthodox (Old Calendar) observed by the Ukrainian, Romanian, Serbian and Macedonian Churches, New Year is on 14 January. This day, under the Old Calendar, was also St Sylvester's Eve (31 December in the new calendar), and in some places, including Switzerland, this day and night are still commemorated with activities symbolising the battles of good and evil. In Polish tradition St Sylvester's Eve is an occasion of rejoicing, marking the avoidance of an ancient end of the world prophecy made in the year 1000. *See also Customs; Foodways; Religious Folklore*

NICKNAMES

Australian nicknames abound, ranging from the generic, such as 'Blue' for a male with red hair, 'Spud' for people named Murphy, through to occupational monickers such as 'The Judge', a waterfront workers' (wharfie) name for someone who spends most of his time sitting on a case, or at the bar. Other characteristically Australian nicknames include a variety of shortened forms, such as 'Dazza' for Darrel or Darren, 'Gazza' for Gary, or 'Lozza' for the female Laurie (though the form is most frequently used with male names). Nicknames are also endemic in all forms of sport, in families, among criminals and wherever Australian is spoken. Buildings may also have nicknames, such as 'The Jesus Hilton' for Sydney's St Vincent's Hospital and 'The Gabba', for the Brisbane Cricket ground, and so on. Taffy Davies produced two collections of nicknames, *Australian Nicknames* (1977) and *More Australian Nicknames* (1978). *See also Folk Speech, Place Names, Sports Lore, Turf Lore*

'NINE MILES FROM GUNDAGAI'

Bush song and recitation, also known as 'Bill the Bullocky', in which the bullocky's team becomes bogged one dark rainy night, during which the famous 'dog sat on the tucker box nine miles from Gundagai'. The dog, of course, did not only sit in the tucker box but shat in it, leading Bill to lament:

> I can forgive the blinking team, I can forgive the rain,
> I can forgive the dark and cold and go through it again.
> I can forgive my rotten luck, but hang me 'till I die,
> I can't forgive that bloody dog, nine miles from Gundagai.

This ballad is the basis for the famous statue of the dog on the tucker box about eight kilometres east of Gundagai. *See also Bullockies; Bush, The; Dog on the Tuckerbox, The; Dogs; Pastoral Industry Folklore*

NOLAN, ARTHUR

Possibly historical jockey from Newcastle (NSW) whose ballad details his death when his horse Sulphide fell in the Sydney Steeplechase. Probably late nineteenth century. As with many such ballads of tragedy, sentiment is a strong element of their appeal. The chorus of this song goes:

> Poor lad, his mother was not there to bid her lad goodbye,
> Poor Archie Nolan stood like stone with a teardrop in his eye.
> 'I'm sorry I ever let him ride', good Mr. Burgo said,
> But alas, kind friends, it was too late, for the jockey lay there dead.

See also Disasters; Robinson, Alec; Stone, Willy

NULLARBOR MUSTER, THE

An event held each year on a weekend in early June at the settlement of Rawlinna, 350 kilometres east of Kalgoorlie (WA). Rawlinna, a railway fettler's settlement of a dozen or so houses on the Nullarbor Plain, services the Transcontinental Railway line ('the Trans') and annually attracts around three hundred souls from the apparent emptiness to participate in the Muster. The main event is racing station horses, but there are also sleeper chopping, steer running, clay pigeon shooting, arm wrestling and beer drinking competitions, as well as steer riding and a bush dance. *See also Customs; Folk Sports; Picnic Races; Sports Weekend*

NURSERY RHYMES

'Sing a song of sixpence', mentioned in the entry relating to the great Aussie meat pie, is only one of the many traditional British nursery rhymes which virtually every English-speaking parent recites to infants and small children. Other family favourites include 'Baa Baa Black Sheep', 'Twinkle Twinkle Little Star', 'Hey Diddle Diddle the Cat and the Fiddle', 'Ride a Cock Horse to Banbury Cross', 'London Bridge is Falling Down' and other reminders of the British heritage common to many Australians. Most adults can recall some nursery rhymes by heart, but may also jog their memories with the many compilations of nursery rhymes published regularly since at least the eighteenth century.

The main purpose of nursery rhymes, which number in their hundreds in the English language, is for entertainment, but there is also a great deal of painless and enjoyable learning of sounds and numbers in rhymes such as:

One two three four five
Once I caught a fish alive;
Why did you let it go?
Because it bit my finger so.

Is there an Australian nursery rhyme? In 1917 the *Bulletin* magazine ran a competition for an Australian nursery rhyme, but none of the winning (or other) entries passed into the Australian tradition, demonstrating that generally, folklore cannot be written to order. Some research done by Gwenda Davey at the Institute of Early Child Development in the 1980s showed that many Australian parents used 'Waltzing Matilda' as a nursery rhyme to soothe or amuse babies and toddlers. They also used 'Kookaburra Sits on an Old Gum Tree':

Kookaburra sits on an old gum tree,
Merry merry king of the bush is he;
Laugh kookaburra,
Laugh kookaburra,
Gay your life must be.

It is interesting to folklorists, who generally acknowledge that it is rare to know the origin of any given piece of folklore, that both 'Waltzing Matilda' and 'Kookaburra' have known authors. The first was written by

Banjo Paterson (author of 'The Man from Snowy River' and many other favourites in the years around 1900), and the latter by Marion Sinclair of Adelaide. Dr Keith McKenry, in the 1980s a member of the Folklife Inquiry, visited Miss Sinclair in Adelaide not long before her death, and she wrote out in a fine hand the words and music of the song, which were published in facsimile in the Inquiry's report, *Folklife in Australia* (1987). Clearly both songs prove that, whatever the origin, if 'the folk' take something to their hearts, it enters the folk tradition, and becomes folklore.

It might be said that nursery rhymes are a major means of maintaining Australia's British heritage, through rhymes such as 'London Bridge is Falling Down', 'Oranges and Lemons' (the bells of St Clemens) and 'Pussy Cat, Pussy Cat, Where have you been?' (I've been up to London to visit the Queen).

However, nursery rhymes are not common only to English-speaking families. The Australian Children's Folklore Collection at Museum Victoria in Melbourne houses sound recordings of nursery rhymes in at least twenty different languages, and international research confirms the almost universal spread of this engaging form of adult–child interaction. The very nonsense included in rhymes such as 'Hey Diddle Diddle, the Cat and the Fiddle' (The cow jumped over the moon) seems to have a function in helping children learn to know what's real and what isn't. The Collection at Museum Victoria includes similar examples of nonsense rhymes in Spanish, Serbian, Croatian, Italian, Greek, French, Russian and Dutch. The Dutch collection includes Prins Joris:

> *Prince Joris was a gentleman,*
> *A gentleman was he;*
> *He had a coat of currants on*
> *And pants of rice pudding…*

The origin of nursery rhymes is a topic of considerable interest, and many individuals in English-speaking countries will theorise that 'Ring a Ring a Rosy' (we all fall down) dates from the Black Plagues of mediaeval or later times. However, the prominent English researchers into child lore Iona and Peter Opie point out that as this rhyme did not appear in print until the nineteenth century, this 'origin', along with most such conjectures, is either suspect or unproven. *See also Australian Children's Folklore Collection, Children's Folklore*

O

OCKER *See Bloke*

OKTOBERFEST
A traditional German event (since 1810 in Munich) involving food, drink (mostly beer), music, song and dance. There are numerous similar events observed throughout Australia, such as in Darwin since 1969 and Townsville since 1984. Perth's first Oktoberfest was held on 28 October 1961 at the Claremont showgrounds. *See also Customs; German Influences on Australian Folklore*

OLD BARK HUT, THE *See Bob the Swagman*

'OLD BULLOCK DRAY, THE'
Humorous bush song in which a bullock driver makes an open proposal of marriage to 'everything that has two legs'. The rollicking chorus of the song probably accounts for its popularity:

> *So, it's roll up your blankets,*
> *And let's make a push.*
> *I'll take you up the country*
> *And I'll show you the bush.*
> *I'll be bound you won't get*
> *Such a chance another day,*
> *So come and take possession of my old bullock dray.*

The song does not record if the bullocky was successful. *See also Bullockies; Bush, The; Bush Ballad*

OLD BUSH SONGS
Term used in the late nineteenth century, and since, to describe ballads of bush life, most of which were then not very old at all. A.B. ('Banjo') Paterson collected a number of these songs (lyrics only) in his 1905 *The Old Bush Songs Composed and Sung in the Bushranging, Digging and Overlanding Days*. This went through five expanding editions, up to

1931. These included songs that have become very well known, such as 'The Wild Colonial Boy', 'The Old Bark Hut' and 'The Stringybark Cockatoo'. While the anthology is usually hailed as the first collection of Australian folksongs, it is not clear if some of the songs included were widely sung, or even sung at all. It also seems that Paterson obtained many of his texts from the verse columns of country newspapers and, according to research by Philip Butterss, the (unacknowledged) collections of others. The title was later used by Douglas Stewart and Nancy Keesing for their 1957 enlargement and revision of Paterson's anthology. In 1984 Graham Seal published a selection of the various editions of *Old Bush Songs* (Angus & Robertson) that included the music to which the lyrics were allegedly sung and/or to which they had become commonly sung. *See also Bush, The; Bush Ballad; Paterson, A.B. ('Banjo')*

OLDFIELD, SNUFFLER

Queensland character about whom many tall tales are told, mostly related to fighting, drinking and the toughness of bush life. Many of the tales told of Snuffler Oldfield are also told of another Queensland figure, Galloping Jones. *See also Folk Humour; Galloping Jones; Yarn*

'OLD KEG OF RUM, THE'

A nostalgic nineteenth-century bush song of working life, especially the 'spree' or drinking session that frequently followed a season or session of hard work. There are two versions of the song, one of which concerns shearers, the other farm workers. Both share the chorus which celebrates the delights of emptying 'the old keg of rum'. *See also Bush Ballads; Grog, Pastoral Industry Folklore, Pub, The*

OPALS

Semi-precious gemstone mined in parts of Australia, especially Coober Pedy. In Australian folk belief opal is often considered to be unlucky. This belief is widespread in Britain, although in former times opals were considered to be lucky in parts of Europe, sometimes depending on the colour of the stone. *See also Folk Belief*

DENIS O'REILLY

Irish hero of a nineteenth-century goldfields ballad also called 'With My Swag All On My Shoulder'. He 'made a fortune in a day and blued it in a week' and then tramped the countryside singing: 'With my swag all on my shoulder, black billy in my hand/I'll travel the bush of Australia like a true-born Irish [sometimes 'native'] man'. *See also Folk Songs; Goldrush Lore; Irish Influences on Australian Folklore*

ORTHODOX CHRISTMAS *See Christmas*

'OVERLANDER[S], THE'
Popular nineteenth-century cattle-droving ballad also called 'The Queensland Drover' and sung in various versions, the best known of which usually features the chorus:

> So pass the billy [or bottle] round, boys,
> Don't let the pint pot stand there,
> For tonight we'll drink the health
> Of every overlander.

See also Bush, The; Bush Ballads, Folk Songs, Pastoral Industry Folklore

OXI DAY
This day commemorates the refusal of Greece, on 28 October 1940, to allow the Italian fascist dictator Benito Mussolini to march his army through the country in his attempt to invade Albania a year after the start of World War II. The telegrammed Greek reply to Mussolini's request was simply 'Oxi' – 'no.' The event is usually celebrated in Greece and in Greek communities throughout the world, especially in Greek Cyprus, on the Sunday closest to 28 October, and involves dance, music, feasting and the laying of wreaths to the memories of those Greeks who died defending their country against Mussolini and, later, Hitler. The eventual result of this conflict was the Battle of Crete, in which Australian forces figured prominently. *See also Customs, Folklore, Greek Folklore in Australia*

P

PALMERSTON, CHRISTY

Historical character of northern Queensland from the 1870s around whom a good many yarns have developed. Most of these centre on his alleged origins as the bastard son of the British Prime Minister, Lord Palmerston; his ability to terrify Aborigines and Chinese; his toughness and ability to live off the land, and his shady, sometimes decidedly criminal activities, including murdering Aborigines. Said to have lived to a considerable age and to have died in New Guinea, Palmerston is commemorated in both folklore and official place -names *See also Folk Humour, Local Lore, Yarns*

PANCAKE DAY

A Christian festival, Shrove Tuesday, also known in England as 'Pancake Tuesday', or just 'Pancake Day'. On this day, pancakes were traditionally cooked and eaten. Pancake races were sometimes a feature of this event, in which women raced each other, tossing pancakes in frying pans as they ran. Many English families in Australia still observe the custom of Pancake Day, though in the privacy of the home, and some schools conduct Pancake Day races. Shrove Tuesday is the Tuesday immediately preceding Ash Wednesday, which marks the start of Lent and so moves around on the calendar. The word 'shrove' refers to the 'shriving' or absolution from confessed sins which takes place during Shrovetide, the three-day period before Lent. Shrove Tuesday is also observed in Germany, where the tradition involves the consumption of special cakes. *See also Customs; Family Folklore; Religious Lore*

PARANORMAL, THE *See Supernatural, The*

PASSOVER (*PESACH*)

Marking the escape of the Jewish people of Israel from slavery in Egypt, the Passover is celebrated over an eight-day period in or near April. The first and second nights of the festival (*Seder*) are marked within the family by a special meal and the telling of the story of the escape. The first and last two days are especially holy. Jewish children generally stay home from school on these days. *See also Customs, Religious Lore*

PASTORAL INDUSTRY FOLKLORE

The cattle, sheep and allied industries have generated a great deal of Australia's better-known folk heritage. Lore of and about shearers, overlanders and other workers in these areas is extensive, often said to be the essence of Australian folklore and national identity. A great deal of the collection of Australian folk traditions has concentrated on associated song, verse, sayings, craft and other practices. A. B. Paterson's *Old Bush Songs* was the earliest influential publication of this type. It was followed by the collections of English folklorist A.L. Lloyd in the 1920s and early 1930s (though these were not made generally known until decades later). Since the 1950s, the work of many independently funded collectors of folksong, music, dance and verse has also added to the growth of interest in bush music and other elements of the rural Australian lifestyle felt to be especially redolent of national identity. There is a considerable body of such lore held in various archives, libraries and private collections around the country, a representative portion of which has been published and recorded in one form or another. The Stockman's Hall of Fame in Longreach (Qld) is a well-known repository of many elements of pastoral industry traditions. *See also Bush, The; Bush Ballads; National Icons; Old Bush Songs; Shearers*

PATERSON, A.B. ('BANJO')

Andrew Barton ('Banjo') Paterson (1864–1941), solicitor, journalist and author, based some of his ballads on bush songs and verse, and many of his compositions (notably 'Waltzing Matilda') became folk songs or recitations, the best known of which is 'The Man from Snowy River'. He was also responsible for what is arguably the first published anthology of Australian folk song, *The Old Bush Songs (Composed and Sung in the Bushranging, Digging and Overlanding Days)*, originally published in 1905. *See also Bush Ballad, Old Bush Songs, Waltzing Matilda*

PATSY FAGAN

Fictional Irish character in a song, probably twentieth century, named after him in which he calls himself 'a harum-scarum devil-may-care-um decent Irish boy'. Patsy celebrates his being 'a decent working man' and good-humouredly threatens to steal an Australian girl away over the sea to Ireland. *See also Irish Influences on Australian Folklore; Migration Lore*

PAVLOVA

Another contender (with the meat pie) for the title of Australia's national dish. The pavlova is a sweet dessert made of a large round meringue base made mainly of egg whites and sugar which is topped or filled with whipped cream and a variety of fresh fruit, usually including passionfruit. kiwi fruit (Chinese gooseberries) and strawberries are also popular today.

The origin of the dessert is much debated, although it is usually acknowledged that it was created in honour of the Russian ballerina Anna Pavlova when she visited Australia in the late 1920s. Michael Symon's authoritative book on the history of eating in Australia, *One Continuous Picnic* (1982), attributes the Pavlova to Perth chef Bert Sachse. Symons acknowledges, however, that New Zealand might have a prior claim, with recipes for a 'meringue cake' or small 'Pavlova Cakes' published in recipe books in 1927 and 1929. Symons' rueful comments on the Aussie/Kiwi problem are worth repeating:

> In those days of sea travel, New Zealand was closer than Perth to Australia's main centres, and had almost joined the Federation. For us to be confident the Pavlova is a truly Australian dish, it's a pity it didn't.

See also Foodways; Lamington Drive; National Icons

PEARLER'S GHOST, THE

A ghost tradition. Abraham Davis, a prominent entrepreneur in the Broome pearling industry and an eminent member of the town's Jewish community around the turn of the twentieth century, owned a fine home in Broome. Davis was drowned, along with all other passengers and crew, in the wreck of the *Koombana* off Port Hedland in 1912. His house later became the palace of Bishop Gerard Trower (1860–1928), the first Anglican bishop of the north-west. One night Trower allegedly awoke to see a ghostly figure, dressed in the garments of a rabbi, standing in a pool of light. When the bishop called to the figure it promptly vanished. The same figure is said to have been seen on numerous later occasions, usually late in the afternoon or early in the evening. *See also Folk Belief; Ghost Lore; Maritime Lore; Pearler's Light, The*

PEARLERS' LIGHT, THE

A ghost tradition. On the foreshore at Broome is an electrical beacon that dims unaccountably from time to time. No cause of this mysterious dimming has ever been found, despite the light having been overhauled on many occasions. No natural phenomenon, such as mist, appears to be the cause of the light's dimming. It is said that the ghosts of drowned pearlers creeping around the beacon on certain nights of the year cause the light to fade. *See also Folk Belief, Ghost Lore, Maritime Lore; Pearler's Ghost, The*

PEMULWUY

Pemulwuy (1756–1802) was an Aboriginal warrior of the Botany Bay (NSW) region who resisted British settlement between 1790 and 1802. A reward for his death or capture was offered in 1801 and he was shot, then beheaded by police in 1802. His heroic legend remains powerful among Aboriginal people and has been the subject of a number of published works. *See also Indigenous Folklore, Jandamurra, Yagan*

PHANTOM MAIL, THE

Supernatural tradition from the Hay (NSW) area. A light that seems to be on a mail-coach was said to be seen travelling across the One Tree Plain. No matter how fast men rode after the light no-one was ever able to catch up with it. Also known locally as 'the Ghostly Coach'. *See also Ghost Lore*

PHAR LAP

Phar Lap, Australia's most famous racehorse, a New Zealand-born chestnut gelding of over seventeen hands, was for a period between September 1929 and his death, never unplaced in any race he ran in, except for the Melbourne Cup of 1931, when he was handicapped with the enormous weight of 68 kilograms. He won the 1930 Melbourne Cup, handicapped. Phar Lap became a heroic animal for many ordinary Australians during the Depression years through becoming a champion despite his undistinguished breeding and looks. Phar Lap died as a five-year-old in California in 1932. As with Les Darcy, Australian folk belief suggested strongly that the 'Yanks' poisoned Phar Lap before he could beat their own horses. The exact cause of the horse's death is still debated. Phar Lap's relics (his out-sized heart was donated to the Museum of Anatomy in Canberra, and his skin mounted and put on display now at Museum Victoria) have become oddly venerated national icons. *See also Folk Heroes; Horses; National Icons; Turf Lore*

PICNIC RACES

These were, and still are, held annually in country areas; their origins have been traced to Goulburn (NSW) in 1830. Here, on a property named 'Tirrana' owned by the Gibson family, a rough track was made for the children to race their ponies. The races, held at lunchtime, grew in popularity and sophistication and soon were followed by a dinner, then a dance or 'ball'. In the early 1870s the Tirrana Picnic Race day was so popular that guests were asked to bring their own food and the ball was held in a hall in Goulburn. By this time the event, often held on public holidays, had caught on and spread throughout the colony and the country. The Bong Bong races near Moss Vale (NSW) were among the most popular of these events.

Held in rather different country on the western side of the continent, but satisfying the same need for sociability, are the Kulin Bush Races, which usually take place in October in this wheatbelt town 300 kilometres from Perth. The Kulin Races began in nearby Jitarning during the 1920s and have continued in one form or another ever since, now featuring, among many other attractions, a bush two-up school after the races.

Other long-established picnic races include the Hanging Rock (Vic.) picnic races, which were established before the 1870s and are held on New Year's Day, Australia Day and the first Sunday in March. Increasingly popular are the Nullarbor Muster (WA)and the Birdsville (Qld) Races in central Australia. A good deal of money often changes hands through betting and other activities, and a portion of the takings is usually donated, it is claimed, to local good causes and community improvements. Bush races and similar events are becoming increasingly important in the economies of many declining rural areas, attracting tourists and allowing the display of customs, crafts and activities distinctive to the local area. *See also Birdsville Races; Customs; Family*

Folklore; Harvest Customs; Horses; Nullarbor Muster, The; Sports Lore; Turf Lore

PICNICS

The usually family-oriented leisure custom of the casual meal taken out of doors, usually in a scenic or otherwise pleasant spot such as a park, beach or river-front, has long been popular in Australia. Encouraged by the climate and the casual lifestyle of most Australians, these convivial folkloric events are popular among many different ethnic groups, and may include favourite sports such as *bocce* and cricket. The picnic has also become a part of other Australian folk customs, such as Picnic Races. *See also Customs; Family Folklore*

PIGEON *See Jandamurra*

PILGRIMAGE

An ancient custom associated with most religions. In Australia a number of Marian pilgrimages have developed to shrines at Berrima (NSW) and Mt Tambourine (Qld). As well, there is a pilgrimage on foot each year between the cathedrals at Ballarat and Bendigo in Victoria, ending on the Feast of the King (last Sunday in October by the Old Calendar). Of course many Australians undertake the great international pilgrimages of various religions, such as those of Christians to Lourdes and those of Muslims to Mecca.

Similar to pilgrimages are the often long journeys made by those observing the celebrations of village saints, a custom transported from a number of southern European countries. Similar journeys are often undertaken by Chinese families at Spring Festival and by Muslim families at Ramadan, though these events generally involve family and community relations as well as religious observance. It might be argued that Australians' visits to Uluru (Ayer's Rock) in Central Australia are pilgrimages to pay tribute to the heart of the Australian continent. *See also Customs, Hajj, Religious Lore, Uluru*

PLACE NAMES

The lore of naming places is extensive, and may apply to natural features such as rivers, mountains, gullies and coasts and to human-made features, especially towns. In Australia these derive largely from names of colonial personages or officials or loved ones the European 'discoverer' wished to honour (Goulburn, Melbourne, Alice Springs, Diamantina), from (often inaccurate) transcriptions of words from Aboriginal languages (Coonabarabran, Waimea), or from local events, incidents or personalities (Dead Horse Gap, Mount Misery, Battle Camp). The often apocryphal stories of how such places were named are important elements of local folklore. *See also Eco-lore; Local Lore; Nicknames*

POEPPEL'S PEG

Coolabah stump marking Poeppel's Corner at the junction of the Queensland, South Australian and Northern Territory borders, originally marked by surveyor Augustus Poeppel in 1879. A spot of legendary significance in the lore of the outback and subject of considerable mythology and controversy in the surveying profession regarding whether or not Poeppel placed the peg in the correct location. *See also Folk Speech*

POINTING THE BONE

A phrase used by many Australians in many contexts. To non-Aboriginals, to 'point the bone' at someone may involve wishing them ill, accusing them of wrongdoing, or perhaps wishing punishment or retribution on them. The origin of the phrase comes from Aboriginal Australia, and J. M. Arthur in *Aboriginal English* (1996, p. 53), defines it as meaning 'To direct a malevolent force against another by the use of a spiritually charged piece of bone'. This act may be carried out against those who have transgressed Aboriginal law. *See also Evil Eye, The; Indigenous Folklore*

POLITICAL LORE

Like other areas of human endeavour, Australian politics has generated a considerable body of occupational folklore. Politicians and those who work with them have extensive traditions similar in genre to those of other occupational groups, including legends – often humorous – of individuals and events. As well, there is a great deal of folklore about politicians and the political processes in the broader community. This includes nicknames for politicians, songs, verse, jokes, anecdotes, legends, e-lore and other usually abrasive, scurrilous and obscene expressions of a popular Australian scepticism about politicians. Often these expressions last only as long as the issues, politicians, their parties and policies are in the limelight, with each generation evolving new folkloric reactions. A number of collections of political folklore have been published, including Fred Daly's *The Politician Who Laughed* (1982); former federal minister Barry Cohen's collections of political anecdotes; and folklorist Warren Fahey's anthologies of political song, old and new. *See also Folk Heroes; Labor Lore; Little Digger, Stump Speech; The; Theodore, 'Red Ted'*

PONGAL

The Tamil Harvest Festival, which takes place over three days in the month of *Thai* (around mid-January by the Christian calendar), the start of the rice harvest. As in the seasonal customs of many cultures, the houses are decorated with plants and leaves, cleaned out and new cookware replaces the old. *See also Customs, Harvest Customs, New Year's Day*

PRAWN NIGHT

A night of conviviality characterised by the consumption of large quantities of prawns and beer. Formerly a favoured pastime of RSL, football and other social clubs in New South Wales and elsewhere with memberships now primarily middle-aged and elderly, the Prawn Night, with its overtones of excess, has become less common since the 1980s. *See also Customs; Foodways*

PROGRESSIVE DINNER

A meal in which each course is eaten at a different location, usually in the participants' homes. Going in and out of fashion, Progressive Dinners are favourites of social clubs and occupational groups, and are also often related to fundraising for community groups. *See also Customs; Foodways*

PROPHET'S BIRTHDAY, THE

This central Muslim celebration commemorates the birth of the prophet Mohammed, c. 571 AD in the Christian calendar, and usually takes place in November. Folklore activities appropriate to this day (the 12th day of *Rabi' al-Awwal*, the third month of the Islamic calendar) include festivities, processions, together with the telling of the story of Mohammed's life as well as the preparation of a ceremonial evening meal for the family group. *See also Customs; Family Folklore; Religious Lore*

PROSH

Annual day of student revel for the University of Western Australia, usually in April, involving dressing up, pranks and collecting money for charity. The term is usually said to derive from the inability of students to pronounce the word 'procession' while under the influence of alcohol. *See also Customs; Leavers; Schoolies' Week; Student Revels*

PUB, THE

Abbreviation of 'public house'. The classic locus of much Australian folklore, especially that of the bush and much of that set in the city and at war in foreign parts. Folklore of pubs, about pubs and about things that are said to have happened in pubs is extensive. A representative sampling can be found in Bill Wannan's *Folklore of the Australian Pub* (1972), which includes some of the many sayings, poems, songs, games, stories and beliefs related to pub life and culture. Pubs are also favoured locations for supernatural traditions, especially hauntings. *See also Chook Raffle; Drinking Games; Grog; Kirup Syrup; Supernatural, The*

PUBLIC HOLIDAYS

Public holidays are part of the official state and religious calendar of Australia and therefore not themselves examples of folklore. However, these numerous days free from work provide many occasions for folkloric activity associated with a characteristically Australian love of leisure and socialisation, including picnics, barbecues, traditional games and sports, cultural activities, drinking and so on. *See also Anzac Day, Customs, Holidays, May Day, New Year's Day*

PUNCH AND JUDY

English folk-puppet play well known throughout Australia, despite being infrequently performed today. The character of Punch, also known as 'Mr Punch', is usually said to derive from the wandering players of the fourteenth-century Italian Commedia dell'Arte and the character of *Pulcinella* (anglicised to Pulcinello or Punchinello), a raucous, hook-nosed, cowardly buffoon. Despite its violence, the show teaches morality by participation: by tradition, the watching children vigilantly shout out 'Oh, yes you did!' whenever Punch lies or denies his misdeeds.

In the puppet play, the hunchbacked and ugly Punch usually beats his wife Judy to death after she complains that he has murdered their baby. His subsequent escapes from the law in the shape of the Policeman, and his defeats of the Doctor, Death and the Devil, have the quality of heroic transgression. In some versions of the play, Punch even tricks Jack Ketch, the hangman, into hanging himself, once again escaping retribution for his acts and demonstrating a trick often encountered in folk tales where the hero fools the villain into killing himself or herself. Punch represents the defiance of regulation and authority that is a feature of much folklore. A still common colloquial expression is to be 'As pleased as Punch'. In Italian, 'Pulcinella's secret' is one that everyone knows. *See also Children's Folklore; Family Folklore; karagiozis*

PURIM (FEAST OF LOTS)

Taking place in February–March, *Purim* precedes the Passover by four weeks and is an important commemoration of the delivery of the Jews of Persia from massacre in the sixth century BC. According to tradition, Haman, vizier of the King of Persia, drew lots to determine the day on which he would murder all the Jews in the kingdom, hence the name for this custom. During this celebration, the story of how Queen Esther saved the Jews is retold, with the children trying to drown out Haman's name whenever it occurs in the story by shouting 'May his name be blotted out.' There are readings from Jewish holy books, and special prayers are said. Within Jewish families gifts are exchanged and special sweet cakes, including *Hamantaschen* – 'Haman's purse' – are consumed at a family feast. Folk features of this celebration also include fancy dress, masking and general enjoyment. *See also Children's Folklore; Customs; Foodways; Religious Lore*

Q

QUILTS

It is sometimes thought that patchwork quilts are essentially an American craft, brought to Australia in the twentieth century by visiting Americans and expatriate Australians who have lived in the United States. In fact Australia has a long tradition of quilt-making, going back at least to the convict quilt (known as the 'Rajah Quilt') made by convict women *en route* to Australia in 1841. This national treasure, now held in the National Gallery of Australia in Canberra, is a very large work that includes an embroidered inscription:

> *To the ladies of the convict ship committee*
> *This quilt worked by the Convicts of the ship Rajah during their voyage*
> *to Van Diemen's Land is presented as a testimony of the gratitude with*
> *which they remember their exertions for their welfare while in England*
> *and during their passage and also as proof that they have not neglected*
> *the Ladies kind admonition of being industrious*
> *June 1841*

The 'Ladies' who supplied the convict women with materials, needles and scissors as well as instruction were philanthropists such as Elizabeth Fry, the noted Quaker prison reformer. Their help turned the genteel pastime of patchwork into a grass-roots activity for poorer women. By the end of the nineteenth century the 'lady's pastime' had become a widespread folk art in Australia, and many quilts survive in galleries and private homes. These quilts tell a great deal about their makers and their customs and beliefs, some expressing an emerging Australian nationalism through the use of Australian motifs such as wild-flowers and native animals. Other women recorded family, district and national events on their quilts. The Australian National Gallery also houses the superb 'Westbury Quilt', made by the Misses Hampson in Tasmania in 1900–03. This unusual quilt is not patchwork, but embroidered in white on red cloth. It has a variety of motifs and symbols, ranging from Queen Victoria to houses in Westbury and family animals (Boz the dog, Barney the rooster, and Polly and Kitty the cows). The quilt also has a number of inscriptions, including 'Good luck to the winner of this', suggesting that it may have been made for a raffle or other competition. Two other national treasures are the 'Changi Quilts', held by the Australian War Memorial. These were made by British and Australian women who were prisoners of war of the Japanese in Singapore during World War II. Quilting is still a popular handcraft today, actively pursued by individuals and in groups. Contemporary quilting may involve not only bed covers and clothing but wall hangings, which may be group projects for display and educational purposes, such as the 'Heritage' and 'Bandicoot' quilts made by the Hamilton Quilters of Western Victoria. *See also Crafts; Embroidery; Wagga Rug; Women's Folklore*

QUING MING (Chinese), THANH MINH (Vietnamese)

This (northern hemisphere spring) festival, the 'Tomb-sweeping Festival', is devoted to tending ancestors' graves and takes place in late April. Twenty-four hours beforehand all household fires are put out and the 'Feast of Cold Food' occurs: only specially prepared cold foods are eaten. The next morning the fires are re-lit. Quing Ming is generally translated as 'clear brightness'. *See also Customs, Foodways, Religious Lore*

QUIZ NIGHTS

Also occurring in Britain and elsewhere, quiz nights have become popular social events throughout Australia in recent years, and have been especially longstanding in Western Australia. Usually they are held in public houses or hotels, where the proprietor makes a room or other area available to the competitors free of charge, expecting a good return from drinks purchased. Questions are assembled, often by a specialised 'quiz master' who may preside at the event itself, and competitors gather around numbered tables. Points for correct answers are generally cumulatively recorded on a black or whiteboard as each 'round' progresses. In between rounds games such as 'heads and tails' may be played, where competitors indicate their choice by putting their hands on heads or behinds – 'tails'. The winner is the last one standing. There may also be special questions to individuals. Prizes are given, often substantial. Quiz nights are generally mounted for charitable or community fundraising purposes and provide a popular mix of socialising, game-playing and general knowledge, although specialised or themed (eg. sport) quiz nights may also be held. Also termed 'trivia night'. *See also Chook Raffle, Customs, Lamington Drive*

R

RACIST FOLKLORE
All folklores have extensive bodies of ethnic and other slurs that mostly revolve around supposedly humorous depiction of negative racial and ethnic stereotypes. Australian folklore is no exception. English-language prejudices and misconceptions about the Irish, Italians, Americans, Poles, the French, 'Asians', Muslims and other ethnic and cultural groups are common, although not exclusive to English. There is also a sizeable body of racist material about Aboriginal people, both in the older traditions of the bush and in more recent urban and various reprographic forms. A selection of Australian racist ballads and related expressions can be heard on the compact disc *White on Black* (2000), compiled and produced by folklorist Keith McKenry. *See also Bawdry; Folk Humour; Walkabout*

RAFFERTY'S RULES
No rules at all, or a mish-mash of confused or invented rules. May be used in a great variety of contexts, from politics to scratch football, sometimes to describe a free-for-all. First recorded 1918 and probably First AIF slang. Also 'Kelly's Rules'. *See also Digger, Folk Speech*

RAGGED THIRTEEN, THE
Group of high-spirited goldminers who travelled from what is now the Northern Territory to the Hall's Creek (WA) gold rush of 1886. Their activities became the stuff of an embryonic Robin Hood legend across the Top End, romanticised by Ernestine Hill in her book *The Territory* (1951), in which she claimed the group were as famous as the Twelve Apostles and described them as 'gentle grafters of the unfenced' and 'soldiers of outback fortune'. *See also Bush, The; Bushrangers; Folk Tales; Goldrush Lore*

RAILWAY LORE
An important form of occupational folklore involving a variety of skills, beliefs, customs, yarns, songs and jargon. Patsy Adam-Smith's *Folklore of the Australian Railwaymen* (1969) provides an Australia-wide survey of

railway verbal traditions, and a number of trade union arts projects have been undertaken. A favourite railway yarn, told in all states, is usually called 'The Slow Train':

> *One day the train was clattering slowly along, stopping and starting. A frustrated woman passenger asked the conductor when the train would reach its destination. 'I must get there as quickly as possible,' said the woman, 'because I'm pregnant.' The shocked conductor said: 'Considering your condition, it's a wonder you boarded the train.' 'When I boarded the train I wasn't in this condition', replied the woman.*

See also Billy Sheehan; Granville Rail Disaster; Sunshine Railway Disaster; Work Lore; Yarns

RAINBOW SERPENT

To non-indigenous Australia, the Rainbow Serpent is one of the best-known figures from Australian Aboriginal mythology. An important ancestral being in Aboriginal lore, it is common to many groups as a Creator and source of fertility, and is generally associated with life-giving water. Aboriginal people tell many different stories about the Rainbow Serpent, mainly in northern Australia, including those about the serpent's role in the creation of rivers. The Rainbow Serpent has become a popular icon of Aboriginality in non-Aboriginal Australia and is sometimes used as an emblem in non-Aboriginal artwork, parades and in schools – more often now with the permission of the tradition's owners. *See also Bunyip; Indigenous Folklore; Yarama*

RAKSHA BANDHAN

A Hindu festival, but also celebrated by many Indians, regardless of faith. '*Raksha*' means to protect and '*bandhan*' to bind or tie. In this custom, which takes place in August, a girl ties a *rakhi* (a red and gold bracelet often having a medallion at its centre) to her brother's wrist as a sign that she trusts him and expects his protection. The boy may in turn give a small gift of flowers, sweets or money, and promises to protect his sister.

Adults as well as children observe this symbolic binding, and special cards bearing appropriate messages may be sent. *See also Customs; Religious Lore*

RAMADAN

The central Islamic observance that takes place in *Ramadan*, the ninth month of the Muslim year (May/June), and commemorates the start of God's revelations to the prophet Mohammed. Muslims fast from sunrise to sunset throughout this period, usually 29 days or until the new moon is sighted, breaking the fast at night with a special meal, *iftar*. *Ramadan* ends with the 'small festival' (*Eid-ul-fitr*), during which families eat a celebratory meal together and give presents of money, sweets and 'small festival' greeting cards to the children. Relatives are visited and the emphasis on family unity is very strong. Under various local names, this festival is celebrated in many Muslim countries, including Malaysia, Indonesia and Pakistan. It is customary for Turkish Muslims to visit friends and relations at this time, often travelling long distances across Australia to do so. *See also Customs, Family Folklore, Foodways, Hajj, Religious Lore*

REBETIKA

Rebetika is sometimes called 'the Greek blues', as this form of music has the same melancholy themes of hardship and lost love as the better known African-American blues. Nevertheless the irresistible sound of this music, usually featuring the Greek stringed instrument the *bouzouki*, has made it popular in Australia as well as in Greece. Melbourne, sometimes known as 'the third largest Greek city in the world', has been since the early 1980s an international centre for the revival of this music. *Rebetika* is an interesting example of the fusion of culture and politics. It came to Greece in the 1920s with the former Greek residents of Turkey who were repatriated to Greece by international agreement, and who subsequently lived often in extreme poverty in areas such as Piraeus, the port of Athens. Because of the music's association with hashish culture and other forms of rebellion, *rebetika* was banned in Greece for some years until rehabilitated by the Papandreou government in the 1970s, after the defeat of the Greek junta. Some Greek-Australian musicians began writing songs in *rebetika* mode about their experiences of migration and living in Australia. Thymios Stathoulopoulos recorded his own composition 'The Bouzouki in Melbourne' in 1985:

In Melbourne's lovely evenings now
In clubs and taverns the bouzouki plays.
And people dance and live it up in the purely Greek way,
Getting merry on Aussie wine and breaking all the plates.
Beautiful Greek girls, full of grace,
Proudly dance zeibekiko,
And so do fine blonde Aussie girls,
They dance away their passions.

See also Folk Music, Greek Influences in Australian Folklore

RECITATION

The reciting of poetry and some other verbal forms such as toasts, stump speeches (a form of folk political parody) and monologues is a characteristic element of Australian folk traditions – especially, though not solely, those of the bush. The 'old bush song' was – and often still is – as frequently recited as sung. Many of the compositions of A. B. ('Banjo') Paterson, Henry Lawson and other bush writers are popular, together with home-grown, local compositions, some of which have become traditional. A favoured style is the ballad and its variants, including parodies. Collectors have also come across monologues and other recited pieces from the music hall and Victorian parlour tradition. Recitations are typically delivered in a laconic, almost deadpan manner, though some modern performers have developed more flamboyant styles suited to the demands and tastes of contemporary audiences. See also Bush Ballad, Folk Poetry; Paterson, A.B. ('Banjo'); Spider from the Gwydir, The

RED DOG

Kelpie–cattle dog cross born in Paraburdoo (WA) in 1971 and also known as 'Tally', Red Dog became a well-known wanderer throughout the Pilbara region, famous for consuming large quantities of food. Many tales were and are told of his amazingly long and arduous journeys and gargantuan appetite, and he was a generally loved character in the region, frequently given lifts by passing vehicles as he made his way from one favourite feeding place to another. Not everyone liked Red Dog, though. He took, or was perhaps given, a strychnine bait in Karratha on 10 November 1979 and died ten days later. Buried between Roebourne and Cossack, Red Dog is commemorated in a statue at Dampier, in verse, in a number of books and especially in Pilbara folklore. The well-known writer Louis de Bernieres published a book of the same name based on this legend in 2001. *See also Dingo; Dogs; Folk Tales; Loaded Dog, The; 'Nine Miles from Gundagai'*

RED STEER, THE

Cryptic term for rural arson, a favoured method of industrial protest and personal revenge in the conflict between rural capital and labour in the late nineteenth and early twentieth century. *See also Bush, The; Folk Speech; Labor Lore*

REEDY RIVER

Stage musical using Australian folk songs collected by actor John Gray and some composed pieces in folk style, with a script by Dick Diamond. First produced by the Melbourne New Theatre in 1953 and frequently revived. *See also Folklorism; Folk Revival*

REGIONAL RIVALRIES

Strong undercurrents of Australian folk values and attitudes revolve around regional and inter-city rivalries. The most famous of these is perhaps that between 'crass' Sydney and 'staid' Melbourne, but there are other such rivalries, often expressed in humorous form that are deeply held. West Australians are thought to have a deep antipathy to and suspicion of 'eastern staters'; the 'Top End' considers the southern states and territory to be 'soft'; Queenslanders sometimes call those from Victoria and New South Wales 'Mexicans' (i.e. from south of the border); Tasmania is, in accord with international folk prejudices about offshore islands, considered to be populated by halfwits and inbreds, and just about everyone thinks the national capital, Canberra, is out of touch with the realities of life experienced by the rest of the country. *See also Folk Speech; Insult and Invective*

RELIGIOUS LORE

While most faiths are institutionalised belief systems, and so not considered folklore, all religions have well-developed bodies of associated customs, beliefs, apocryphal stories, songs and similar that are clearly folkloric. Folk periodic customs frequently cluster around major religious calendar feasts, fasts and festivals, including the Christian Easter, Christmas and Halloween, the Islamic *Eid-ul-adha*, and the Jewish

Rosh Hashanah and *Sukkoth*, the Hindu *Diwali* and *Raksha Bandhan*, to mention only some. Individual folk customs or rites of passage related to birth, coming of age, marriage and death are intimately associated with religious belief, as are the many pilgrimages undertaken by devout Australians, both within Australia and elsewhere in the world. Apocryphal tales and songs about the reputed – often humorous – doings and sayings of religious figures are found throughout the world's traditions and amongst the many religious and cultural groups making up modern Australia's multicultural community. *See also Blessing of the Fleece; Blessing of the Fleet; Chanukah or Hannukkah; Chinese New Year; Christening; Christmas; Dawn Service, The; Diwali or Divali; Double Ninth Festival; Easter; Eid-ul-adha; Evil Eye, The; Feast of the Hungry Ghosts; Fo dan; Folk Belief; Funerals; Hajj; Halloween; Harvest Customs; Islamic New Year; Krishna Janmashtami; Mid-Autumn Moon Festival; Pancake Day; Passover; Pilgrimage; Prophet's Birthday, The; Purim (Feast of Lots); Quing Ming; Rainbow Serpent; Raksha Bandhan; Ramadan; Roadside shrines; Rosh Hashanah; St Patrick's Day; Satanism; Shab-e-bharat; St Valentine's Day; Sukkoth, Thanksgiving; Village Saints' Processions, Wetting the Baby's Head,*

RHYMING SLANG

Rhyming slang as used in Australia is often called 'Cockney rhyming slang' and probably originated in England among Cockneys, working-class people living in the East End of London. Many Cockneys came to Australia either as convicts in the late eighteenth and early nineteenth centuries or as free settlers. However, no rhyming slang was included in either of two nineteenth-century compilations of Australian and British convict slang (by Vaux and Grose, and so it may have arrived later. The Australian folklorist John Meredith's book on the subject, *Learn to Talk Old Jack Lang* (1984), argues that 1900 is a more likely focus for the growing popularity of rhyming slang, as it was particularly influenced by popular theatre and music hall comedians.

Some examples of rhyming slang which are still used today are plates of meat (feet), eg. 'I've walked so far that my plates of meat are hurting', and Noah's Ark (shark), eg. 'you shouldn't swim in Sydney Harbour because of the Noah's Arks.' Rhyming slang in Australia is almost exclusively used by males, mainly in informal contexts and among friends or work-mates, and also in prisons. It may well be considered a form of male verbal display, a true folk performing art. *See also Folk Speech*

RING, THE

Probably mythical secret society of convicts on Norfolk Island, much romanticised by writers. According to the sketchy legendry of the Ring it was organised on principles similar to those of many secret societies, with varying circles of membership, from the outer 'Nine' to the inner 'One', with the appropriate number of members for each circle. The members of each circle were known only to each other and did not know the members of the next circle in. Consequently no one knew who was 'the One'. Only the most recalcitrant convicts were admitted to membership, which on Norfolk Island meant that they were likely to be especially irredeemable. Indeed, the Ring's purpose was not to protect or assist the convicts but to take control of the regime of tyranny and terror that characterised Norfolk Island. There is an eight-verse chant usually known as 'The Convict Oath' that contained the codes of conduct, or misconduct of the Ring, beginning:

> Hand to hand
> On earth, in hell.
> Sick or well,
> On sea or land,
> On the square ever.

and ending:

> Stiff or in breath,
> Lag or free,
> You and me,
> In life, in death,
> On the Cross never.

The Ring, it is said, effectively ran the penal station, dispensing punishment in accordance with the organisation's perverse principles, to anyone who acted too fairly, including guards and officers. The organisation also allegedly administered the murder–suicide pacts that desperate convicts used to escape, forever, the horrors of Norfolk Island. *See also Convict Lore; Transportation Ballads*

ROADSIDE SHRINES AND MEMORIALS

Commemorative plaques, cairns and other monuments to saints, travellers and to particular historical events are a familiar feature along many roads. In recent years the custom of placing flowers, wreaths or other commemorative items such as white wooden crosses at the spot of road fatalities has become increasingly common. These unofficial tributes are usually placed by the victim's family and friends, or sometimes by sympathisers within the community. Such shrines can sometimes become constructions of considerable size and permanence. Probably the best-known observation of this custom is the annual service and placing of flowers at the site of the Granville (NSW) rail disaster of 1977.

By 1998, so widespread had roadside shrines, memorials and other markers become that authorities in some states, notably New South Wales, began actively discouraging them, claiming that they are both illegal and a dangerous distraction for drivers. Two councils in Western Sydney had banned roadside markers by September 1998. Also in that year, researchers at the University of New South Wales revealed that 75% of roadside memorials studied were for young men. However, researchers at Newcastle University and the University of New South Wales have claimed that such markers are a deterrent to fast driving. A South Australian authority of the town of Millicent (SA) reported a 50% fall in road fatalities after police officially approved an organised program of roadside markers following a triple fatality in 1993. However, such official activities are a formal extension of the folk custom. *See also Customs; Disasters; Funerals; Granville Rail Disaster; Religious Lore*

ROBINSON, ALEC

Probably fictional jockey whose often-collected song laments his death when his horse, Silvermine, fell. The sentimental words of the chorus are:

> *Gather round, jockey boys, hang down your heads,*
> *Sad tears will silently fall.*
> *We'll all shed a tear for the boy who was dear,*
> *The best and the bravest of all.*

See also Disasters, Nolan, Arthur; Stone, Willy

ROSH HASHANAH

Celebrated for ten days in September or early October around the time of the Equinox, this Jewish New Year celebration ends with *Yom Kippur*, the Day of Atonement. *Rosh Hashanah* is the holiest period of the Jewish year. It is customary to send greeting cards with the message 'May you be written down for a good year.' Special foods are prepared for consumption within the family at this time, including *lekach* or honey cake, symbolising the hoped-for sweetness of a good year, rounded bread called *challah* and glazed carrots, or *tzimmes*. See also Customs, Foodways, Religious Folklore

RUNNING NAKED WITH THE COWS

On the first Sunday after the first rain of 'the Wet' (the Wet Season in northern Australia), the adult males of Weipa (Qld) meet around 3am, take off all their clothes and run naked through the herds of local cows. This unusual custom began as something of a drunken joke in the early 1990s and seems to have become popular, growing larger each year. In 1998, for instance, around one hundred men took part. Like many recent customs and revivals of older events, this activity seems partly related to a desire to generate local tourism. See also Customs; Folk Humour; Folklorism

'RYEBUCK SHEARER, THE'

Well-known nineteenth-century shearing ballad, sung in various versions, in which a shearer aspires to be the best – that is, the ryebuck – shearer in the shed. He aims to beat the fastest shearer, or 'ringer', saying 'While the ringer's shearing five, I'll be shearing ten/And I'll prove I'm a ryebuck shearer.' See also Bush, The; Pastoral Industry Folklore, Shearers

S

ST PATRICK'S DAY

Celebrated since at least the 1680s by the Irish (and many others) throughout the world, St Patrick's Day, 17 March, is Ireland's National Day, honouring the National Saint. A shamrock or the colour green may be worn, and copious quantities of alcohol, known as 'Patrick's Pot', are traditionally consumed in mainly male drinking traditions known as 'drowning the shamrock'. Many Australian pubs serve green beer on this day. Officially recognised by 1810, St Patrick's Day has long been a favourite celebration in Australia. The event was first recorded here in 1795, though had no doubt been observed by the Irish from the first years of settlement. Bound up closely with religious, political and ethnic divisions in Australian society, the day has experienced the ups and downs of popularity, excess and containment typical of many major festivals. An Australian feature has been a strong component of competitive sports, including foot racing, athletics and cycling. Since the 1980s there has been an increasing interest in Irish and 'Celtic' cultural activities, and St Patrick's Day has benefited accordingly. *See also Customs; Grog; Irish Influences on Australian Folklore*

ST VALENTINE'S DAY

Celebrated by the ancient Greeks as the day of the goddess Hera, symbolic of femininity and marriage. The Romans continued the custom in relation to their deity, Juno. The day, then, already had associations with love and marriage when a priest named Valentine defied the command of the Emperor Claudius that soldiers should not marry. Claudius believed that marriage made soldiers unwarrior-like. Valentine was executed on 14 February 296 AD, thus becoming the patron saint of lovers.

St Valentine has a long history of commemoration within the Christian church. Like St Agnes' Eve, St Valentine's Day is popular for folkloric predictions about the future of one's love life. It is also widely observed by the wearing of a yellow crocus, the flower of St Valentine. Yellow birds seen flying on St Valentine's day are also believed to be a good omen. However, the 'St' is often dropped nowadays, a reflection of the day's secular and almost totally folkloric significance for young – and not so young – lovers. On 14 February cards bearing traditional messages (sometimes insulting) are exchanged, or increasingly printed in the form of advertisements in newspapers, and gifts of flowers and sweets may also be exchanged. Unsigned cards from unknown admirers may also be received. *See also Customs; Marriage; Religious Lore*

SANDGROPERS
Folk name for residents of Western Australia, from the great amount of desert in that state. Probably from the 1890s. Often simply 'gropers'. *See also Folk Speech; Regional Rivalries*

SANTA CLAUS *See Father Christmas*

SATANISM
Ancient beliefs about Satan are as current in modern Australia as they are elsewhere in the world. The 1980s and 1990s saw a number of such beliefs result in legal proceedings against groups and individuals for alleged Satanic Ritual Abuse (SRA). Beliefs about 'The Great Beast' and the number or mark of the Beast – 666 – have been collected, including the delusion that human beings are having bar codes embedded in their bodies, through which device the Great Beast will achieve his ultimate ambition of ruling the world. Beliefs about Satan, sacrifices and 'black magic' were also widely invoked during the Azaria Chamberlain affair. The recent consequences of such beliefs in Australia were tracked by R. Guilliatt in *Talk of the Devil: Repressed Memory and the Ritual Abuse Witch-hunt* (1996). *See also Chamberlain, Azaria; Evil Eye, The; Folk Belief, Urban Legends, Witchcraft*

SAUSAGE AND BUN TEA
A now obsolete and mainly West Australian custom in which participants enjoyed a simple meal. Often associated with group activities such as fundraising, bingo nights and similar. *See also Customs; Chook Raffle; Foodways; Lamington Drive*

SAVVATOVRATHI
In Greek wedding tradition, the groom and friends may share a specially prepared rice dish. They may then go to the bride's house and burn

incense to 'smoke' the bride's clothing. This custom is sometimes known as *savvatovrathi*. *See also Customs, Greek Folklore in Australia, Weddings*

SCANLON, CONSTABLE

Member of the police party murdered by Ned Kelly at Stringybark Creek in 1878 and featuring in Kelly folklore. *See also Kelly, Ned*

SCHOOLIES' WEEK

The annual celebration of secondary school students who have finished their final examinations, 'Schoolies' Week', more accurately 'weeks', takes place on the Gold Coast of Queensland and is a time of riotous behaviour and excessive drinking in the tradition of earlier student revels of Europe. While celebrations of the end of school life have long been a feature of this time of the year around the country, Schoolies' Week grew into a spontaneous national festival during the 1980s, attracting ever-increasing numbers of young adults – approximately 80,000 students aged 17 to 18 years old took part in 1994. The riotous nature of the event has sometimes been marred in recent years by serious injury, violence and death.

Similar activities take place elsewhere, such as Rottnest Island off Perth and in other West Australian locations, where graduating high school students, often mingling with university students, have in recent years caused considerable police and community concern about escalating violence and damage to property and the environment (including killing the small marsupial quokkas native to Rottnest, often it is charged, by playing 'quokka soccer'). In this part of the country the Schoolies' tradition is known as 'Leavers'. *See also Customs; Leavers; Prosh; Student Revels*

SCREENSOUND AUSTRALIA

ScreenSound Australia, the National Screen and Sound Archive, was formerly known as the National Film and Sound Archive. Based in Canberra, ScreenSound collects and preserves Australia's moving images and sound recordings, including commercially produced films, videos, compact discs and other recordings. It has valuable archival footage of Australia's first films and sound recordings, as well as the latest productions. ScreenSound also has substantial holdings of folk music, including field recordings of well-known collectors such as John

Meredith and Rob Willis. *See also* CHRONICLE; *National Library of Australia*

SERGEANT SMALL
Allegedly historical Queensland or northern New South Wales policeman notorious for ill-treatment of vagrants during the 1930s depression. 'Tex Morton' (Robert Lane) composed a song about the man and recorded it in 1938 . The chorus 'I wish I were about fourteen stone and only six foot tall/I'd take the train back north just to beat up Sergeant Small' ensured that the song passed into oral tradition and made the song a favourite of singers, old and young. *See also Folk Songs; Great Depression, The*

SEWING BEE
Communal occasion in which women gather to sew, or otherwise construct, garments or other items intended for a common, usually charitable purpose. Also a 'quilting bee'. A 'working bee' is a less gender-specific event in which men, women and perhaps children will join together to perform some communal charitable or useful function, often for a local school or community group. *See also Crafts; Customs; Federschleissen; Women's Folklore*

SEXIST FOLKLORE
Male and female folk traditions have a great deal of folklore that revolves around gender prejudice. As with racist folklore, these attitudes are generally expressed in allegedly humorous forms, such as jokes, reprographic material and occasionally in story. Much of the material circulated among males is misogynist and obscene in nature. *See also Bawdry; Folk Humour; Racist Folklore*

SHAB-E-BHARAT
A Muslim celebration anticipating the month of Ramadan (May/June in the Christian calendar). In many Muslim communities special sweet foods may be prepared and distributed to family, friends and the poor. *See also Customs; Ramadan; Religious Folklore*

SHAUVOT
Sometimes referred to as the Jewish 'Pentecost' because it falls fifty days after Passover, *Shauvot*, celebrated in late May or June, is thought to have

originally been an agricultural festival. This aspect is still present in the custom of decorating the synagogue with greenery, though the day is now primarily associated with the giving of the *Torah* (Law) to Moses. Meat is avoided, and readings from various holy books take place throughout the night. *See also Customs; Religious Folklore*

SHEARERS

The men who shore the wool from the backs of the sheep that Australia once rode upon are the focus of a large body of bush folklore, much of which celebrates the shearers' lifestyle, emphasising the difficult nature of their work and often revolving around the 'sprees' that followed a season's work, in which the shearers would traditionally 'knock down their cheques'. Having spent all their hard-earned money, or 'tin', the shearers would return to the sheds for another season, a work pattern common in the bush during the nineteenth and early twentieth centuries and very similar to that of sailors in the days of sail, also recorded in a number of sea songs. The shearer is an iconic figure in the lore of the bush and in popular notions of national identity. *See also Bush, The; Bush Ballad; National Icons; Pastoral Industry Folklore; Work Lore*

SHED *See Backyard*

BILLY SHEEHAN

Fictional railway engine driver hero of a parody of the American railway song 'Casey Jones', itself based on a Mississippi riverboat song called 'Steamboat Bill'. Sheehan tries to outrun the Spirit of Progress express in a steam train but the steam engine's boiler explodes, killing him and the fireman. Thought to have originated among railway workers in Hughenden, Queensland, c. 1937. *See also Disasters; Railway Lore; Work Lore*

SHERRITT, AARON

Close sympathiser of the Kelly gang of bushrangers, murdered by Joe Byrne, once his best friend, on 26 June 1880 as a prelude to the Glenrowan Station incident. The gang suspected Sherritt, probably correctly, of being a double agent. Sherritt appears in Kelly folklore as a Judas figure whose 'life [for] the treachery paid', claims the ballad 'Kelly Was Their Captain'. *See also Kelly, Ned*

SHINJU MATSURI

Broome (WA) festival held in late August–early September. Originally known as 'Bon-Matsuri' (Festival of Lanterns), this was mainly a mourning custom for the souls of dead Japanese ancestors, especially pearlers. Traditional food, dancing and prayers accompanied lanterns lit in the cemetery and offerings to the spirits of the dead. This Japanese custom declined until 1970, when local community groups resolved to re-establish a community festival that would involve everyone in the town. The Japanese term 'Shinju Matsuri' ('Pearl Festival') was chosen as the name for the festival. Held for eight to ten days each year, it is a large, organised event attended by most of the local population and about three times as many tourists, and it also incorporates the Chinese feast of Hung-Tiang for the commemoration of the dead. As well, there is a range of traditional activities including an Aboriginal corroboree, sports and competitions, dancing, street parades, displays and consumption of prodigious quantities of food and drink. See also Chinese Folklore in Australia, Customs, Indigenous Folklore

SHOUTING DRINKS

'Shouting' or 'standing a round' is an essential, mainly male, drinking custom in Australia. Although the term 'shout' dates from the 1850s, the custom is probably much older, perhaps having its origins in the convict period. While the custom (though not the term) is also known in Britain, it is adhered to with a peculiar egalitarian ferocity in Australia, anyone who fails to 'shout' when his turn comes round being in danger of social ostracism. The custom is enshrined in at least one uncomplimentary folk phrase 'He wouldn't shout if a shark bit him.' See also Customs; Grog; Pub, The

SHOWER TEA

Also known as a 'Kitchen Tea', 'Wedding Shower', Bridal Shower' or just a 'Shower'. Apparently derived from American usage, this is an event organised for the bride-to-be by the bridesmaids and her friends. Usually held on a weekend, it is a women-only event to which guests usually bring a small present for the kitchen of the bride, or for her trousseau. The bride may be advised about domestic affairs.

The Greek krevatti, as traditionally practised in Castellorizo and elsewhere, is equivalent to the 'shower tea' and may be followed by the bed-making ceremony, in which bride and bridesmaids make the marriage bed, singing and sprinkling the bedspread with aromatic herbs and sugared almonds. The bed may be blessed, and it was traditional for a male child to be thrown onto the bed, symbolic of a wish that the bride might bear sons.

To some extent, the 'shower tea' has been either replaced or joined in recent and more liberated years by the custom of 'hens' night', an event that parallels the male 'bucks' night' or 'stag night'. *See also Customs, Weddings*

SHROVE TUESDAY *See Pancake Day*

'SICKIE', THE

Properly, sick leave. A day or more off work taken as sick leave even though the worker may or may not be medically unfit. The 'sickie' is an Australia-wide occupational institution that has become increasingly frowned upon as an anti-productive work practice in times of economic rationalism. Nevertheless, the custom persists, as does the term, although research conducted in 2002 suggested that it was in decline as a result of workplace reform. *See also Customs, Work Lore*

SIKH FOLKLORE IN AUSTRALIA

Sikhs are perhaps among the most conspicuous of Australia's diverse Indian communities because of the distinctive turban still worn by many, usually older, members. Similarly, Sikh women may still wear the *salwar kamiz* (loose trousers and tunic), the traditional dress of all Punjabi women, which is usually worn with a long scarf. The best-known, and the largest, rural community in Australia is in Woolgoolga (NSW), which has two *gurdwaras*, or places of worship, and there are substantial Sikh communities in Melbourne, Sydney and Shepparton (Vic.). The *gurdwaras* remain important religious and social centres for Sikhs in Australia, especially for celebrations and festive days, and worship will sometimes be followed by a procession. Songs and hymns are an important part of Sikh attendance at the *gurdwaras*, and folk dances for men and women, such as *bhangra* and *gidha*, are popular on celebratory occasions. National Sikh sports are held annually. *Baisakhi*, the Spring Harvest Festival, and *Divali*, the Festival of Light, are two important celebrations in Australian Sikh communities. *See also Customs; Diwali; Migration Lore*

SILVER REEF, THE

'The Silver Reef', as told by Bill Beatty, is a fabulously rich lode said to be somewhere in the Wyndham and King Sound region of Western Australia's remote north. It was discovered by a Malay merchant, Hadji Ibrahim, sometime before European colonisation. After selling a load of silver ore from the trove in Macassar, Ibrahim returned for more, only to be shipwrecked and drowned. But Ibrahim kept a journal of his voyages and recorded all the details of his find, except for the location. The saga continued when a local – colourfully named 'Mad Jack' – was found dead in his cutter near Yampi Sound in 1909, with his body pierced by several spear wounds and his head split open with a tomahawk. The discoverers of the body found a few ounces of gold in the cabin, and a kerosene tin full of silver ore. Some years later an employee of Ibrahim's great-grandson became obsessed with the legend of the silver reef and made many visits to the area to find it. According to Beatty's version of the tale in his *A Treasury of Australian Folk Tales and Traditions* (1960, p. 76), 'he ended his days there and was last seen in 1939 travelling with a treacherous tribe of wild natives in the Kimberley country'. *See also Gardiner's Gold; Lasseter's Reef; Lost Treasures*

SIMPLY AUSTRALIA

Online magazine established in 2001 to showcase Australian folklore and social history. *See also Australian Folklore; Folk Revival; Websites*

SIMPSON AND HIS DONKEY

John Simpson Kirkpatrick (1892–1915), under the name 'Simpson', was a stretcher-bearer with the 3rd Field Ambulance, Australian Army Medical Corps, on Gallipoli in the early weeks of the campaign. He was probably the first to use donkeys and mules from the ammunition trains to carry the wounded along the highly dangerous gullies for treatment. He was mortally wounded by Turkish sniper fire on 19 May 1915, aged 22. War correspondent C.E.W. Bean, and others, wrote adulatory articles about Simpson and his undoubted bravery which appeared in Australian and Maltese newspapers and made the man and the donkey an overnight national hero. However, as Peter Cochrane details in his book *Simpson and the Donkey* (1992) on Gallipoli, Simpson's fellow ambulance workers had no particular celebration of 'Simpson's' bravery; to the Anzacs he was just another soldier doing his duty. When subsequent drafts of troops landed at Gallipoli with words of wonder about Simpson, the original

Anzacs were amazed at all the attention given to the man in the Australian press. Since then, Simpson and his donkey have become firmly fixed in Anzac mythology through being taught to generations of schoolchildren and through the statue of him at the Australian War Memorial, Canberra. *See also* ANZAC, *Digger, Folklorism, Gallipoli*

'SIXTEEN THOUSAND MILES FROM HOME'

Nineteenth-century emigration ballad sung to a jaunty tune, telling of the hardships faced by migrants who must earn a living breaking stones for road sub-contractors. The song begins:

> *Oh, I'm sixteen thousand miles from home*
> *And my heart is fairly achin',*
> *To think that I should humble so*
> *To come out here stone breakin'...*

See also Folk Songs; Migration Lore

SKIPPING

Skipping, or 'skippy' as it is more commonly known in Australia, is both an individual and group pastime for children, usually of primary-school age. For group skipping, a light rope of about three metres (nine to ten feet) is turned at varying speeds by a child at each end. Different games are accompanied by such popular chants as:

> *Teddy bear, teddy bear, go upstairs;*
> *Teddy bear, teddy bear, say your prayers.*
> *Teddy bear, teddy bear, say goodnight,*
> *Teddy bear, teddy bear, turn out the light.*

Any child missing or touching the rope is immediately 'out', and, depending on the game, may have to replace one of the rope turners. The rope may be shortened for a fast sequence such as Pepper, and two ropes may be used for French and English or Double Dutch. Skipping was played by both boys and girls in the nineteenth century, but is largely a girls' game today. Individual skipping has similar games and rhymes to group skipping, and may use a commercially produced skipping rope with wooden (or plastic) handles. The American term 'jump rope' is not in common use in Australia. *See also Australian Children's Folklore Collection; Children's Folklore*

SKIPPY, THE BUSH KANGAROO

A television program popular with children and families in the 1960s and 1970s, its central character was a gifted kangaroo named 'Skippy' who solved problems and rescued lost children in a similar manner to the wonder dog, Lassie. The program's constant reruns in Australia and overseas have ensured that Skippy the Bush Kangaroo has become an Australian icon and has passed into Australian mythology. *See also Kangaroo; National Icons; Skips*

SKIPS

Based on the popular television character *Skippy the Bush Kangaroo*, the term skips, or skippies, to mean Anglo-Australians is thought to have been popularised by 'non-Anglo Australians' as a means of fighting back against their own common labelling as 'wogs'. *See also Kangaroo, Racist Folklore*

SLEDGING *See Barracking*

SLEEPOVER

Children from about eight years of age may take part in a sleepover, an overnight social visit to a friend's house. A sleepover is essentially a group activity, so that often more than one visitor is required. These are often associated with birthdays. A more organised sleepover may also involve indoor overnight camping in a Scout or Brownies hall, or at school. Older teenagers and even adults may take part in more spartan outdoor sleepovers, usually to raise funds for the homeless, Community Aid Abroad or other charities supporting the disadvantaged. *See also Children's Folklore; Customs; Family Folklore*

SLOUCH HAT, THE

Usual name for a well-known World War I digger yarn in which a slouch hat (the characteristic broad-brimmed rabbit-felt uniform hat of the Australian digger) is seen floating on the mud. On investigation it is found that there is a digger underneath the hat. A rescue attempt is made but after about ten minutes of trying to get the mud-bound digger out he says, 'It's no good. I've still got me feet caught in the stirrups.' This is an

Australian version of an internationally distributed folk tale. *See also Digger; Folk Humour; Folk Tales; Yarn*

SMOKER, SMOKE NIGHT

A usually all-male evening involving dinner, alcohol, speech-making, toasting and performances of various kinds, sometimes risqué. Smoke nights were especially popular in the 1920s and 1930s, particularly with returned soldiers. They persisted into the 1940s and 1950s when they were largely superseded by the 'Prawn Night', a social occasion to which women were also invited. *See also Customs; Foodways; Prawn Night*

SMOKO

The Australian-originated occupational custom of breaking from work long enough to roll and smoke a cigarette and, often, brew a billy of tea. The term is first noted in print in 1865, but the custom is no doubt considerably older, the practice beginning as an unsanctioned halt to work, though it has now also become institutionalised in the 'tea-break' or 'morning/afternoon tea'. Today, the American term 'take ten' may be used, or even 'take five', although the actual amount of time mentioned should not be taken literally. *See also Customs; Work Lore*

SOUTHERLY BUSTER

Folk name for the cool and strong southerly breeze that blows through the south-east coastal regions of New South Wales. First documented in 1850, and certainly older in folk usage. *See also Brickfielder; Cockeye Bob; Eco-Lore; Folk Speech; Fremantle Doctor*

SOUTHERN CROSS, THE (flag)

Flag of white stars on a blue background representing the Southern Cross constellation, sewn by the wives and sweethearts of gold diggers for the Eureka Stockade uprising of 1854. The central icon of the Eureka Stockade mythology, the original Eureka flag is a national treasure held in the Ballarat Fine Art Gallery. Its design has been appropriated by various dissenting organisations, such as the Builders' Labourers' Federation (BLF) and, in more recent years, the Construction, Forestry, Mining and Energy Union (CFMEU). *See also Eureka Stockade; The, National Icons*

SPEEWAH (SPEEWA)

Mythical region somewhere in the outback where the trees are so tall they have to have hinges on their uppermost branches so they can be lowered to let sunlight in and the sheep are so large that the shearers have to carry ladders to shear them, and so forth. The equally mythic character 'Crooked Mick' is associated with the Speewah, as are a number of other characters, most of whom seem to owe their existence to literary rather than folkloric origins. Bill Wannan's book *Crooked Mick of the Speewah* was published in 1966. *See also Big Burrawong, Crooked Mick, Pastoral Industry Folklore, Shearers*

SPIDER FROM THE GWYDIR, THE

Subject of a popular verse recitation, probably from the early twentieth century, in which a drunken shearer is saved from losing 'fifty smackers of the best' from his wallet by a redback spider living in 'a rusty Jones's jam-tin' at the Moree (NSW) Showground. *See also Folk Poetry; Recitations*

SPLIT-NOSE JACK

A possibly fictional north Queensland Aboriginal outlaw who, in a song of this name collected in the 1890s, is murdered by a stockman. *See also Bushrangers, Folk Heroes, Indigenous Folklore*

SPORTS LORE

All sports have extensive folk traditions known to all or most of their participants and followers. These typically cluster around noted players or practitioners, past and present ('the Don' in cricket, Cazaly in Australian Football League, Les Darcy in boxing), the specialised language associated with the sport (including barracking and, latterly, sledging), customs, special events such as Grand Finals, dress (scarves, jumpers, hats) and regalia (large paper banners through which football players run, made by club supporters), anniversaries and, of course, the songs and chants of teams, clubs and codes. Nicknames such as 'The Shark' (Greg Norman, golfer) and 'Thorpedo' (Ian Thorpe, swimmer) are very common in most of the popular codes, as are team nicknames such as 'The Magpies', or just 'Pies' (Collingwood) and 'The Bulldogs' (Footscray) among Melbourne AFL clubs, a practice echoed in all football codes around the country. Communal crowd behaviour of mass joviality is also a feature of sporting tradition, such as the singing of club songs and 'the Mexican wave'. Anecdotes are also common in most sports, as in this example about the rivalry between Rugby League and Australian Football: In response to a question from a man who had never been to Melbourne about whether AFL was like rugby, a travelled northerner replied that the games were very different indeed. 'In AFL', he said, 'there are thirty-six players and thirty-six thousand umpires'. *See also Folk Sports; Melbourne Cup, The; Sports Weekend; Turf Lore*

SPORTS WEEKEND

A weekend gathering, usually held in the rural and outback areas of Australia, where competitive sports of all kinds are featured, along with socialising, eating, drinking and dancing. Sports weekends may often take on the character of the region in which they are held. In the Northern Territory, for instance, there may be spear-throwing competitions as well as football games. *See also Customs; Folk Sports; Sports Lore*

'SPRINGTIME IT BRINGS ON THE SHEARING, THE'

Well-known late nineteenth-century folk song existing in several versions, all probably derived from a poem by E.J. Overbury titled 'On the Wallaby Track', published in 1865, the chorus of which, in its most common version, is:

> Oh, the springtime it brings on the shearing
> And it's then you will see them in droves,
> To the west country stations all steering,
> Seeking a job off the coves. [bosses]

See also Bush Ballad; Folk Songs; Pastoral Industry Folklore; Shearers; Wallaby Track

STAG NIGHT

An all-male event usually involving drinking, smoking, gambling and perhaps risqué entertainment, such as a stripper. The term seems to be an American import. *See also Bucks' Night; Customs; Folk Speech; Smoke Night*

STAWELL GIFT, THE

Properly the Stawell (pron. 'Stall') Easter Gift. At each Easter since 1878 'the Melbourne Cup of Footrunning' has been held in what was originally the mining town of Stawell (Vic.). Initially a miners' holiday sports event and fete, the 'Gift' developed into a 130-yard professional handicap foot race involving prize money and considerable gambling. A rich body of lore and customs is associated with the race, including deception as to a runner's true form and other nefarious practices. *See also Customs; Sports Lore*

STIRRING THE POSSUM

'Stirring the possum', 'shit-stirring' or simply 'stirring' is an Australian term for a custom strongly, though not solely, associated with work. Stirring can take a variety of forms, including rumour-mongering, bantering, horseplay and various expressions and actions designed to good-humouredly vex one's co-workers or, just as frequently though not necessarily so good-humouredly, the management. Stirring is essentially provocation of one kind or another. *See also Customs, Folk Speech, Work Lore*

STONE, WILLY

Historical jockey whose song celebrates his bravery and laments his death in a racing accident in Brisbane when his mount, Crusoe, fell on him and killed him in December 1892:

> *With the coffin and the wreath they've laid him down to sleep*
> *Where the lilies will be growing o'er his grave.*
> *In the graveyard at Toowong where the river rolls along*
> *Sleeps Willy Stone, so trusted, true and brave.*

See also Disasters; Folk Heroes; Nolan, Arthur; Robinson, Alec

STORYTELLING

Storytelling is one of the most ancient of folk arts, and is still alive and well in the twenty-first century, whether in the home ('tell us about when you were a little girl, grandma') or in organisations devoted to this pastime, such as the Storytelling Guild. At a weekend of storytelling organised by the National Library of Australia in 1997, Ernest Grant, an elder of the Jirrbal tribe in North Queensland, spoke of storytelling in traditional Aboriginal culture as 'a much-loved way of teaching our children'. Children will ask for the same story again and again, he said, and with each retelling, particularly as children grow older, the story is embellished and becomes more complex, to teach increasingly adult moral lessons. Stories play this role in non-Aboriginal societies too, and the almost universal story of 'the boy who cried wolf' is a classic, if simple, example.

Although some Australian adults may tell their children stories from the classic 'fairy tale' repertoire, such as *Cinderella* and *Little Red Riding Hood*, most storytelling between adults is in the shorter mode which Australians call the yarn. Yarns are often about personal experiences, and are presented as entertainment or to instruct the listeners. A popular form of cautionary tale is the urban legend, usually presented as true, and as having happened to 'a friend of a friend'. One urban legend which periodically appears in the media concerns the couple who receive two free tickets to the theatre – and return home to find their house has been burgled.

John Thompson from the National Library had the last words at the National Library's 1997 storytelling weekend. It was, he said, highly significant that the first major recommendation in *Bringing Them Home*, the Report of the National Inquiry into the Separation of Aboriginal and Torres Strait Islander Children from their Families (1997), concerned stories. The Report recommended a major oral history project to record and preserve the stories of indigenous people and others involved in the removal of children. This oral history project, the largest ever undertaken in Australia, was carried out by the National Library of Australia. It has published a book about the stories titled *Many Voices* (2002). *See also* Folk Tales; Urban Legends; Yarns

STRING GAMES

String games are sometimes known generically as 'cat's cradle', although this is only one of many complex figures which Australian children make with a piece of string looped between their two hands. Other popular figures are parachute, Eiffel Tower, cat's whiskers and cup and saucer. String figures are a popular pastime in many parts of the world, in Europe and Asia, from Africa to the Inuit (Eskimo) and are made by adults as well as children. This writer mentioned string games in a seminar with senior arts administrators in Korea in 1999 – the next day, with the help of some string, Vietnamese, Japanese, Korean and Zimbabwean women were all digging into their childhood memories to produce elaborate string figures. Australian Aboriginal people, both adults and children, make string figures, traditionally using string made from twisted hair or bark fibre. Both males and females play string games, although in Australia they are most commonly a girls' pastime. Some expert practitioners, both children and adult entertainers such as Australia's Kel Watkins, produce amazing performances involving moving elements – all with a piece of string. *See also Australian Children's Folklore Collection, Children's Folklore*

'STRINGYBARK COCKATOO, THE'
Nineteenth-century bush ballad in which a 'broke alluvial miner' finds work reaping for a stringybark cockatoo farmer whose penny-pinching, harsh treatment and eventual jealousy drives the miner away. A song very much in the tradition of the tough, miserly 'cockatoo farmer', such as 'The Cockies of Bungaree'. *See also Bush Ballad; Cocky; 'Cockies of Bungaree, The'; Goldrush Lore*

STROUD INTERNATIONAL BRICK AND ROLLING PIN THROWING CONTEST
Held in New South Wales on the third Saturday in July. Since 1960, the towns of Stroud, UK and Stroud, Oklahoma, USA, have held a brick-throwing competition. Both the British and the American Strouds have large brickmaking industries. In 1961, Stroud in Canada and Stroud in NSW were invited to join the competition. The Australian Stroud is known for the manufacture and export of wooden rolling pins and so, in 1962, throwing rolling pins was added as a ladies' event. The events are held more or less at the same time in each location, with results being telephoned to each of the four participating Strouds. The Australian Stroud also features a procession, dancing, music, tug-o-war and woodchopping on the day itself. *See also Customs; Folklorism*

STUDENT REVELS
A European tradition dating from the establishment of the mediaeval university in which students, usually on some significant date or period in the academic or ecclesiastical calendar, do not attend classes, but drink, sing, and generally indulge themselves in horseplay and misrule. In their modern, comparatively mild Australian form such events may be associated with the university's, school's or college's foundation date, and

often involve collecting for charity. *See also Customs; Leavers; Prosh; Schoolies' Week; Work Lore*

STUMP SPEECH

A form of recitation that humorously parodies the inanities mouthed by many politicians, usually employing rhyme, rhythm and other poetic devices within a prose framework. *See also Folk Humour; Folk Poetry; Recitations*

'SUCH IS LIFE'

Reputedly Ned Kelly's last words when he was hanged on 11 November 1880. It is more likely that, if anything, he said, 'I suppose it had to come to this.' However, the more resonant 'Such is life' has become part of Australian folklore and literature, given wide currency through Joseph Furphy's novel of that name (1903). *See also Folk Speech; Kelly, Ned; Lowry, Fred; National Icons*

SUKKOTH

Taking place in late September–October, *Sukkoth* or *Succoth* ('Rejoicing in the Law') is an eight-day festival commemorating the wandering of the Jewish people in the desert after their escape from Egypt, and also celebrating the northern hemisphere harvest. Family and communal meals are shared with friends, with fruit often being served as a symbol of the festival's agricultural significance. The last day of *Sukkoth* is a day of joy, *Simchat Torah*, to mark the ending of the Reading of the Law for the year and the starting again from the Book of Genesis. The folkloric aspects of this Jewish occasion include the giving of sweets, cakes and fruit to children who form a procession, carrying flags topped with apples. *See also Customs, Religious Lore*

'SUNSHINE RAIL DISASTER, THE'

On 20 April 1908 two passenger trains collided at Sunshine station just outside Melbourne. The trains, from Ballarat and Bendigo, were packed with Easter holiday-makers. Forty-four were killed and over four hundred injured. A ballad about the incident was still current in the 1960s, with the chorus:

> If those trains had only run
> As they should, their proper time,

There wouldn't have been a disaster
At a place they call Sunshine.
If those brakes had only held
As they did a few hours before,
There wouldn't have been a disaster
And a death-roll of forty-four.

See also Disasters; Granville Rail Disaster, The

SUPERNATURAL, THE
Folk beliefs may include some deference to supernatural and paranormal phenomena, and many individuals will talk about experiences including premonitions, ESP (Extra Sensory Perception), and extra-sensory communication between closely related people such as twins, or experiences of predicting death or danger involving close family members. Clairvoyants become the subject of attention when terrifying or inexplicable incidents capture the attention of the public and the authorities, such as the disappearance of the three Beaumont children in Adelaide in 1966. In-between times clairvoyants write columns and give advice in some women's magazines. See also Evil Eye, The; Folk Belief; Satanism; UFOs; Witchcraft

SUPERSTITIONS See Folk Belief

SWAG See Swagman

SWAGMAN
A swagman is an itinerant bush worker, usually found travelling country roads on foot in search of work, who 'carries a swag', 'humps a drum' or 'bluey' or, more rarely, 'waltzes matilda'. The swag is generally a roll of blankets, equipment and a few personal belongings, usually completed with a billy. A favoured and sometimes romantic character of bush lore, swagmen and swag feature in song, verse and yarn, and are the iconic focus of the song 'Waltzing Matilda'. The swagman, or 'swaggie', is rarely, but still occasionally, seen today. See also Battler; Folk Speech; Great Depression, The; National Icons; Tank Messages, Waltzing Matilda

SWEEPS

Many people who otherwise never gamble will take part in the workplace 'sweep', usually organised by a volunteer (or conscript), especially at Melbourne Cup time. For a fixed and usually modest sum of money, each participant takes the chance of winning the whole pot, or a major part of it. In a Melbourne Cup sweep, horses are allocated to participants by drawing names out of a hat. In many sweeps with numerous participants, more than one person may win a horse, but this means a smaller share of the money available to the winners. *See also Melbourne Cup, The; Turf Lore*

SWEET ALICE *See Black Alice*

SWY *See Two-Up*

SYDNEYSIDERS

Today used to mean residents of Sydney, though in earlier times, probably from the mid-nineteenth century, the term could also mean non-Aboriginal people living in New South Wales. *See also Folk Speech*

T

TANK MESSAGES

Messages, often in verse, left by overlanders and other outback travellers at tanks and waterholes. *See also 'Overlander(s), The'*

'TANTANOOLA TIGER, THE' *See Legendary Animals*

TAPESTRY

An ancient folk art, usually practised by women, tapestry involves constructing a pattern or picture with coloured threads stitched into a linen or other cloth base. Tapestries (and stitch size and thread density) may range from very small, such as in a *petit point* purse, glasses case or footstool cover, to medium size such as a *gros point* chair seat, cushion or wall-hanging (often framed), to very large, such as the wall-sized tapestry, based on an Arthur Boyd painting, which hangs in Australia's new Parliament House in Canberra. The last was made by the Victorian Tapestry Workshop, a world-renowned team enterprise in Melbourne which has produced large tapestries for public places including the National Library in Canberra and Melbourne Airport. These tapestries may be considered fine art, but the process of tapestry making is a time-honoured folk craft, and many individuals will make a tapestry at some time during their lives, even if (as for this writer) once is enough. *See also Crafts, Women's Folklore*

TASMANIAN TIGER

A carnivorous marsupial known as the native 'Thylacine'. This striped wolf-like creature is probably the best known of a number of fabulous beasts, especially cats, populating Australian lore and legend. Unlike most other such animals, the Tasmanian tiger, or wolf, is known to have existed: the last known Tasmanian tiger died in captivity in Tasmania's Hobart Zoo in September 1936. Although it is now believed extinct, reported sightings, and searches, are regular occurrences. *See also Legendary Animals; Nannup Tiger, The; National Icons*

TASWEGIANS
Residents of Tasmania, c. mid-twentieth century. *See also Folk Speech; Regional Rivalries*

'TEN THOUSAND MILES AWAY'
In this London music hall song of the 1840s that became a folk song, a young man's sweetheart is transported 'ten thousand miles away'. He follows her 'taking a trip on government ship, ten thousand miles away'. Other related songs include 'A Thousand Miles Away', a late nineteenth-century overlanding song, and the slightly earlier 'Old Palmer River Song', in which the singer is bound for the Palmer River (Qld) gold strikes which began in 1873. *See also Goldrush Lore; Migration Lore; Transportation Ballads*

TENTERFIELD HIGHLAND GATHERING
Since 1888 this festival of Scots highland music, dance, games, sports, crafts and traditions, held on the second Saturday in February at Tenterfield (NSW), has been an important highlight of the year for Scots-Australians. A similar event has been held at the same time in Ross (Tas) since 1958. *See also Annual Highland Gathering, Customs, Folk Sports, Maclean Highland Gathering*

THANKSGIVING
An important American occasion, observed in Australia by many Americans, and Australians with American connections, on the fourth Thursday in November. The first Thanksgiving feast was held in Massachusetts by the 'Pilgrim Fathers' in 1621, to celebrate their first bountiful harvest after a winter of starvation and sickness. Traditional Thanksgiving food is turkey, cranberry sauce, corn, sweet potatoes and dishes such as pumpkin pie. The date on which Thanksgiving was celebrated varied considerably until fixed by Congress in 1941 as the fourth Thursday in November. *See also Customs; Migration Lore*

THATCHER, CHARLES
Popularly known as 'The Goldfields Minstrel' and 'The Colonial Minstrel', Charles Thatcher (1831–78) migrated from England to Australia in 1853. He was well known on both the Australian and New Zealand goldfields, specialising in humorous parodies of popular songs, his new lyrics reflecting the lifestyle and attitudes of the gold diggers.

Many of his songs passed into folk tradition, including 'The Chinaman' and 'Look Out Below'. *See also Digger; Goldrush lore*

THEODORE, 'RED TED'

Folk name of E. G. Theodore (1884-1950), Labor Premier of Queensland from 1919 to 1925, and subsequently a federal MP and Treasurer who was noted both for his radical reforms of the Queensland political system and for his radical economic prescriptions during the Great Depression. *See also Folk Heroes; Great Depression; Labor Lore; Political Lore*

THUNDERBOLT

The bushranger hero Frederick Wordsworth Ward was born in Windsor, (NSW), in or around 1836. A bushman and stockman of high calibre, Ward was imprisoned for horse-stealing in 1856 and sentenced to prison on Cockatoo Island, the gaol which was claimed to be escape-proof. In company with another inmate, highway robber Fred Britten (with whom 'Thunderbolt' is often confused in folklore), Ward escaped the island. The escapees, who had probably been assisted by Ward's lover, Mary Ann Bugg or Budd, stole clothing and headed north towards the New England area, where Ward officially began his career as a bushranger. Between then and his eventual shooting down by a trooper policeman in May 1870, 'Thunderbolt', 'Captain Thunderbolt' and 'Captain Ward', as he was variously known, managed to pursue a career of intermittent robbery and become a local hero. He was said to have handed money back to those whose need was greater than his, and ballads about him indicate that he was perceived by many to operate in a style and manner befitting the bushranging and highwaymen heroes of the past. One version of a toast or poetic introduction attributed to Ward himself goes:

> My name is Frederick Ward, I am a native of this isle;
> I rob the rich to feed the poor and make the children smile.

Folk traditions regarding 'Thunderbolt' include his alleged return of gold to some children at Moonbi, his hidden treasure, and the belief that he escaped death in 1870 and lived in either Australia, New Zealand, America or Canada – a delusion also attached to other bushranger heroes, including Dan Kelly. Stephan Williams has investigated the extensive legendry of this bushranger in *A Ghost Called Thunderbolt* (1987). *See also Black Mary; Bushrangers; Folk Heroes*

TIN KETTLING

Said to have originated in the Latin cultures, 'tin kettling' is an old marriage custom found in one form or another in many parts of the world, and is often referred to generically as the 'shivaree'. In France it may be known as a 'charivari', in the United States as a 'shivaree' and in other parts of Australia and New Zealand as 'tin canning', 'tin tattling' or 'rantanning'. Occurring mostly in rural areas, the essentials and purpose of the custom are universal. Generally, the people of the neighbourhood meet secretly and quietly at night outside the house of a newly married couple. At a given signal they throw rocks upon the roof, bang metal pots and make a dreadful din. Then the tin kettlers are invited inside the house for a drink, a snack, games, perhaps singing. This social custom is used both as a means of welcoming the new couple into the community and of introducing them to the other people who live in the area. It may also act as a friendly reminder that no matter how isolated and sparsely populated an area may be, there are always neighbours somewhere!

Tin kettling, in one or more of its many versions, is still practised in rural Western Australia, and was still being carried out in the 1960s among the German-descended communities of South Australia's Barossa Valley. There the custom was traditionally observed on the night before the wedding, and involved the firing of guns as well as other raucous forms of noise-making. The custom is known in Barossa Deutsch as *Polter Abend*, meaning 'noisy evening'. The term 'Tin kettling' or one of its variants, may also be used as a general term for going out and having a good time, as in 'going out on the rantan', as on New Year's Eve or other occasions. *See also Customs, German Folklore in Australia, Weddings*

TOASTS

Like many formal observances, toasting has its folkloric aspects. A toast is usually given at customary social gatherings such as weddings, funerals, birthdays and anniversaries. There is a large repertoire of traditional, mostly satirical, toasts. One well-known version still quite often heard is:

> *Hooray for Bruce*
> *Hooray at last*
> *Hooray for Bruce*
> *For he's a horse's arse!*

This may be followed by the response:

> Don't be mistaken
> Don't be misled
> He's not the horse's arse
> He's the horse's head.

Less well known these days are bush toasts, such as those associated with swagmen:

> A little bit of sugar and a little bit of tea
> And a little bit of flour for you and me
> A little bit of meat you can hardly see:
> It's a bugger of a life, by Jesus!

There are many other traditional toasts in circulation, and most nationalities have characteristic versions wishing health or luck to all present. *See also Customs; Folk Humour; Folk Poetry; Recitations*

'TOMAHAWKING FRED'

Parody of English music hall song 'Fashionable Fred the Ladies' Man'. Tomahawking Fred is a boastful shearer, though in reality his fast shearing cuts the sheep. Another version is titled 'Tambaroora Ted' and there is also a version known as 'The Big Gun Shearer' in which Fred claims he is both fast and clean and in which 'the tar boys say I never call for tar' (to seal any cuts made on the sheep). *See also Bush Ballads, Pastoral Industry Folklore, Shearers*

TOM'N'OPLESS

Trickster-like character who appears in a number of lengthy humorous stories collected in Sydney during the early 1980s. Tom usually outwits or dupes his unsuspecting victims into making themselves look foolish. *See also Folk Humour*

TOODLEMBUCK

A children's game which has passed into history, although many older adults will have memories of playing with the 'Toodlembuck', especially at Melbourne Cup time. Some schools banned the object, as 'encouraging gambling'. Made from a wooden cotton reel and a piece of cardboard cut into a disc or octagon and threaded onto a wooden butcher's skewer, the device was spun with string like a top. The cardboard disc or octagon was divided into segments and each labelled with, say, the name of a horse running in the Melbourne Cup. The segment on which the Toodlembuck came to rest denoted the winner. Children (mainly boys) would bet on the result, sometimes with cherry bobs (cherry stones), and a fine collection of cherry bobs was much prized. See also Australian Children's Folklore Collection; Children's Folklore

TOOTH FAIRY, THE

The 'tooth fairy' seems to be a relatively recent extension of an ancient and widespread belief that it is necessary to properly dispose of a tooth to avoid – unspecified – bad luck. The money paid for the child's milk tooth is an inducement to the child to deliver the tooth to the parents for proper disposal or safekeeping.

The tooth fairy exists in mainland Italian tradition and in Sicily, and while not traditional to Greece, the custom is making some inroads into modern Greek culture. In Maltese tradition the tooth is buried in a flower pot, and in some parts of Germany it is placed beneath a stone. The Australian practice is generally to leave the tooth overnight either under the child's pillow or beside the bed in a glass of water, in one of which locations the child finds payment in the morning, left by the fairy in return for the tooth. The tooth fairy was known in English-language tradition during the 1920s and may well in fact be of nineteenth-century origin, though L. Kanner's Folklore of the Teeth (1928), an otherwise extensive international survey of the various customs involving the casting away of milk teeth, makes no reference to the tradition. See also Children's Folklore; Customs; Family Folklore; Folk Belief

TOP ENDERS

Residents of the 'Top End' – the northern part of the Northern Territory, the north of Western Australia and Far North Queensland. Probably early twentieth century. See also Folk Speech; Regional Rivalries

TOPPING OUT

A custom still observed in many parts of Europe, as well as in Australia, 'topping out' is a ceremony that takes place at the end of large building projects. When the job is complete, it is customary for a tree, a branch or other piece of greenery to be hoisted to the top of the building.

Sometimes this is lashed to the highest point and all who have been involved with the project will celebrate with an alcoholic drink. While the greenery is a traditional element of this custom, often only the drinking aspect is retained nowadays. *See also Customs; Work Lore*

'TOWNSVILLE COUGAR, THE' *See Legendary Animals*

TRAD & NOW
The Australian folk music magazine, established 2002.

TRANSPORTATION BALLADS
Songs about the transportation of convicts from Britain. Generally composed in Britain, though many were transmitted to, and sung in, Australia. Some typical examples include 'Judges and Juries', 'Johnny Troy', 'Van Diemen's Land', 'The Black Velvet Band' and 'Maggie May'. The street ballad form of the transportation ballads had a continuing influence on the development of later folksong, especially the bush ballad and other forms of popular versification. Important studies and anthologies of such songs have included Geoffrey Ingleton's *True Patriots All* (1952), Ron Edwards' *The Convict Maid* (1985/7) and *The Transport's Lamentation* (1988), and Hugh Anderson's *Farewell to Judges and Juries* (2000). *See also 'Black Velvet Band, The'; Bushrangers, Convict Lore, 'Convict Maid, The'; Frank the Poet, 'Isle de France, The'; Treason Ballads*

TRASH AND TREASURE *See Markets*

'TRAVELLING DOWN THE CASTLEREAGH'
Also known as 'A Bushman's Song' in the verse version by A. B. ('Banjo') Paterson. An often-collected nineteenth-century song celebrating the itinerant lifestyle of the bush worker who is always moving 'further out' at 'the old jig-jog'. Finally, he gives up on civilisation altogether, saying:

> *Farewell, I must be going, I've a long way to go*
> *To where they drink artesian water from a thousand feet below.*
> *I'll meet the overlanders with their cattle coming down,*
> *Then work a while and make a pile and have a spree in town...*

Usually sung to variants of the humorous Irish song 'Pat from Mullingar'. *See also Bush, The; Irish Influences on Australian Folklore, Pastoral Industry Folklore; Paterson, A. B. ('Banjo')*

TREASON BALLADS
A group of songs believed by their singers and others to bring legal sanction due to their supposedly subversive sentiments. Various songs are said to be 'treasonous', including 'The Wild Colonial Boy', among others. No legislation outlawing such songs has yet been discovered. There are similar folk beliefs about songs elsewhere, including Ireland ('The Wearing of the Green' and 'The Rising of the Moon', to mention two), and in the British Army ('McCafferty') and the Royal Navy. *See also Bush Ballads; Folk Belief; Folk Songs*

TREE OF KNOWLEDGE, THE
Ghost gum at Barcaldine (Qld), a meeting and speaking place for the town, beneath which many strike meetings were held during the early 1890s. In May 1891 several thousand striking shearers marched beneath the Southern Cross flag to protest working conditions and wages. Thirteen of the leaders were subsequently tried for conspiracy and gaoled. Said to be called 'the tree of knowledge' as a consequence of all that had passed beneath its branches, the tree has a central place in Labor lore. (There is also a 'tree of knowledge' in Darwin, though this has no direct link to the Labor movement.) *See also Eureka Stockade; The; Labor Lore; Political Lore; Southern Cross, The*

TRICK OR TREAT
'Trick or Treat' is an American Halloween custom that has become popular with Australian children since the 1970s. While the more developed aspects of Halloween common to Britain and the United States are not generally followed here, the practice of children dressing up in ghoulish costume and threatening the neighbours with a 'trick' if they are not given a 'treat' is well established. The custom is controversial for various reasons. Parents, having heard horror stories from America (and possibly urban legends) of children being given razor blades embedded in apples, or adulterated sweets, etc while trick or treating, are generally uneasy about it. Although most of these stories are unproven. Also, some neighbours do not take kindly to being disturbed by small ghosts and ghouls, or to the 'Americanisation' of Australian life.

The Christian church is decidedly antagonistic to such 'pagan' activities on the night of All Hallows, 1 and 2 November. *See also Customs; Halloween; Religious Folklore*

TROUSSEAU

In earlier generations girls were expected to have a 'glory box', 'box' or 'hope chest' in which to store their own embroidery and other bought objects (such as fine linen and crystal) in preparation for marriage. The 'trousseau' particularly refers to clothing such as embroidered night-gowns, and girls could start 'collecting' whilst still in their teens, even if no young man was in sight (hence the 'hope'). Much of the handwork, such as the embroidered bed linen made by young women from villages in Italy or Greece, for example, was of a high order. Such fancy work may have been brought to Australia when the young woman came to meet a fiancé who had migrated earlier, or when she came, often having married by proxy, to join a man she had never met. The trousseau is an important element of the wedding traditions of many cultures, especially in Greece, where the bride's 'dowry', as it is often translated, may be worth considerable sums of money in total. The trousseau is also important in Turkish, Italian, Chinese, French, German and American traditions.

Today's changes in women's roles mean that young Australian working women do not have the leisure to produce elaborate handcraft, although some sewing, by hand and machine, may still be done. In addition, more young people are living together, and do not regard 'marriage' as the goal it once was. In recent years, though, some elements of the trousseau have tended to be created more or less at once through the 'shower' or 'kitchen tea', held sometime between the formal announcement of engagement and the wedding. *See Customs; Engagement/Betrothal; Family Folklore; Shower Tea; Weddings*

TURF LORE

The folklore of horseracing, in its various forms, is rich and diverse, as might be expected in a country that is famous for enjoying a bet. The turf has its own language, or argot ('gee-gees', 'ring-in', 'mug punter'), legends and yarns of great – and not-so-great – horses, jockeys, punters, trainers and other characters, usually with equally colourful nicknames (Perce 'The Prince' Galea, 'Harry the Horse' and 'Hollywood George'), and an extensive body of folk belief involving luck. A number of folk songs including 'Arthur Nolan' and 'Tommy Corrigan' deal with horseracing, mainly tragedies in which jockeys and/or their mounts were killed. One racing identity, Edgar Britt, has been honoured in general folk speech with the use of his name in rhyming slang – an Edgar Britt is 'a shit'. The national obsession with the turf is reflected in one of our most significant customs, the Melbourne Cup, on which millions of Australians who do not usually bet will traditionally 'have a punt'. The legendry of the racehorse Phar Lap is yet another example of the power of the turf in Australian folk consciousness. *See also Horses; Horses' Birthday; Folk Belief; Melbourne Cup, The; National Icons; Phar Lap; Sports Lore; Sweeps*

TWO-UP

A popular and famous pastime, two-up is derived from a German gambling game (hence its folk name 'swy', from the German *zwei*, meaning two) where the player bets on which way two tossed coins will fall. A version of two-up was probably played by convicts transported to New South Wales in the late eighteenth century, but the modern form of the game became established during the late nineteenth century. The preferred game of World War I diggers, it has since been especially associated with popular notions of Australian identity and nationalism, with kits consisting of the two pennies and wooden 'kip' traditionally required for playing being sold as tourist souvenirs. Historically, in conjunction with alcohol, it has been an easy way for shearers, canecutters and other rural workers to be parted from their pay cheques at the end of a season. Normally illegal nowadays, the game is generally tolerated on Anzac Day and may be otherwise played only in government-controlled gaming premises, usually casinos. Unofficial two-up 'schools' may still exist around the country, and the game can generally be enjoyed at country events such as races and shows. An elaborate jargon has developed around what is a very simple gambling game, an indication of the extent to which two-up has been an important element of Australian folk culture for a very long time. *See also Anzac Day; Customs; Digger; Fair Go; German Influences on Australian Folklore; National Icons*

TYSON, JAMES ('HUNGRY')

Nickname of James Tyson (1819–1898), a wealthy squatter renowned for his meanness and dour manner, characteristics that feature in various yarns about him and in a poem by A.B. ('Banjo') Paterson. In one such yarn Tyson, rather than pay a ferryman's high fee, swims across the Murrumbidgee River. He is also commemorated in the folk phrase 'meaner than Hungry Tyson'. *See also Folk Humour; Folk Speech; Yarns*

U

UFOs

'Unidentified Flying Objects' have given rise to many stories and folkloric beliefs, both about flying objects in the sky and about terrestrial signs of the presence of UFOs, such as crop circles (unexplained circles cut in, say, a corn or wheat field). Many of these stories have been disproved, but the degree of conviction among believers is strong, and there are organisations (particularly in the United States) devoted to the subject. *See also Folk Belief*

ULURU

Uluru, also known as Ayer's Rock, the great stone monolith in central Australia, is one of Australia's foremost tourist attractions and an icon of considerable importance in Australia's folk beliefs. To many Australians, visiting Uluru is a once-in-a-lifetime pilgrimage to the very heart of Australia, although attitudes to 'The Rock' encompass many of Australians' contradictory attitudes towards Australian Aboriginality. *See also Chamberlain, Azaria; Pilgrimage*

URBAN LEGENDS

Urban legends are sometimes known as urban myths or contemporary legends. The first two labels, though popular, are slightly misleading, as this highly contemporary form of storytelling is not necessarily confined to urban centres, and some of the legends require rural settings. Contemporary legends differ from yarns, tall stories or jokes in that, rather than simply being told to entertain, they are usually told by people who believe them to be true, and usually are believed to have happened to an acquaintance of someone they know – the 'friend of a friend', or FOAF, as some folklorists have entitled this elusive source.

Jan Brunvand, of the University of Utah, is the world's best-known pioneer and researcher into contemporary legends, through books such as *The Vanishing Hitchhiker* (1981) and *The Choking Doberman* (1983). Brunvand has identified about 500 different legends with innumerable variations, and in 1990, in a personal communication with this writer, classified them into ten major categories, namely:

Legends about automobiles
Legends about animals
Horror legends
Accident legends
Sex and scandal legends
Crime legends
Business and professional legends
Legends about governments
Celebrity rumours and legends
Academic legends

The Australian filmmakers Nadia Tass and David Parker employed one legend – tongue in cheek – in their prize-winning film *Malcolm* (1986): the character Malcolm's unquestioning acceptance of it was used to illustrate his apparent simplicity to humorous effect.

This story is set on a lonely country road where a father and his child run out of petrol, and the father leaves the child to sleep in the car while he walks to a distant garage. All night the child hears a terrifying 'thump, thump' on the roof of the car, and later is rescued by the police, who warn the child not to look back. The child disobeys and sees his father's headless body thumping on the car roof, having been hung on a tree by the murderer, an escaped maniac from a nearby criminal asylum.

It is not hard to see the derivation of the instruction to not 'look back' from the classical Greek legend of Orpheus and Eurydice, or the Biblical story of Lot's wife. In all cases, the disobedient one suffers terrible consequences – Lot's wife is turned into a 'pillar of salt'. Contemporary legends incorporate the same fundamental themes as those in ancient mythology, such as death, violence, sex, obedience or transgression of society's norms. The modern stories, however, are generally firmly set in the present day (or if based on older stories, are updated in context), and are international in their circulation.

It is hard to identify a specifically Australian contemporary legend. Amanda Bishop, in *The Gucci Kangaroo* (1988), published the story of the travellers who knocked down a kangaroo with their car and, believing it to be dead, dressed it in one of their number's expensive sports coat – whereupon the kangaroo revived and thumped away, never to be seen again. Graham Seal's more recent book, *Great Australian Urban Myths* (1995), includes the story of 'The Exploding Dunny' – where a cigarette is thrown into a toilet which has mistakenly been disinfected with petrol. However, both writers acknowledge that these very Aussie-sounding stories have many international versions. Many stories gain currency in response to current events: recent Australian bushfires have seen a recurrence of the story about a man in a scuba diving outfit being found in a treetop in a national park after water-bombing planes had been in use – this story is also current in California.

As can be seen from Brunvand's categories, the origins of modern legends can be sought in society's preoccupations, fears and anxieties, including fears about new technology. Some current examples concern razor blades in water slides; used, AIDS-infected needles being found in cinema seats; babies (or pets) in microwave ovens; and cement mixers dumping cement into an alleged sexual transgressor's car.

One of the most common themes for urban legends concerns the dangers of hitchhiking, for both hitchhikers and drivers. A popular legend concerns the narrow escape of a (usually) female driver, who picks up a 'little old lady', luckily identifying 'her' in time as a male murderer/rapist, by 'her' unusually hairy hands or muscular wrists. In one version of this story a handbag is later found in the car, 'containing nothing but a large knife'.

As well as being transmitted orally, urban legends are frequently spread by journalists in newspapers and radio, and increasingly, over the Internet and by electronic mail. In addition to *Great Australian Urban Myths: Granny on the Roofrack* (1995), Graham Seal has published *Great Australian Urban Myths: The Cane Toad High* (2001). Bill Scott, who pioneered the study of urban legends in this country, has also published his collections in *The Long and the Short and the Tall* (1985) and *Pelicans and Chihuahuas and Other Urban Legends* (1996). Other folklorists, including Ron Edwards and Gwenda Davey, have also published on these intriguing modern folk expressions. *See also Folk Belief; Folk Tales; Satanism; Storytelling; Yarns*

V

VALENTINE'S DAY

Valentine's Day, February 14, is widely observed as the day for young and not-so-young lovers. Despite various theories linking Valentine's Day with the customs of ancient Greece and Rome and the martyrdom of a Christian named Valentine, scholars have found no evidence to link the modern Valentine's Day with the Roman, far less the Greek eras. The origins of the modern observance of Valentine's Day are in medieval France and England as an aristocratic expression of the doctrine of courtly love popular at that period. The custom has evolved and, probably in the nineteenth century became widely observed throughout English society, from where it was brought to Australia.

Here, as in other English-language versions of the custom, cards bearing traditional messages of love (sometimes insulting) are exchanged, or increasingly printed in the newspapers and on the World Wide Web. Gifts of flowers, sweets and so on are also given. Valentine's Day is a popular one for folkloric predictions about the future of one's love life and may be observed by the wearing of a yellow crocus, said to be the flower of Saint Valentine (a number of Christian martyrs have this name). Yellow birds seen flying on Valentine's Day are believed by some to be a good omen.

Valentine's Day is also observed widely in Japan.

VAN DIEMEN'S LAND

First European name for Tasmania, given by Dutch mariner Abel Tasman in 1642 in honour of Anthony Van Diemen, Governor-General of the Dutch East Indies. In folklore it is the most common title of an early nineteenth-century transportation ballad detailing the horrors and harshness of convict life at Port Arthur: 'If you knew the hardships we endure, you'd never poach again.' 'Van Diemen's Land', in one of its various versions or another, was frequently reprinted by the British broadside press and probably inspired a number of other broadsides on similar themes and using many of the same lines and similar plots, complete with inaccuracies of geography, flora and fauna. *See also Convict Lore, Transportation Ballads*

VANE, JOHN

Member of the Frank Gardiner–Ben Hall gang of bushrangers mentioned in ballads and lore. Vane was the only gang member to survive to a reasonable age. *See also Bushrangers; Gardiner, Frank; Hall, Ben*

VEGEMITE

A commercial product which has entered the folk tradition for reasons which are inexplicable except for the folklorist's usual explanation that 'if the folk take something to their hearts, it can become folk culture'. Vegemite has become an Australian icon, associated with Australian identity and used for symbolic purposes in various contexts, including the Office of Multicultural Affairs poster bearing the slogan 'It's as

Australian as Vegemite', and the popular Men at Work song 'I come from the land down under' (in which the singer, when not chundering, offers his listeners 'a Vegemite sandwich') that was revived for the Sydney Olympic Games in 2000. Vegemite's marketing strategy featured its benefits for children 'it puts a rose in every cheek', and like 'Aeroplane Jelly', the catchy theme song for its radio show – 'We're happy little Vegemites' – has made it memorable. Only Australians seem to consume it with gusto; many other nationalities regard it with horror, when not mistaking it for axle grease. *See Foodways; National Icons*

VICTORIAN FOLKLIFE ASSOCIATION

The Victorian Folklife Association was formed in 1991 to incorporate a number of separate folk organisations in the state. It has carried out a vigorous program promoting folklore in Australia, including a number of large conferences. Particularly significant were the 1994 National Folklife Conference, *Tradition and Tourism: the good, the bad and the ugly*, and the 2001 Congress of the International Society for Folk Narrative Research, whose meeting was hosted by the Victorian Folklife Association in Melbourne. As at late 2002, the future existence of the VFA is in doubt, due to the withdrawal of government financial support. *See also CHRONICLE*

VICTORIAN FOLK MUSIC CLUB, THE

Founded in 1959 to preserve and popularise Australia's folklore heritage of traditional songs, poetry and dance, and to encourage the composition of works in the folk idiom. *See also* CHRONICLE; *Folk Dance; Folk Revival*

VILLAGE SAINTS' PROCESSIONS

Some celebrations of the patron saints of various Italian, Maltese and Greek villages are continued in some locations throughout Australia every year. Often these events are the focus of major reunions of migrants (and their children) from the originating village or region. Typically, a statue of the saint is carried in procession around the town or suburb and is then taken to a local church, where it is blessed. A church service follows and there is usually a feast, accompanied by general merrymaking. The Feast of San Rocco, mounted by the Italian community in the Perth suburbs of Leederville, Mt Hawthorn and North Perth, is an example of this custom: a procession, followed by a service in St Mary's Church, Leederville takes place around November every second year. Another is the Blessed Virgin of the Rosary held in Donvale (Vic.). *See also Customs; Italian Folklore in Australia; Migration Lore;Religious Lore*

WAGGA RUG

A classic example of 'making do' in earlier generations of Australian life, the Wagga Rug was commonly made out of discarded clothing, blankets and other fabrics sewn onto chaff bags or other base fabric to provide a warm cover for a bed. The grandparents of one of the writers of this book had a relative who was a tailor, and the family made Waggas from the swatches of (woollen) sample fabrics he provided. Margaret Rolfe, writing in the *Oxford Companion to Australian Folklore* (1993), states that Wagga Rugs were not only made by the poorest people but by many who valued thrift. The name for the rugs seems to be clearly taken from the New South Wales town of Wagga Wagga (known within Australia as Wagga), a major wheat (and therefore chaff) producing area. *See also Crafts; Making Do; Quilts*

WAKES *See Funerals*

WALKABOUT

The term 'walkabout' is commonly used in Australia in various contexts: someone who has not been seen for a while (such as through going on holidays), for example, may be said to have 'gone walkabout'. The original term is from Aboriginal English. Dixon, Ramson and Thomas in their book *Australian Aboriginal Words in English* (1990, p. 215), in the section on 'Aboriginal objects and concepts in English', define 'walkabout' as follows:

> A journey on foot, as undertaken by an Aborigine in order to live in the traditional manner (especially one undertaken as a temporary withdrawal from white society). Originally a 'walkabout' referred to a hunting and gathering trip that would last from a few hours to a few days and involve return to the place of origin (often a semi-permanent camping place). 'To go walkabout' is to make such a journey.

The term 'walkabout', however, has also been used in Australia to denigrate Aboriginal people by implying a racist narrative about shiftlessness, unreliability and evasion of responsibility, usually in relation to jobs, characteristics which many non-Aboriginal Australians attribute to the indigenous population. These characteristics are only part of the denigration of Aboriginal people in Australia which underpins much of our troubled race relations and which expresses itself in a thousand different ways in Australian life. *See also Folk Speech; Racist Folklore*

WALLABY BRIGADE, THE

Term for itinerant bush workers carrying their swags in search of work. Also the title of a nineteenth-century bush song which, tongue-in-cheek, extols the rigours of this lifestyle and includes firing the fences of station-owners unwilling to provide the swagman with rations, and stealing sheep – 'You've only to sport your Dover [knife] and knock a monkey [sheep] over/That's cheap mutton on the Wallaby Brigade.' *See also Bush Ballads; Dover; Folk Speech; Red Steer, The; Swagman*

WALLABY TRACK, THE

To 'go on the wallaby' or 'on the wallaby track' was a colonial phrase for taking to the road in the manner of a swagman, usually in search of work. A poem titled 'On the Wallaby Track' was composed and published by E.J. Overbury in 1865, variations of which have coalesced into a related and often-collected song usually known as 'The Springtime it Brings on the Shearing'. A number of other folksongs turn on the term, including 'The Wallaby Brigade', emphasising the hardships and delights of the itinerant life. A song titled 'Australia's on the Wallaby' is very similar to Henry Lawson's famous radical poem 'Freedom on the Wallaby' (published 1891), and is often sung to the same tune: possibly it formed the basis of Lawson's poem. *See also Bush, The; Folk Speech; 'Springtime it brings on the Shearing, The'; Swagman; Wallaby Brigade, The*

WALTZING MATILDA

Poem written by A. B. ('Banjo') Paterson in 1895 on Dagworth Station near Winton (Qld). Allegedly based on recent incidents in the area, and set to the music of a Scottish tune known as 'Thou (or 'The') Bonnie Wood of Craigielea', versions of the song quickly passed into Queensland oral tradition. In 1903 the song, with a new musical setting of the original tune by Marie Cowan and slightly adapted lyrics, was used as an advertisement for Billy Tea and became more widely known in its most popular version. Since then the song has become Australia's unofficial national anthem. *See also Folklorism; Jolly Swagman, The; National Icons; Paterson; A. B. ('Banjo'); Swagman*

WAR LORE

The folklore of Australia at war is extensive, including songs and yarns of conflicts in New Zealand (1863–1872), the Sudan (1884), and South Africa (1899–1902). The Dardanelles campaign and the combined Australian and New Zealand actions on Gallipoli began a rich body of tradition associated with the figure of the 'digger' (although this word was not used with its present significance until 1917). From the beginning, the First AIF (Australian Imperial Force) was an intermingling of bush and city men who created a body of folk speech, verse and song that depended heavily on the nineteenth-century traditions of pioneering and rural life and fused these with the traditions of the city. Digger lore is an amalgam of bush slang, bush ballad style, bush yarns and the culture of the urban centres, especially that usually associated with the larrikin. The tradition of anti-authoritarianism, egalitarianism, toughness and sardonic humour associated with the digger ever since is a wartime extension of the bushman hero of the previous century. Subsequent conflicts have extended and deepened this tradition of the volunteer footsoldier.

As well as digger lore and its powerful connection to national mythology, there is also a body of home front traditions. In World War I these dealt mainly with political events surrounding the conscription issue. In World War II there was a good deal of home front lore relating to the American presence in Australia, including 'When They Send the Last Yank Home', a parody of the popular song 'When They Sound the Last All-Clear'. The Korean War generated relatively little folklore, but the Vietnam War continued the irreverent traditions of digger lore with songs like 'The Tunnel Tigers', about underground tunnel fighting, and 'Christmas in Vietnam', a classic example of soldiers complaining. The Vietnam War also generated some home front lore related mainly to the anti-war movement, including versions of Lyall Sayer's song about the F-111 aeroplane. Subsequent conflicts have no doubt generated their own folklore, though this remains largely uncollected at present. There has often been a strong connection between soldier slang and folk speech, with terms and idioms moving from the civilian to the military sphere and vice versa – especially, though not exclusively, during the two world wars. Wartime experiences have also generated items of material culture such as the Changi Quilts, made by female prisoners of the Japanese during World War II, and beliefs about such items as the Lone Pine Seedlings from the Gallipoli campaign of World War I. *See also ANZAC; Digger; Folk Speech; Gallipoli; Lone Pine Seedlings; National Icons*

'WATERFORD PANTHER, THE' *See Legendary Animals*

WATTLE

Folk name of the native plant species *Acacia*. Wattle is a popular Australian icon, and is also favoured in folksong and popular verse for romantic and sentimental death scenes. Possibly due to this association, some people believe it is unlucky to have wattle in the house. It appears in the bush song 'The Stockman's Last Bed':

> *They laid him where wattles*
> *Their sweet fragrance shed,*
> *And the tall gumtrees shadowed*
> *The stockman's last bed.*

See also Eco-lore, Folk Belief, National Icons

WEATHERLORE

The extensive traditions relating to the weather, and especially to predicting it, are an important element of bush lore and of sailor lore. Beliefs about weather may involve sayings and ditties of the type 'Red sky at night, sailor's delight'; signs and portents contained in the activities of birds, snakes, ants, and other animals and insects; and the appearance of natural phenomena such as rings or haze around the moon. In farming communities, such beliefs may also be related to beliefs about the right time to plant or harvest crops, often involving the phases of the moon. The late Nancy Keesing collected a good deal of such Australian lore, published as *Just Look Out the Window* (1985). Some folk sayings relate to the climate in particular locations: for example, changeable Melbourne is said to have 'four seasons in one day'. By contrast, the Northern Territory is often held to have four unique seasons in a year, namely the Build-Up, the Wet, the Knock-em-Downs, and the Dry. *See also Ants; Cockatoos; Eco-lore; Folk Belief*

WEBSITES

The growth of the Internet since the mid-1990s has led to the development of many folklore-related websites. These include pages and sites established and maintained by individuals with a particular interest in an aspect of folklore, such as urban legends, folk music or dance, as well as resource sites such as Folklore Australia. Organisations involved in the collection, study, preservation or performance and dissemination of folklore, plus the various folk festivals and state and national organisations such as the Folk Federations, the Folk Alliance Australia and the Australian Folklore Network also maintain sites, as do major cultural institutions such as the National Library of Australia and those universities with an involvement in folklore studies. *See also DOCUMENTATION OF AUSTRALIAN FOLKLORE; Simply Australia*

WEDDINGS

The marital union of, usually, a man and a woman is a life cycle event celebrated in all cultures and is the focus of considerable folklore. This begins with beliefs and customs that may be observed in the lead-up to the wedding day. For example, in many Christian or European societies it is widely believed to be unlucky for the bride and groom to see each other for twenty-four hours – sometimes more, sometimes less – before the wedding. The wedding car may be decorated with streamers and also, of late, with a Barbie Doll, dressed in the same material as the bridesmaids' dresses, attached to the bonnet. Other mascots and forms of decoration are also common, including the traditional white ribbons.

Beliefs and customs relevant to the wedding day itself vary widely. In Lithuanian tradition, for instance, it is a popular custom to prevent the bride and groom from entering the reception. The groom must convince the guardians at the door and the guests that he and his bride should be allowed in. Gifts are offered as an inducement. Barring the way to the fully wed state, with all its attendant rights and obligations, is a widespread facet of wedding customs, a rite of passage that marks the transition of the newlyweds from unmarried to married. Barring customs are also reported in British, American, Breton, Japanese and Carpathian tradition.

There are many interesting and colourful wedding customs observed in different ethnic and religious groups in Australia, such as stamping on a drinking glass (Jewish), linking ribbon coronets worn by bride and groom (Greek), the groom arriving at the wedding on horseback (Indian), and sugared almonds being given to wedding guests (Greek, Italian and many other ethnic groups). The custom of giving sugared almonds has also been reported in France, Wales, England, Scotland, Israel and Belgium. In other places, raw nuts are considered appropriate food and/or gifts at weddings, a continuation of the widespread association of nuts and fertility, though in Italian tradition the nuts are generally said to symbolise good luck.

Almost always, an Australian wedding ceremony is followed by a reception, supper or party for the newlyweds and their friends and families. Often held at a reception centre or other public facility hired for the purpose, wedding receptions may also take place in the home of the bride or groom. Characteristic elements include music, dance, song, food and drink, and speeches and toasts by the father of the bride, best man and groom. It is the duty of the best man to read out telegrams, letters, cards and faxes from absent well-wishers on this occasion. In the past, these messages may have been of a playfully suggestive nature, though this feature seems to have faded from the contemporary observance of the custom. The gifts to the newlyweds are usually displayed at the reception.

It is important to note the dramatic changes in marriage practices in Australia even in the last twenty years, and their consequent effect on wedding customs. These changes have been documented by the Australian Bureau of Statistics, and the 2001 Census shows changes such as the rise in non-church weddings. Civil celebrants performed 53% of marriages in 2001, and of all marriages, 32% are estimated to end in divorce. In the same census, 72% of couples stated that they had cohabited before marriage, although this does not stop many of these couples eventually celebrating a legal marriage, sometimes with their children present, in simple or elaborate ceremonies which may be devised by the bride and groom themselves. Another marked change in Australian society is the high rate of intermarriage between couples of different ethnic origins. All of these changes suggest that folklorists, with other social commentators, need to be cautious about making pronouncements about marriage, or weddings, in Australia. *See also Customs; Engagement/Betrothal; Family Folklore; Foodways; Going Away; Religious Lore; Women's Folklore*

WEDDING RECEPTION *See Weddings*

WESTERN AUSTRALIAN FOLKLORE ARCHIVE

Founded in 1985 at Curtin University of Technology, Perth (then the Western Australian Institute of Technology), this archive has considerable holdings of West Australian and some other materials. It aims to collect, preserve, research and disseminate the state's folk traditions through publication and community activity. It is the only state folklore archive in Australia and the only one that collects all forms of folklore. *See also CHRONICLE*

WETTING THE BABY'S HEAD

A common Australian folk custom to celebrate the birth of a new baby, usually among male family members or friends, by the consumption of alcohol. This may involve a drink at home, at the pub, or a modest party after a formal christening in a church, usually at the home of the child's parents or other relative. *See also Christening; Customs; Family Folklore; Grog*

WHALER

A 'whaler' was a swagman who followed the courses of creeks and rivers. 'Whalers' and 'whaling' are referred to in a number of bush ballads, including 'Three Little Johnny-Cakes'. Each major river system of eastern Australia had a local term for these men, including 'Murray Whalers', 'Darling Whalers' and 'Murrumbidgee Whalers'. Not to be confused with the now-obsolete 'Waler', being short for a person from New South Wales, and 'waler', an early term meaning an Australian (or New South Wales) horse bred for the army. *See also Folk Speech; Swagman*

WHITE WOMAN OF GIPPSLAND, THE

This legend concerns a white woman supposedly captured by Aboriginal people in Gippsland, Victoria, formerly known as Gipps Land. It is a variant of many frontier stories from different countries about captivity of whites by indigenous groups such as North American Indians. The captive white woman legend became widespread in Victoria (then the settlement of Port Phillip) from about 1840, being spread by explorers and settlers in Gippsland such as the land agent Angus McMillan. It may be interpreted as an attempt to promote a view of Aborigines as fearsome and brutal, justifying the taking of Aboriginal lands by white settlers.

Despite both private and public-funded rescue expeditions in 1846 and 1847, no trace of a captive white woman was found.

The legend has been maintained in circulation by occasional newspaper reports or recapitulations throughout the nineteenth and twentieth centuries. The story has also been continued in numerous literary and artistic versions, up until the present day. Sidney Nolan's 1945 painting 'Gippsland Incident' is a notable work interwoven with this legend, and Liam Davison's 1994 book *The White Woman* is a critical account of frontier violence and colonial Australia. In 2001 Melbourne University Press published Julie Carr's book *The Captive White Woman of Gipps Land: In pursuit of the legend. See also Folk Belief; Local Lore*

WHITSUN

The third most important festival of the Christian year, Pentecost or Whitsuntide (celebrated by the Catholic, Protestant and Armenian Apostolic churches in mid to late May) is a moveable feast marking the founding of the Christian church. Pentecost – fifty days after Easter – is believed to be the day when the Holy Spirit descended upon the Twelve Apostles and sent them to preach the word of God.

In Britain, Pentecost was also known as Whitsuntide, and Whitsunday in England was an important day for baptisms, feasting, fairs, games and general festivity. Whit Monday and Whit Tuesday were observed in Melbourne until well into the 1880s and are still observed by some Australians today. In Ireland, Whitsunday is a particularly unlucky day, associated with the malign activities of fairies. *See also Customs; Religious Folklore*

WIDGEGOARA JOE

Hero of a song also called 'The Backblocks Shearer' in which Joe laments that despite the many sheds he has shorn and the celebrated shearers he has worked with, 'I never became a gun' (fastest shearer in the shed). Probably from the early 1890s. *See also Pastoral Industry Folklore; Shearers; Work Lore*

WIGWAM FOR A GOOSE'S BRIDLE *See Children's Folklore*

WILD COLONIAL BOY, THE

Largely fictional character, based to a considerable extent on earlier traditions surrounding the historical bushranger Jack Donohoe, who figures in an Australian ballad celebrating the activities of an outlaw hero type. The defiance and bravery of the 'Wild Colonial Boy' are expressed in the lines that claim that he would rather die than 'live in slavery, bound down with iron chains'. This ballad is also widely sung outside Australia – in New Zealand, the United States, Canada, Ireland, England, Scotland and Wales. *See also Bushrangers; Donohoe, Jack*

WITCHCRAFT

Despite fears of witchcraft expressed at the beginning of the twenty-first century by some religious persons and bodies due to the craze among children for the Harry Potter books, most Australians probably regard witchcraft, witches and wizardry as subjects for humour and scepticism rather than for concern. However, there are those who take these matters seriously, and some who identify themselves as wizards and witches. The most well-known self-styled witch in Australia was the artist Rosaleen Norton who courted publicity in Sydney in the 1940s. While witchcraft may be treated in many quarters as absurd and irrational, folk belief in such matters is often persistent, as demonstrated during the Azaria Chamberlain affair. *See also Chamberlain, Azaria; Evil Eye, The; Satanism; Supernatural, The*

WOMEN'S FOLKLORE

Women's own folklore is normally transmitted from female to female, both between and within generations. Some of its major forms are handcrafts, foodways, folk beliefs, communication skills and verbal lore. In 1982 Nancy Keesing published *Lily on the Dustbin: Slang of Australian Women and Families*, a good account of the special slang used in a number of female and family contexts, including the woman who 'puts on her face' before going to work in the morning, using cosmetics resting on the 'duchess set' (lace doileys) on the dressing table, anxious to look her best even if she has 'the curse'. The 'Sheilaspeak' and 'Familyspeak' which Keesing describes has a variety of functions, including instructing children ('Were you born in a tent?'), commenting on male behaviour ('The wandering hands society') or on other women ('Mutton dressed up as lamb'). Much of this slang is used to enhance female solidarity and for the pleasure of colourful idioms such as 'a lick and a promise' or 'a canary's bath' to describe hasty ablutions.

Women's traditional handcrafts frequently embody the values and beliefs of their makers. This may range from expressing affection for family (as in a gift of a hand-knitted jumper) to their deep-seated and ideological beliefs. In the 1980s, for example, women parishioners from St John's Anglican Cathedral in Parramatta (NSW) made a notable series of tapestry covers for seats and kneeling pads. These tapestries featured the church itself and other historic buildings in Parramatta.

The handcrafts made by women (and men) from non-English speaking backgrounds, whether recent immigrants or from old-established communities, have greatly enriched Australian life and have been the subject of a number of exhibitions, such as *Arti e Mestieri* organised in Melbourne by the Co.As.It (Italian Assistance Association).

Some aspects of women's folk beliefs and practices in contemporary Australian multicultural society have been the subject of controversy. Public debate has been particularly agitated about 'female circumcision', or genital mutilation of females as practised by older women in some African/Islamic communities, although some senior medical personnel regard this practice as uncommon in Australia and it has not been authoritatively documented. Debate has also occurred in Australia about the traditional headscarf worn by many Muslim women and female children, although public acceptance of this practice seems to be growing. It is not uncommon today to see young Muslim women wearing the headscarf – and jeans.

A number of women's folk beliefs are beliefs about themselves. Contemporary debate frequently focuses on the 'glass ceiling' and the scarcity of women in high positions in Australia life, whether in academia, business or politics. Some of the reasons for this situation are practical (eg child-bearing and rearing) and some are thought to be the results of derogatory male beliefs about women's competence. Undoubtedly, too, some reasons are to do with women's lack of self-belief or assertiveness. The opposite side of this situation is more positive; traditional women's culture is often marked by cooperative and conciliatory attitudes and good communication skills.

Some changes are occurring in aspects of women's folklore. Traditionally, women have taken the main responsibilities for cooking in the domestic arena, while professional cooks have almost all been males, but both areas are moving, albeit slowly, towards greater gender equality. Marriage and childbirth have changed dramatically; birth out of wedlock is no longer a stigma in Australia, and a number of women, both with and without children, are declining to enter into legal marriage with their partners. Despite these changes, the elaborate 'white wedding', largely a female-instigated custom, still flourishes in Australia. *See also Crafts, Crochet, Making Do, Quilts, Sewing Bee, Weddings*

WOODCHOPPING

Deriving from the skills developed in the Australian timber industry, woodchopping ('woodchop') competitions and exhibitions remain a characteristic feature of fairs, shows and other events throughout Australia. Involving prodigious feats of strength, speed, stamina and skill, woodchopping is also seen in cities when the country comes to town at the Agricultural Shows. *See also Agricultural Shows; Customs; Folk Sports; Work Lore*

'WOOLLOOMOOLOO LAIR, THE'

Also known as 'My Name it is McCart(h)y', a song that celebrates the larrikinesque lifestyle of late nineteenth-century Sydney. The chorus goes:

> *My name it is McCarty and I'm a rorty party,*
> *I'm rough and tough as an old man kangaroo.*
> *Some people say I'm lazy, and others call me crazy*
> *And I hang around with the boozy crowd in the pub at Woolloomooloo.*

See also Folk Songs; Larrikin

WOOLSHED DANCE *See Dance*

WORKING BEE *See Sewing Bee*

WORK LORE

A general term for the great variety of folklore associated with work, including initiation customs and pranks; stirring; April Fool's Day hoaxes; faxlore, xerox lore or e-lore; jokes, rumour and gossip; stories about 'the worst/best job I ever had', and a variety of social customs such as the 'whip-around', the office party, the retirement dinner and the like. In earlier times much of the lore of work revolved around the celebration of bush occupations, especially shearing, bullock-driving and overlanding, and the lifestyles that accompanied them. These activities were the subject of a large body of nineteenth- and early twentieth-century folk song, poetry and yarns. Worklore of the contemporary variety is frequently critical of authority, especially 'the boss', occupational hierarchies, paperwork and bureaucracy ('red tape'), and other aspects of workplace culture. It tends to be distributed globally, though is usually adapted and modified in various ways to suit Australian circumstances. *See also Bastardisation, E-lore, Faxlore, Initiation, Labor Lore, Railway Lore, 'Sickie', The; Smoko, Stirring the Possum*

WORLD'S GREATEST WHINGER, THE
Popular and lengthy yarn, probably of World War II vintage though often said to be older. The World's Greatest Whinger is exactly that. He complains long and loud about everything – food, weather, the war, the economy, etc. When the whinger dies, surprisingly perhaps, he goes to heaven where even in that place of perfection he complains about the quality of the haloes and the necessity of attending angel choir practice. *See also Folk Humour; Yarn*

WU LAN/VU LAN
Celebrated in late August, Chinese Buddhist *Wu Lan* and Vietnamese Buddhist *Vu Lan*, or 'Wandering Souls' Day', occurs on the fifteenth day of the seventh month of the Chinese lunar year. Prayers are said for the souls of ancestors and various offerings and propitiations are traditionally made. *See also Chinese Folklore in Australia; Customs; Religious Lore*

X

XEROX-LORE *See E-lore; Work Lore*

XIN NIAN *See Chinese New Year*

Y

YAGAN

West Australian Aboriginal warrior who led resistance to European settlement in the 1830s. He was treacherously murdered by an adolescent friend in 1833, then skinned and beheaded, his skull sent to England for scientific purposes. His skull has recently been returned for burial with the rest of his remains in a secret location in his country. Yagan is celebrated by the Nyungar people as a great hero and his statue stands on Herrison Island in the Swan River, Perth. *See also Folk Heroes; Indigenous Folklore; Jandamurra; Pemulway*

YALLINGUP CAVE SPIRITS

South-west West Australian Nyungar tradition preserves the story of a battle between an evil spirit named Wolgine and a good spirit called Ngilgi. Wolgine lived in Yallingup Cave and made anyone who entered the cave ill and afraid. The good spirit Ngilgi challenged Wolgine for control of the cave and after an epic struggle the good spirit triumphed, forcing Wolgine to the back of the cave, where he begged for mercy. Ngilgi granted him that, but banished him forever to another cave, taking over what is now called Ngilgi Cave and making it a place of goodness rather than evil. *See also Ghost Lore, Indigenous Folklore*

YARAMA

Mythical creatures of Aboriginal origin inhabiting Queensland's tropical coastal forests, yaramas are evil beings about a metre tall, with huge heads, mouths, throats and bellies. Their green and red skin is scaly, and instead of fingers and toes they have cup-shaped suckers. The yaramas like to perch in fig trees and pounce on passing humans, fastening their suckers and draining the victim's blood, then eating what's left. According to legend, should a victim be tough enough to survive and be regurgitated, the yarama will get revenge by drinking the community's water supply. As in European vampire lore, victims always become yaramas themselves. *See also Folk Belief; Indigenous Folklore; Legendary Animals*

YARNS

A widely used term often referring to humorous anecdotes, sometimes with a 'sting in the tail' or a point to make about individuals, events or actions. In common with many other traditions, such anecdotes or folk tales are extremely common in Australian tradition, especially in the genre known as the 'bush yarn'. Such tales about swaggies, bushmen, bullockies and the like are often popularly associated with notions of national identity. Examples in this book include stories about outback characters like Ah Foo and Cornelius Kenna, and the elaborated yarn, or humorous anecdote, such as 'The World's Greatest Whinger'. The term is also used to refer to tall stories, outright lies ('they spun us a yarn') and to simple conversation, as in the phrase 'having a yarn'.

A number of Australian folklorists, notably Bill Scott, Ron Edwards and Patsy Adam-Smith, have collected and published yarns. In *Fred's Crabs and Other Bush Yarns* (1989), Ron Edwards followed a classification method for yarns based on the Irish folklorist Sean O'Suilleabhain's adaptation of the Swedish Uppsala system. O'Suilleabhain divides folk tales into eleven categories: Livelihood, Historical Tradition, Physical Activities and Pastimes, Transport and Communications, Human Life, Community, Behaviour, Events, The Spoken Word, Nature and Myths and Superstitions. Within each category are a number of sub-sections, so that under Historical Tradition there is provision for stories about 'the early days', 'historical calamities' and 'personalities and famous people'. As with all such folklore classification systems, room is allowed for additions of newly distinguished and/or newly developing forms. Folklorists around the world have developed such techniques to allow organisation, classification and comparison of the great amount and variety of information carried in traditional narratives. *See also Ah Foo, Jimmy; DOCUMENTATION OF AUSTRALIAN FOLKLORE; Folk Humour; National Icons*

YOWIE

A fierce, hairy creature of unknown gender derived from Aboriginal belief. The earliest mention of the yowie seems to be 1835, though no one claimed to have seen one until 1871. Since then there have been many reported sightings, though the term 'yowie' does not appear to have come into general use until 1975. *See also Folk Belief; Folk Tales; Indigenous Folklore; Legendary Animals*

Z

ZAC

A pre-decimal currency term for sixpence from at least the late nineteenth century and still heard occasionally, as in the phrase 'I haven't got a zac.' Also used in underworld argot to mean a prison term of six months or six years. *See also Folk Speech*

ZAMBUK

Folk name for a St John's Ambulance Brigade worker. Derived from the name of a brand of antiseptic ointment, it probably became attached to field ambulance workers in Word War I. Rarely heard today. *See also Folk Speech, War Lore*

ZWARTE PIETER *See Father Christmas*

The Australian Folk Year

T his section presents a reasonably comprehensive calendar of the Australian folk year. It combines numerous religious calendars, the civic calendar and the folk calendar, and incorporates obsolete as well as current customs. The Dictionary section of the Guide contains more detailed information on many of the observances noted here. The calendar provides an overview of the diversity of observance in Australia and also highlights the concurrence of many folkloric, religious and civic events. As some observances are moveable there may be discrepancies in dates, especially when the observances have been referenced to the Christian calendar. Some observances are therefore only approximately dated.

JANUARY

2ND FRIDAY IN JANUARY *Festabend*, Barossa Valley (SA).

2ND SATURDAY IN JANUARY *Schutzenfest*, Barossa Valley (SA).

CIRCA MID-JANUARY *Pongal*, or Tamil harvest festival

1 JANUARY New Year's Day. Both a folk celebration and a secular holiday, marks the start of a new year according to the Christian calendar.

6 JANUARY Epiphany Eve (Twelfth Night) according to the Christian calendar.

6-7 JANUARY Orthodox (Old Calendar) Christmas Eve and Christmas Day. Celebrated by those churches that follow the Old Calendar – mainly Macedonian, Serbian and Egyptian – at this time.

7 JANUARY Greek Orthodox observance of the feast of St John the Baptist. Marks the baptism of Jesus Christ by John. Traditional observances include wetting with water and being dipped in the sea and may also involve the custom of diving for the cross.

10 JANUARY Guru Gobind Singh's Birthday . A Sikh celebration of the last and most important of the ten gurus of Sikhism. Observance lasts for up to two days and involves the reading aloud of the Sikh holy book, the *Granth Sahib*.

14 JANUARY Orthodox (Old Calendar) New Year

19 JANUARY Orthodox (Old Calendar) Epiphany (Twelfth Night)

25 JANUARY Burns Night. Commemorates the birth of Scotland's national poet, Robert Burns (1759-1796).

26 JANUARY Australia Day. The Tamworth (NSW) Country Music Festival takes place on the the Australia Day weekend.

27 JANUARY St Sava's Day. Patron Saint of Serbia, and closely associated with the unification of the Serbian state.

30 JANUARY Day of The Three Hierarchs. Greek Orthodox commemoration of the patron saints of schoolchildren.

LATE JANUARY/EARLY FEBRUARY *Xin Nian/Tet*. Spring Festival, marking the start of the first lunar month of the Chinese calendar.

FEBRUARY

FEBRUARY Pancake Day, Shrove Tuesday, according to the Christian calendar. Tuesday immediately preceding Ash Wednesday, which marks the start of Lent

FEBRUARY Lesbos festival, Melbourne (Vic). An Australian Greek festival held since early 1980s

FEBRUARY Blessed Virgin of the Rosary, Donvale (Vic). Italian pilgrimage.

FEBRUARY *Rosenmontag* or 'Rose Monday'. Part of traditional German carnival of the period preceding Lent.

1 FEBRUARY St Brighid's (St Bride's, St Bridget's) Day, according to the Christian calendar. Commemoration of a secondary patron saint of Ireland, and, in the northern hemisphere, the first day of spring.

9 FEBRUARY St Maroun's Day. Commemorates foundation of the Lebanese Maronite Church in the 4th Century AD.

12 FEBRUARY Hobart Regatta Day (Tas.)

14 FEBRUARY St Valentine's Day, according to the Christian calendar

FEBRUARY/MARCH *Purim* (Feast of Lots). Celebration of the delivery of the Jews of Persia from massacre, sixth century BC.

MARCH

MARCH *Holi* (Hindu Spring Festival). Traditionally marks the coming of Spring. A three to ten day festival of street processions, bonfires, dancing and the throwing of coloured powder and water.

EARLY MARCH Gay and Lesbian Mardi Gras, Sydney (NSW)

MARCH (DATE VARIES) *Nowruz.* 'New day' or New Year for the Zoroastran Parsee people and the Bahai of Iran.

FIRST MONDAY IN MARCH Labour Day (WA).

SECOND MONDAY IN MARCH Labour Day, formerly 'Eight Hours Day' (Vic). Labour Day (ACT). Moomba Parade and opening of Moomba, Melbourne (Vic.)

SECOND SATURDAY IN MARCH Tenterfield (NSW) Highland Gathering

1 MARCH St David's Day, according to the Christian calendar. David (*Dewi*) is the patron saint of Wales.

17 MARCH St Patrick's Day, according to the Christian calendar. Ireland's National Day, honouring one of three National Saints.

19 MARCH Feast of St Joseph, according to the Christian calendar. Italian Catholic commemoration .

25 MARCH Independence Day (Greece). Marks the beginning of Greece's successful struggle against the Turks in 1821.

MARCH/APRIL Palm Sunday. A Catholic, Protestant and Armenian Apostolic observance taking place on the Sunday before Easter and marking the start of Holy Week, the most significant week in the Christian year. In recent times also marked by marches in support of world peace and an end to armed conflicts.

APRIL

SATURDAY BEFORE EASTER Start of Sydney Royal Easter Show, Sydney (NSW). Bendigo Easter Fair (Vic.)

THURSDAY BEFORE GOOD FRIDAY Holy Thursday ('Maundy Thursday' in England). Observed by the Armenian Apostolic, Catholic and Protestant churches, marks the night of the Last Supper. The Orthodox observance of Holy Thursday takes place seven days later.

LATE MARCH – EARLY APRIL Easter, according to the Christian calendar. The National Folk Festival held annually in Canberra (ACT) at this time.

EASTER SUNDAY Blessing of the Fleet (various locations)

GOOD FRIDAY AND EASTER SATURDAY Maclean (NSW) Highland Gathering

EASTER MONDAY Barossa Valley (SA) Vintage Festival. The Stawell Easter Gift, Stawell (Vic.).

1 APRIL April Fools' Day

APRIL (*Pesach*) (Jewish). Passover.

APRIL *Shab-e-Bharat* (Islamic). Precedes the month of Ramadan

APRIL *Mi'raj/Isra* (Islamic). Anniversary of Ascent of the Prophet Mohammed to heaven, especially important to the Sufi sect. The night is marked in mosques and at home by the re-telling of the story of the Prophet's ascent.

APRIL (DATE VARIES) Day of Outing. Last day of Iranian thirteen-day New Year celebrations, known as *Nowruz* (see March). It is unlucky to work or to stay indoors on this day.

MID-APRIL Prosh activities, University of Western Australia, Perth (WA). Student revels, University of Adelaide, Adelaide (SA).

LATE APRIL *Quing Ming* (Chinese); Thanh Minh (Vietnamese). Tomb sweeping festival.

23 APRIL St George's Day (Greece)

25 APRIL ANZAC Day

30 APRIL May Eve

MAY

1ST MONDAY OF MAY Labour Day (Qld.). May Day (NT). Bangtail Muster, Alice Springs (NT).

1 MAY May Day

6 MAY *Gurgouden* (Romany Day)

SECOND SUNDAY IN MAY Mother's Day. First Day of Summer in northern hemisphere and Middle Eastern countries.

MID-MAY (ODD YEARS ONLY) *Kernewek Lowender*, Moonta Peninsula (SA

MID-LATE MAY Pentecost or Whitsuntide (Catholic, Protestant, Armenian Apostolic churches)

24 MAY Empire Day (obsolete)

LATE MAY *Shauvot* (Jewish)

MAY/JUNE *Ramadan* (Islamic)

JUNE

JUNE *Mnarja*, Maltese harvest festival

EARLY JUNE Nullarbor Muster (WA).

1ST MONDAY IN JUNE Foundation Day (WA)

2ND MONDAY IN JUNE Queen's Birthday (except WA)

16 JUNE Bloomsday. Celebration of Irish author James Joyce's literary achievement, particularly in relation to his masterwork, Ulysses.

23 JUNE Midsummer Eve

24 JUNE St John's Day, according to the Christian calendar

LATE JUNE Dragon Boat Festival (Chinese)

JULY

JULY *Hajj*. Islamic pilgrimage

JULY Christmas in July

3RD SATURDAY IN JULY International (Stroud) Brick and Rolling Pin Throwing Contest

25 JULY Santiago Apostle (Spain). Associated with pilgrimage.

LATE JULY Royal Darwin Show (NT)

31 JULY Mt Kembla Mine Explosion Commemoration, Mt Kembla (NSW)

ONE SUNDAY IN JULY OR AUGUST (depending on neap tide) Darwin Beer Can Regatta, (NT)

AUGUST

1 AUGUST Horses' Birthday. Lammas Day, according to the Christian calendar

EARLY AUGUST Picnic Day (NT)

1ST MONDAY IN AUGUST Wattle Day (not all states). Bank Holiday (NSW, ACT). Henley-on-Todd Regatta, Alice Springs (NT). Festival of Our Lady of Terzito (Observed principally by families from the Isle of Salina, Italy) Hawthorn (Vic.)

AUGUST Feast of the Hungry Ghosts (Chinese)

AUGUST Feast of the Seven Sisters (Chinese)

MID-AUGUST Show Day, Brisbane (Qld)

LATE AUGUST *Wu Lan* (Chinese Buddhist) *Vu Lan* (Vietnamese Buddhist). 'Wandering Souls Day'

LATE AUGUST *Eid-ul-Adha*, Festival of Sacrifice (Islamic). Festival in memory of the prophet Abraham

AUGUST-SEPTEMBER Double Ninth Festival (Chinese)

LATE AUGUST-EARLY SEPTEMBER *Shinju Matsuri*, Broome (WA)

SEPTEMBER

SEPTEMBER *Rosh Hashanah* (Jewish New Year)

FIRST SUNDAY IN SEPTEMBER Father's Day. Wattle Day (not all states)

8 SEPTEMBER Feast of Our Lady of Victories (Maltese). Commemoration of the defeat of Turkish invaders of Malta in 1565

ON OR AROUND 11 SEPTEMBER *El-Nayroz* (Coptic Orthodox). Egyptian observance of the New year according to the Coptic calendar. Also known as the 'Feast of the Martyrs'.

MID TO LATE SEPTEMBER Islamic New Year

LATE SEPTEMBER Show Day, Melbourne (Vic)

LATE SEPTEMBER Queen's Birthday (WA). Celebrated at this time in WA because that state's foundation day is in June, the month when the other states and territories observe the monarch's birthday.

LATE SEPTEMBER-OCTOBER *Sukkoth* (Jewish)

LATE SEPTEMBER-EARLY OCTOBER Mid-Autumn Moon Festival (Chinese, Vietnamese)

SEPTEMBER-OCTOBER AFL (Perth, Melbourne) and Rugby League (Sydney) football Grand Finals.

SEPTEMBER-OCTOBER *Yom Kippur* (Jewish Day of Atonement). Ten days after the start of *Rosh Hashanah*, a fast day for the Jewish people and a time for remembering the dead.

OCTOBER

OCTOBER *Simchat Torah* (Jewish)

OCTOBER Lygon St Festa, Melbourne (Vic.) (Italian)

OCTOBER Blessing of the Fleet Geraldton (WA)

OCTOBER *Oktoberfest*. German drinking festival.

OCTOBER Royal Perth Show

OCTOBER Launceston Show People's Day (Tas.)

1ST MONDAY IN OCTOBER Labour Day (NSW and ACT).

2ND MONDAY IN OCTOBER Canadian Thanksgiving Day. Labour Day (SA.)

THIRD WEEK IN OCTOBER Hobart Show (Tas.)

28 OCTOBER *Oxi* Day (Greece)

LAST WEEKEND IN OCTOBER (Friday, Saturday, Sunday) McLaren Vale Wine Bushing Festival, McLaren Vale (SA).

LATE OCTOBER (Bi-annual) Festival of Leadlights Subiaco (WA)
LATE OCTOBER Blessing of the Fleet, Fremantle (WA)
31 OCTOBER Halloween

NOVEMBER

NOVEMBER The Prophet's Birthday (Islamic)
FIRST TUESDAY IN NOVEMBER Melbourne Cup Day (Vic. and elsewhere)
4 NOVEMBER Recreation Day (Northern Tasmania)
5 NOVEMBER Guy Fawkes Day and Night
SECOND SUNDAY IN NOVEMBER Feast of San Rocco, Perth suburbs of
  Leederville, Mt Hawthorn, N. Perth (WA) (Italian)
11 NOVEMBER Remembrance Day (previously Armistice Day).
  Commemorates the end of World War I on this day in 1918 .
AROUND MID-NOVEMBER *Diwali* Hindu Festival of Lights. Held on the
  first day of the month of *Kartik* on the Hindu calendar.
FOURTH THURSDAY IN NOVEMBER Thanksgiving (American)

DECEMBER

DECEMBER *Chanukah* (Jewish). Beginning on the 25th day of the Jewish
  month of *Kislev*.
5 DECEMBER St Nicholas Eve (Dutch)
13 DECEMBER St Lucia's Day (Swedish). Celebrates a martyred Italian
  saint of the fourth century.
19 DECEMBER St Nicholas (Orthodox Old Calendar). Observance of St
  Nicholas day. *See 6 December*
24 DECEMBER Christmas Eve, according to the Christian calendar
25 DECEMBER Christmas Day, according to the Christian calendar
26 DECEMBER Boxing Day, St Stephen's Day, according to the Christian
  calendar
27 DECEMBER St Stephen's Day (Greek Orthodox)
30 DECEMBER Proclamation Day (SA) (Exact date of observance varies)
31 DECEMBER New Year's Eve

Regional Traditions

T his gazetteer groups traditions according to state and territory, but does not include those common to the whole country. Some entries relevant to more than one state or territory will appear in two or more categories.

AUSTRALIAN CAPITAL TERRITORY
Folk Festivals
Ghost Lore
Holidays
Simpson and his Donkey

LORD HOWE ISLAND
Lost Treasures

NEW SOUTH WALES
Albury Ram, The
Annual Highland Gathering
Black Mary
Blessing of the Fleece
Blessing of the Fleet
Cabbage Patch
Cash, Martin

Click Go the Shears
Coo-ee
Cornstalks
Curlew
Currency
Donohoe, Jack
Dunn, John
Eumerella Shore, The
Female Factory, The
Feste
Free Selector
Gardiner, Frank
Ghost Lore
Goldrush lore
Goorianawa
Granville Train Disaster, The
Great Depression, The

Kennedy, Sergeant
Legendary Animals
Mahogany Ship, The
Melbourne Cup, The
Morgan, Daniel 'Mad Dog'
Picnic Races
Pilgrimage
Stawell Gift, The
Victorian Folk Music Club, The
Village Saints' Processions

WESTERN AUSTRALIA
Alkimos Ghosts
Bell-ringing
Blessing of the Fleet
Blue Lady of New Norcia
Bushrangers
'Catalpa, The'
Cockeye Bob
Corn Dollies
Curtin's Cowboys
Doyle, Tom
Feste
Fremantle Doctor, The
Festival of Leadlights
Folk Belief
Folk Sports

Funerals
Ghost Lore
Goldrush Lore
Jandamurra
Jarrah Jerker's Jog, The
Kirup Syrup
Legendary Animals
Lollybagging
Maritime Lore
'Maryborough Miner, The'
Moondyne Joe
Museum of Childhood
Nannup Tiger
Nicknames
Nullarbor Muster, The
Picnic Races
Prosh
Ragged Thirteen, The
Red Dog
Sandgropers
Shinju Matsuri
Silver Reef, The
Tin Kettling
Top Enders
Village Saints' Processions
Western Australian Folklore
    Archive

BIBLIOGRAPHY

This bibliography has been prepared to provide an accessible and representative listing of writing about folklore in Australia. A few nineteenth-century and other older references have been included because of their historical importance, but most books are more recent, and can be found in major libraries around Australia. A few individuals have produced a very large number of works, such as Anderson, Edwards, Factor, Seal and Wannan – only a selection of their writings have been included. These selections include their most recent work, as well as attempting to show the range of topics in Australian folklore that they have addressed. Some titles may appear to have little to do with Australian folklore; they have been included because they have been referred to in this book. Insights about folklore can be found in many different places.

Anderson Hugh, 'Farewell to Judges and Juries': The Broadside Ballad and Convict Transportation to Australia, 1788–1868, Red Rooster Press, Hotham Hill (Vic.) 2000.

A Plan for Cultural Heritage Institutions to Reflect Australia's Cultural Diversity, Consultative Committee on Cultural Heritage in a Multicultural Australia, Canberra 1991.

Adams, Phillip and Newell, Patrice The Penguin Book of Australian Jokes, Penguin Books Australia, Ringwood (Vic.) 1994.

Adam-Smith, Patsy Folklore of the Australian Railwaymen, Macmillan, Melbourne 1964.

American Folklife Preservation Act (1976), Public Law 94-201, 94th Congress, H.R. 6673, 2 January 1976.

Anderson, H. *Colonial Ballads:* Rams Skull Press, Ferntree Gully (Vic.) 1955.

Anderson, H. *Australian Song Index 1828–1956* (decorations by Ron Edwards) Rams Skull Press, Ferntree Gully (Vic.) 1957.

Anderson, H.M. (ed.) *Goldrush Songster* (decorations by Ron Edwards) Rams Skull Press, Ferntree Gully (Vic.) 1958.

Anderson, H.M. (ed.) *The Colonial Minstrel* (1955) F.W. Cheshire, Melbourne 1960.

Anderson, H. and Meredith, J. *Folk songs of Australia and the men and women who sang them* Ure Smith, Sydney 1968.

Anderson, H.M. *The Story of Australian Folksong* (illustrations by Ron Edwards) Hill of Content, Melbourne 1970.

Anderson, H.M. *Time Out of Mind: Simon McDonald of Creswick* National Press, Melbourne 1974.

Anderson, H. *George Loyeau: The Man Who Wrote Bush Ballads* Red Rooster Press, Ascot Vale (Vic.) 1991.

Anderson, H and Anderson, D. *On the Track With Bill Bowyang* (Part 1) Red Rooster Press, Ascot Vale (Vic.) 1991/2.

Andrews, S. *Take Your Partners: Traditional Dancing in Australia (c. 1974)* Hyland House, Melbourne 1979.

Andrews, S. *Take Your Partners: Traditional Social Dancing in Colonial Australia* Victorian Folk Music Club, Melbourne 1979.

Ankatell, J. *Walker in the Wilderness: The Life of R J Ankatell* Hesperian Press, Carlisle (WA) 1998.

Arthur, J. M. *Aboriginal English: A Cultural Study* Oxford University Press, Melbourne 1996.

Arthur, S. (ed.) *To Wear a Convict's Chains* (no publisher given) Brisbane 1961.

Australian Children's Folklore Newsletter (see Play and folklore)

The Australian Folk Directory 1982/83 Australian Folk Trust, Canberra 1982.

Australian Folklore Department of English, University of New England, Armidale (NSW) annually since 1987.

'Australian Nursery Rimes', *Bulletin*, Sydney 1917.

Australia's Hidden Heritage, Office of Multicultural Affairs, Canberra 1989.

Baker, Sidney *Australia Speaks: A Supplement to 'The Australian Language'* Shakespeare Head Press, Sydney 1953.

Baker, S.J. *The Australian Language* Sun Books, Melbourne 1945, 2nd edn Angus & Robertson, Sydney 1966.

Barber, V. et al. *Blue Bags, Bloodholes and Boomanoomana: Folklore of the Southwestern Riverina* Finley High School (NSW) 1987.

Baring-Gould, W. and Baring-Gould, C. *The Annotated Mother Goose* (1962) Bramhall House, New York (c.1967).

Bausinger, H. *Folklore in a World of Technology* (translated by Elke Dettmer) Indiana University Press, Bloomington 1990.

Beatty, W.A. *Come A-Waltzing Matilda* Ure Smith, Sydney 1950.

Beatty, W.A. *A Treasury of Australian Folk Tales and Traditions* Ure Smith, Sydney 1968.

Beilby, P. and Roberts, M. (eds) *Australian Music Directory* Australian Music Directory Pty Ltd, North Melbourne 1981.

Bell, D. & Hawkes, P. *Generations* McPhee Gribble/Penguin, Fitzroy (Vic.) 1988.

Bishop, A. *The Gucci Kangaroo and Other Australian Urban Legends* The Australasian Publishing Company, Hornsby (NSW) 1988.

Blair, S. (ed.) *People's Places: Identifying and Assessing Social Value for Communities* Australian Heritage Commission, Melbourne 1994.

Blanchette, J.F. *From the Heart: Folk Art in Canada* McClelland and Stewart, Toronto 1983.

Burton, C. et al. 'North Fremantle Community Map, Stage 1 Cultural Heritage Project 1992–1993: Draft Final Report' 1993.

Butterss, P. *Songs of the Bush: The First Collection of Australian Folk Song* (illustrated by Ron Edwards) Rams Skull Press, Kuranda (QLD) 1991.

Byron, K. *Lost Treasures in Australia and New Zealand* Angus & Robertson, Sydney 1964.

Carr, J. *The Captive White Woman of Gipps Land: In pursuit of the legend* Melbourne University Press, Carlton (Vic.) 2001.

Cave, D. *Percy Jones: Priest, Musician, Teacher* Melbourne University Press, Melbourne 1988.

Cooke, E.A. *Fresh Evidence From Early Goldmining Publications 1851–1860* Australian Language Research Centre, University of Sydney, Sydney 1966.

Cooke, E.A. *The Early Goldmining Terms and Popular Collocations* Australian Language Research Centre, University of Sydney, Sydney 1966.

Covell, R. *Australia's Music: themes for a new society* Sun Books, Melbourne 1967.

Covell, R. and Brown, P. *Music Resources in Australian Libraries: A Report Prepared for the Australian Advisory Council on Bibliographical Services,* Canberra 1970.

Cowham, Bill (Comp.) *Lego Lingo: The Cadets' Language* Australian Defence Force Academy, Canberra n.d.

Cronin, M. and Adair, D. *The Wearing of the Green: A History of St Patrick's Day* Routledge, London and New York 2002.

Cumes, J.W.C. *Their Chastity Was Not Too Rigid: Leisure Times in Early Australia* Longman Cheshire/Reed, Melbourne 1979.

Cusack, F. *The Australian Christmas* Heinemann, Melbourne 1966.

Davey, G. 'Nursery Lore and the Functions of Folklore' *Australian Folklore* No. 2, pp. 3–24, 1988.

Davey, G. Beed *Snug as a Bug: Scenes from Family Life* Oxford University Press, Melbourne 1990.

Davey, G. Beed *Duck Under the Table: More Scenes from Family Life* Oxford University Press, Melbourne 1991.

Davey, G. Beed *Presentation and Paradox: Folklore and Tourism* CAS Applied Folklore Research Studies 2, Curtin University, Perth (WA) 1992.

Davey, G. Beed and Seal, G. (eds) *The Oxford Companion to Australian Folklore* Oxford University Press, Melbourne 1993.

Davey, G. Beed and Faine, S. *Traditions and Tourism: The Good, the Bad and the Ugly* Proceedings of the Sixth National Folklife Conference, National Centre for Australian Studies, Monash University, Melbourne 1994.

Davey, G.B. 'Ethnicity isn't the only thing that matters: Reflections from the Moe Folklife Project' *Australian Folklore* 11, pp. 211–16, 1996.

Davey, G. *The Moe Folklife Project: A final report prepared for the Department of Communication and the Arts and the National Library of Australia* National Centre for Australian Studies, Monash University, Melbourne 1996.

Davies, T. *Australian Nicknames* Rigby, Adelaide 1977.

Davies, T. *More Australian Nicknames* Rigby, Adelaide 1978.

Delbridge, A. (gen. ed.) *Aussie Talk: The Macquarie Dictionary of Australian Colloquialisms* The Macquarie Library Pt. Ltd, McMahons Point (NSW) 1984.

Denholm, D. *The Colonial Australians* (c. 1979), Penguin Australia, Ringwood (Vic.) 1980.

Dixon, R.M.W., Ramson, W.S. and Thomas, M. *Australian Aboriginal Words in English: Their Origin and Meaning* Oxford University Press, Melbourne 1990.

Eagleson, R. *Australianisms in the Early Migrant Handbooks 1788–1826* Australian Language Research Centre, University of Sydney, Sydney 1964.

Eagleson, R. *Australianisms in the Early Migrant Handbooks 1827–1830* Australian Language Research Centre, University of Sydney, Sydney 1965.

Eagleson, R. *The Bibliography of Writing on Australian English* Australian Language Research Centre, University of Sydney, Sydney 1967.

Eagleson, R. and McKie, Ian *The Terminology of Australian National Football* Australian Language Research Centre, University of Sydney, Sydney 1968–69.

Edwards, R. (ed.) *The Overlander Songbook: a selection of 58 early Australian bush ballads* 1st edn. Rams Skull Press, Ferntree Gully (Vic.) 1956; 2nd edn Holloways Beach (QLD) 1969; revised edn Adelaide 1971.

Edwards, Ron *Bushcraft 1: Australian Traditional Bush Crafts* Rams Skull Press, Kuranda (QLD) 1975.

Edwards, Ron (ed.) *Australian Folklore Society Journal* Rams Skull Press, Kuranda (QLD) first published September 1984.

Edwards, R. *Two Hundred Years of Australian Folk Song Index 1788–1988* Rams Skull Press, Kuranda (QLD) 1988.

Edwards, R. *The Wealthy Roo and Other Bush Yarns* (originally published as *Yarns and Ballads of the Australian Bush*, Adelaide 1981); Rams Skull Press, Kuranda, Queensland 1988.

Edwards, R. *Traditional Torres Strait Cooking* Rams Skull Press, Kuranda (QLD) 1988.

Edwards, R. *Mud Brick Techniques* Rams Skull Press, Kuranda (QLD) 1990.

Edwards, R. *Great Australian Folk Songs* Ure Smith, Sydney 1991.

Edwards, R. *The seafaring tradition in Tasmania: traditional crafts in the Maritime Museum, Hobart* Rams Skull Press, Kuranda (QLD) 1994.

Edwards, R. *The Australian Yarn*, University of Queensland Press, Brisbane 1977; 2nd edn Rigby, Adelaide 1996.

Edwards, R. *Leather lacing manual* (illustrated by Ron Edwards) 10th edn Rams Skull Press, Kuranda (QLD) 2000.

Edwards, R. *Stockmen's plaited belts* (illustrated by Ron Edwards) 11th edn Rams Skull Press, Kuranda (QLD) 2001.

Elliott, B. *Singing to the Cattle and Other Australian Essays* Georgian House, Melbourne 1947.

Ely, R. 'The First Anzac Day: Invented or Discovered?' *Journal of Australian Studies* No. 17, pp. 41–58, November 1985.

Factor, J. 'Fragments of children's play in Colonial Australia' The Colonial Child papers presented at the 8th Biennial Conference of the Royal Historical Society of Victoria, Melbourne 12–13 October 1979; RHSV, Melbourne 1981.

Factor, J. *Far Out, Brussel Sprout! Australian children's chants and rhymes* (illustrated by Peter Viska) Oxford University Press, Melbourne 1983.

Factor, J. *All Right, Vegemite! A new collection of children's chants and rhymes* (illustrated by Peter Viska) Oxford University Press, Melbourne 1985.

Factor, J. *Childhood and Children's Culture* Australian Children's Television Foundation, North Melbourne (Vic.) 1985.

Factor, J. *Children's Folklore in Australia: An Annotated Bibliography* Institute of Early Childhood Development, Kew (Vic.) 1986.

Factor, J. *Unreal, Banana Peel! A third collection of children's chants and rhymes* (illustrated by Peter Viska) Oxford University Press, Melbourne 1986.

Factor, J. *Captain Cook Chased a Chook: Children's Folklore in Australia* Penguin, Ringwood (Vic.) 1988.

Factor, J. *Real Keen, Baked Bean! A fourth collection of children's chants and rhymes* (illustrated by Annie Marshall) Hodder & Stoughton, Sydney 1989.

Factor, J. *Roll Over, Pavlova! A fifth collection of children's chants and rhymes* Hodder & Stoughton, Sydney 1992.

Factor, J. and Viska, Peter *Far Out book of ooey gooey stuff* Hodder Headline, Sydney 1998.

Factor, J. *Kidspeak: A Dictionary of Australian Children's Words, Expressions and Games* Melbourne University Press, Melbourne 2001.

Fahey, W. *Joe Watson: Australian Traditional Folk Singer* Australian Folklore Unit, Paddington (NSW) 1975.

Fahey, W. *Eureka: The Songs That Made Australia* Omnibus Press, Sydney 1984.

Fahey, W. *The Balls of Bob Menzies: Australian Political Songs 1900–1980* Angus and Robertson, North Ryde (NSW) 1989.

Fahey, W. *When Mabel Laid the Table: the folklore of eating and drinking in Australia* State Library of NSW Press, Sydney 1992.

Fahey, W. *Diggers' songs: songs of the Australians in eleven wars* Australian Military History Publications, Loftus (NSW) 1996.

Fahey, W. *Ratbags and rabblerousers: a century of political protest, song and satire* Currency Press, Sydney 2000.

Fahey, W. *Classic bush yarns: Australian outback humour, tall yarns and bulldust* Harper Collins, Pymble, (NSW) 2001.

Fearn-Wannan, W. (Bill Wannan) *Australian Folklore: A Dictionary of Lore, Language and Popular Allusions* Lansdowne, Dee Why West (NSW) 1976.

Freeland, J.M. *Architecture in Australia: A History* F.W. Cheshire, Melbourne 1968.

Folklife: Our Living Heritage Committee of Inquiry into Folklife in Australia, Australian Government Publishing Service, Canberra 1987.

Gauntlett, S. 'Folklore and populism: the "greening" of the Greek blues' *Proceedings of the 4th National Folklore Conference,* University of New England, Armidale (NSW) 1990.

Gilbert, L. *A Grave Look at History: Glimpses of a Vanishing Form of Folk Art* John Ferguson, Sydney 1980.

Glassie, H., in Vlach, J.M. and S.J. Bronner *Folk Art and Art Worlds* UMI Research Press, Ann Arbor/London 1986.

Greenway, J. 'Folklore Scholarship in Australia' *Journal of American Folklore* Vol. 74 pp. 440–48, 1961.

Greenway, J. *The Last Frontier: A Study of Cultural Imperatives in the Last Frontiers of America and Australia* Lothian, Melbourne 1972.

Grose, F. *Dictionary of the Vulgar Tongue: A Dictionary of Buckish Slang, University Wit and Pickpocket Eloquence* first published as *A Classical*

Dictionary of the Vulgar Tongue 1795; under new title 1811; this edn Macmillan, London and Basingstoke 1981.

Gunn, J.S. *The Terminology of the Shearing Industry* Australian Language Research Centre, University of Sydney, Sydney 1965.

Gunn, J.S. *An Opal Terminology* Australian Language Research Centre, University of Sydney, Sydney 1971.

Gunn, J.S. *Distribution of Shearing Terms in New South Wales* Australian Language Research Centre, University of Sydney, Sydney 1971.

Haswell, G. *Ten Shanties Sung on the Australian Run 1879* Antipodes Press, Mt Hawthorn (WA) 1992.

Hiddens, L. *Explore Wild Australia with the Bush Tucker Man* Viking, Ringwood (Vic.) 1999.

Hogbotel and Ffuckes (eds) *Snatches and Lays* 1st edn Melbourne 1962; revised edn Sun Books, Melbourne 1993.

Hollinshead, K. (ed.) *The Possum Stirs: Proceedings of the 2nd National Folklore Conference* Kuringai CAE, Sydney 1987.

Hornadge, Bill *The Australian Slanguage: a look at what we say and how we say it* Mandarin, Richmond (Vic.) 1989.

Howard, D. 'Folklore of Australian Children' *Journal of Education* Vol. 2, No. 1, pp30–35, March 1955.

Hults, D. 'Australian Craft: Within A Folkloric Context' in Ioannou, N. (ed.) *Craft in Society: an Anthology* Fremantle Arts Centre Press, South Fremantle (WA) 1992.

Hults, D. *A Bibliography of Australian Folklore 1790 to 1990* Black Swan Press, Perth 1995.

Ingleton, G. *True Patriots All: or, News from early Australia as told in a collection of broadsides* C.E. Tuttle, Rutland Vt 1988.

Ioannou, N. *Ceramics in South Australia 1836–1986: From Folk to Studio Pottery* Wakefield Press, Adelaide 1980.

Ioannou, N. *The Barossa Folk: Germanic Furniture and Craft Traditions* Craftsman House, Sydney 1995.

Ioannou, N. *Masters of their craft: tradition and innovation in the Australian contemporary decorative art* Craftsman House, Sydney 1997.

Ioannou, N. *Barossa Journeys: Into a Valley of Tradition* (1997) New Holland, French's Forest (NSW) 2000.

Isaacs, J. *Bush Food: Aboriginal Food and Herbal Medicines* Lansdowne, Sydney 1987.

Isaacs, J. *The Gentle Arts: 200 years of Australian women's domestic and decorative arts* Lansdowne, Sydney 1990.

Jacobs, Joseph (ed.) *More English Fairy Tales* David Nutt, London 1904.

Janke, T. *Our Culture: Our Future* Report on Australian Indigenous Cultural and intellectual Property, prepared for Australian Institute of Aboriginal and Torres Strait Islander Studies and the Aboriginal and Torres Strait Islander Commission, Canberra 1998.

Johansen, L. *The Penguin book of Australian slang: a dinkum guide to Oz English* Penguin, Ringwood (Vic.) 1988.

Johnson, C. 'Australian Folk Material Culture: An Annotated Bibliography', *Australian Folklore* No.5, 1990.

Jones, I. 'Foothills Connection: A Shire of Kalamunda Multi-Arts Oral History Project', first pub. Oral History Association Newsletter 11, 1989; *Australian Folklore* No.7, 1992.

Jones, Percy (collector and arranger) *Burl Ives' Folio of Australian Folk Songs* Southern Music Publishing Co., Sydney 1953.

Keesing, N. *Lily on the Dustbin: Slang of Australian Women and Their Families* Penguin, Ringwood (Vic.) 1982.

Keesing, N. *Just Look Out the Window* Penguin, Ringwood (Vic.)1985.

Kempster, C. (ed.) *The Songs of Henry Lawson with music* Viking O'Neil, Ringwood (Vic.)1989.

Lahey, John (ed.) *Great Australian Folk Songs* Hill of Content, Melbourne 1965.

Langker, R. *Flash in New South Wales 1788–1850* Australian Language Research Centre, University of Sydney, Sydney 1980.

Lawson, Will *Australian Bush Songs and Ballads* Frank Johnson, Sydney 1944.

Lewis, M. *Victorian Primitive* Greenhouse , Carlton, Victoria 1977.

Lindesay, Vane *Aussie-osities* Greenhouse, Richmond (Vic.) 1988.

Lindsay, P.L. and Palmer, D. *Playground Game Characteristics of Brisbane Primary School Children* Australian Government Publishing Service, Canberra 1981.

Lowenstein, W. *Shocking, Shocking, Shocking: The Improper Play Rhymes of Australian Children* Fish and Chips Press, Melbourne 1974.

Lowenthal, D. *The Heritage Crusade and the Spoils of History* Viking, London 1996.

Loyau, George E. 'An Old Explorer' *The Queenslander's New Colonial Camp Fire Song Book*, Sydney 1865.

Magoffin, R. *Waltzing Matilda, Song of Australia: A Folk History* Mimosa Press, Charters Towers (QLD) 1983.

Makeshifts: Home-Made Furniture from Kerosene Cases New Settlers League of Australia (Victorian Division), Melbourne 1924.

Manifold, J. *The Violin, the Banjo and the Bones: An Essay on the Instruments of Bush Music* Rams Skull Press, Ferntree Gully (Vic.) 1957.

Manifold, J. *Who Wrote the Ballads? Notes on Australian Folksong* Australian Book Society, Sydney 1964.

Manifold, J.S. (ed.) *The Penguin Australian Song Book* Penguin, Ringwood, Victoria 1964.

May, S. *The Story of 'Waltzing Matilda' 1944*; rev. edn W.R. Smith, Brisbane 1955.

Mapping Culture: A Guide for Cultural and Economic Development in Communities Commonwealth Department of Communications and the Arts, Canberra 1995.

McCredie, A.D. 'German musical traditions in South Australia' in I. Harmstorf and P. Schwerdtfeger (eds) *The German Experience of Australia 1833–1938*, Association of Von Humboldt Fellows, Flinders University of South Australia 1988.

McPhee, J. *Australian Folk and Popular Art in the Australian National Gallery* Australian National Gallery, Canberra 1988.

Mendelsohn, O. *A Waltz with Matilda: On the Trail of a Song* Lansdowne, Melbourne 1966.

Meredith, J. (ed.) *Songs from the Kelly Country Bush Music Club*, Bush Music Club, Sydney 1955.

Meredith, J. *The Wild Colonial Boy: Bushranger Jack Donahue 1806–1830* Red Rooster Press, Ascot Vale (Vic.) 1960.

Meredith, J. and Scott, A. (eds) *Authentic Australian Bush Ballads* Southern Music, Sydney 1960.

Meredith, J. and Anderson, H. *Folksongs of Australia (And the Men and Women Who Sang Them)* Ure Smith, Sydney 1967.

Meredith, J. and Whalan, R. *Frank the Poet: the life and works of Francis MacNamara* Red Rooster Press, Melbourne 1979.

Meredith, J. *Duke of the Outback* Red Rooster Press, Ascot Vale (Vic.) 1983.

Meredith, J. *Learn to Talk Old Jack Lang: a handbook of Australian rhyming slang* Kangaroo Press, Kenthurst (Vic.) 1984.

Meredith, J., Brown, P. and Covell, R. *Folksongs of Australia Vol. 2* University of New South Wales Press, Sydney 1987.

Newall, V. 'The Adaptation of Folklore and Tradition (Folklorismus)' *Folklore* 98, ii, 1987.

Palmer, K. *Indigenous and other Styles of Australian Bush Cooking* Aboriginal Studies Press, Canberra 1999.

Palmer, V. and Sutherland, M. *Old Australian Bush Ballads* Allan & Co., Melbourne 1951.

Parker, K. Langloh *Australian Legendary Tales 1896 and 1898*; new edn The Bodley Head, Sydney 1978.

Pascoe, Robert *Buongiorno Australia: Our Italian Heritage* Greenhouse Publications, Richmond (Vic.) 1987.

Paterson, A.B. (ed.) *The Old Bush Songs (Composed and sung in the Bushranging, Digging and Overlanding Days)* Angus & Robertson, Sydney 1905 (and revised edns).

Pearce, H.H. *On the Origins of Waltzing Matilda: expression, lyric, melody* Hawthorn Press, Melbourne 1971.

Pearce, H.H. *The Waltzing Matilda Debate* Rams Skull Press, Holloways Beach (QLD) 1974.

Play and Folklore Newsletter (formerly *Australian Children's Folklore Newsletter*) Museum Victoria, Melbourne.

Povah, F. *You Kids Count Your Shadows: Hairymen and Other Aboriginal Folklore in New South Wales* self-published, Tenterfield (NSW) 1990.

Queensland Centenary Pocket Songbook, The Federation of Bush Music Groups, Brisbane 1959.

Radic, T. (ed.) *Songs of Australian Working Life* Greenhouse, Elwood (Vic.) 1989.

Ramsay, Jim *Cop it Sweet! A Dictionary of Australian Slang and Common Usage* Allegheney News Service, Darlinghurst (NSW) 1977.

Ramshaw, J. (ed.) *Folklore in Australia: Proceedings of the Inaugural National Folklore Conference* Australian Folk Trust, Paddington (QLD) 1985.

Reed, A.W. *Aboriginal Words and Place Names, c. 1977*; A.H. & A.W. Reed Pty Ltd, French's Forest (NSW) 1982.

Report of the Working Party on the Protection of Aboriginal Folklore Department of Home Affairs and Environment, Canberra 1981.

Robinson, R. *Aboriginal Myths and Legends* Sun Books, Melbourne 1966.

Rolfe, M. *Patchwork Quilts in Australia* Greenhouse, Richmond (Vic.) 1987.

Rooney, R. *Skipping Rhymes: A Collection of Australian Skipping Rhymes* Moonflower Press, Melbourne 1956.

Roper, M. 'Inventing Traditions in Colonial Society: Bendigo's Easter Fair 1871–1885' *Journal of Australian Studies* No. 17, pp. 31–40, November 1985.

Russell, H. *Play and Friendships in a Multi-Cultural Playground* Australian Children's Folklore Publications, Institute of Early Childhood Development, Melbourne 1986.

Russell, H. *Carmen Out to Play: A Collection of Children's Playground Games* Oxford University Press, Melbourne 1989.

Russell, H. *Coming, Ready or not! A new collection of children's playground games* Hodder Children's Books Australia, Rydalmere (NSW) 1995.

Ryan, J. (ed.) *Australian Fantasy and Folklore* University of New England, Armidale (NSW) 1981.

Sandercock, L. and Turner, Ian *Up where, Cazaly? the great Australian game* Granada, London and Sydney 1982.

Saulwick, I. 'Documenting Tradition Through Survey Research Techniques: The Tenacity of Tradition' in Davey, G. Beed and Faine, S. (eds) *'Traditions and Tourism: The Good, the Bad and the Ugly' Proceedings of the Sixth National Folklife Conference 1994*, Clayton (Vic.) 1966.

Saxby, M. (ed.) *Through Folklore to Literature* Papers presented at the Australian National Section of IBBY Conference on Children's Literature 1978, IBBY Australia, Sydney 1980.

Scott, A. (ed.) *A Collector's Songbook: words and music of thirty-one traditional songs collected in Australia* Bush Music Club, Sydney 1970.

Scott, W. (ed.) *The Second Penguin Australian Songbook* Penguin, Ringwood (Vic.) 1980.

Scott, W. (Bill) *The Penguin book of Australian humorous verse* Penguin, Ringwood (Vic.) 1984.

Scott, Bill *The Long and the Short and the Tall: A Collection of Australian Yarns* Western Plains Publishers, Sydney 1985.

Scott, W. (Bill) *The Complete Book of Australian Folklore* 3rd Edition, PR Books, Frenchs Forest (NSW) 1988.

Scott, Bill *Pelicans and Chihuahuas and Other Urban Legends: Bill Scott Talking About Folklore* University of Queensland Press, St Lucia (QLD) 1996.

Seal, G. *Ned Kelly in Popular Tradition* Hyland House, Melbourne 1980; rev. edn *'Tell em I Died Game': The Legend of Ned Kelly* Hyland House, Melbourne 2002.

Seal, G. (ed.) *Banjo Paterson's Old Bush Songs* Angus & Robertson, Sydney and London 1983.

Seal, G. *The Hidden Culture: Folklore in Australian Society* Oxford University Press, Melbourne 1989.

Seal, G. and Davey, G. B. *The Oxford Companion to Australian Folklore* Oxford University Press, Melbourne 1993.

Seal, G. *The Bare Fax* Angus & Robertson, Sydney 1996.

Seal, G. *The Outlaw Legend: A Cultural Tradition in Britain, America and Australia* Cambridge University Press, Cambridge and Melbourne 1996.

Seal, G. *The Lingo: Listening to the Australian English* University of New South Wales Press, Sydney 1998.

Seal, G. *The Cane Toad High* (first published as *Great Australian Urban Myths 1995*) rev. edn, HarperCollins, Pymble (NSW) 2001.

Seal, G. *Encyclopedia of Folk Heroes* ABC Clio, Santa Barbara (CA), and Denver (CO), Oxford 2001.

Smith, M. *Bunyips and Bigfoots: in Search of Australia's Mystery Animals* Millennium, Alexandria (NSW) 1996.

Smith, G. *Playing Australian: Folk, Country and Multicultural Musics* Fremantle Arts Centre Press, Western Australia, forthcoming.

Spearitt, P. and Walker, D. (eds) *Australian Popular Culture* Allen & Unwin, Sydney 1979.

Stewart, D. and Keesing, N. (eds) *Australian Bush Ballads* Angus & Robertson, Sydney 1955.

Stewart, D. and Keesing, N. (eds) *Old Bush Songs and Rhymes of Colonial Times* Angus & Robertson, Sydney 1967.

Stubington, J. *Collecting Folk Music in Australia:* Report of a Forum held at the University of New South Wales, 4–6 December 1987 University of New South Wales Press, Sydney 1989.

Sutherland, Margaret *Old Australian Bush Ballads* (collected by Vance Palmer, music restored by Margaret Sutherland) Allan & Co., Melbourne, Adelaide and Bendigo 1950.

Symons, M. *One Continuous Picnic: A History of Eating in Australia* Penguin, Ringwood (Vic.) 1984.

Symons, P and Symons, S. *Bush Heritage, an introduction to the history of plant and animal use by Aboriginal people and colonists in the Brisbane and Sunshine Coast areas* 2nd edn, self-published, Nambour (QLD) 1996.

Tate, B. *The Bastard from the Bush: Obscene Songs and Ballads of Australian Origin* Rams Skull Press, Kuranda (QLD) 1982.

Tate, B. *Down and Outback*, Popinjay, Woden, (ACT) 1988.

Totaro, P. *Maintenance and Transmission of Italian Culture in Australia: Realities, Myths, Dilemmas* Ethnic Affairs Commission of New South Wales, Sydney 1980.

Totaro, P. *Italian folklore in Australia: discussion notes* Ethnic Affairs Commission of New South Wales, Sydney 1981.

Turner, I.A.H. (ed.) *Cinderella Dressed in Yella: Australian Children's Play-Rhymes*, Heinemann Educational Australia, South Yarra (Vic.)1969.

Turner, I., Factor, J. and Lowenstein, W. (eds) *Cinderella Dressed in Yella* (revised edn) Heinemann Educational Australia, South Yarra (Vic.) 1978.

Union List of Anthologies of Australian Folksongs National Library of Australia, Canberra 1966, supplement 1972.

Vaux, James Hardy *Memoirs of James Hardy Vaux Vol. II* W. Clowes, London 1819.

Walker, M. *Making Do: Memories of Australia's Back Country People* Penguin, Ringwood (Vic.) 1982.

Wannan, W. (ed.) *The Australian (1954)*; Viking O'Neil, Ringwood (Vic.) 1988.

Wannan, W. (ed.) *Crooked Mick of the Speewah* Lansdowne, Sydney 1965.

Wannan, W. (ed.) *Bill Wannan's Folk Medicine* Hill of Content, Melbourne 1970.

Wannan, W. (ed.) *Folklore of the Australian Pub* Macmillan, South Melbourne 1972.

Wannan, W. *The Bill Wannan book of Australian Yarns* Lansdowne, Melbourne 1974.

Wannan, W. *Bill Wannan's great book of Australian humour* Rigby, Adelaide 1977.

Wannan, W. *Folklore of the Irish in Australia* Currey O'Neil, Melbourne 1980.

Wannan, W. *A dictionary of Australian folklore: lore, legends, myths and traditions* Viking O'Neil, Ringwood (Vic.)1987.

Ward, R. *The Australian Legend*, new illustrated edn, Oxford University Press, Melbourne 1978.

Watkins, K., *Readin', 'Ritin' and 'Rithmetic: stories of school and school days from the Coomandook and Coonalpyn areas* Warrendi Project, Coomandook Area School, Coomandook (SA) 1987.

Watkins, K. *Send 'er Down, Hughie* Greenhouse, Richmond (Vic.) 1987.

Watson, E. *Country Music in Australia* 2nd rev. edn, Rodeo Publications, Kensington (NSW) 1976.

Western Australian Folklore Archive 'Catalogue of Holdings' 1993.

Wilkes, G. A. *A Dictionary of Australian Colloquialisms* Oxford University Press, South Melbourne 1996.

Williams, S. *Fisher's Ghost and Other Australian Tales of Ghosts and Murder* Popinjay, Woden (ACT) 1990.

Yarrow, S. and Batchelor, L. *Every Name Tells a Story: the origins of major town names in Western Australia* Regency Publications, Perth (WA) 1979.

INDEX

NB: Where there are multiple references, the main entry reference is in bold.

Names are generally listed under the surname, except for fictional characters such as Jimmy Sago, Paddy Malone.